SPENSER'S WORLD OF GLASS

SPENSER'S WORLD OF GLASS

A Reading of The Faerie Queene

by

KATHLEEN WILLIAMS

UNIVERSITY OF CALIFORNIA PRESS

Berkeley and Los Angeles

University of California Press
Berkeley and Los Angeles, California

© Kathleen Williams 1966
California Library Reprint Series Edition 1973
ISBN: 0-520-02369-2
Library of Congress Catalog Card Number: 72-95300

Printed in the United States of America

To
MY FATHER

CONTENTS

	ACKNOWLEDGMENTS	*page* viii
	INTRODUCTION	xi
1	THE WARRIOR SAINT	1
2	THE IMAGE OF MORTALITY	34
3	THE TERMS OF MORTAL STATE	79
4	INVIOLABLE BANDS	122
5	HEAVENLY JUSTICE	151
6	ALL GIFTS OF GRACE	189
	CONCLUSION: THE LAWS OF NATURE	224
	INDEX	235

ACKNOWLEDGMENTS

MUCH of the reading and preparation for this book was done at the Johns Hopkins University, to whom I am grateful for the award of the Bissing Fellowship for 1959 to 1960 which made it possible for me to take advantage of the resources of the library there. It is a pleasure to express my more particular gratitude to Professor D. C. Allen and Professor Earl R. Wasserman, whose encouragement and help contributed so largely to a rewarding year. I am glad also to thank the Huntington Library for a grant-in-aid which enabled me to work there during the summer of 1960, and to express my appreciation of the unfailing helpfulness of the staff in making the library's remarkable collection readily available to readers. To those whose work has contributed so largely to the present renaissance in Spenser scholarship I have expressed indebtedness in the notes to this book; for the further stimulus of conversation I am grateful to many friends.

The substance of an article, 'Venus and Diana: Some Uses of Myth in *The Faerie Queene*', which was published in ELH, Vol. 28, No. 2, June 1961, is included in the discussion of discordia concors, and of the parallel stories of Britomart, Amoret, and Florimell, in Chapters III and IV, and the substance of 'Courtesy and Pastoral in *The Faerie Queene*, Book VI', published in the *Review of English Studies*, n.s., Vol. XIII, No. 52, November 1962, is included in Chapter VI. I wish to thank the editors of these journals for their kind permission to use this material. The conception of *The Faerie Queene* as a cumulative structure expressive of unity in multiplicity, which underlies the whole of this

ACKNOWLEDGMENTS

book, was first outlined in 'Eterne in Mutabilitie: the Unified World of *The Faerie Queene*', published in *That Soueraine Light*, edited by William R. Mueller and Don Cameron Allen, Baltimore, 1952.

K.W.

hucine mortalis progressa potentia curae?
iam meus in fragili luditur orbe labor? . . .
aemula naturae parva reperta manus.
Claudian, *In sphaeram Archimedis*

INTRODUCTION

NOT so many years ago, it would have seemed necessary to explain one's reasons for writing at any length on *The Faerie Queene*, which critical orthodoxy had agreed to regard as a poem that nobody reads. But lately we have regained the old delight in Renaissance art, whether in words or paint or stone, and regained it, enriched, through the acquisition of knowledge. Our Spenser, like our Botticelli and our Michelangelo, is in some sense made new. We stress in him not the painter of ravishing pictures or the spellbinder who can draw us with him deep into wandering woods of fancy, but the maker, the creator of his own coherent universe, the serious, mature, and dedicated poet whose work is a personal vision of truth. The old Spenser was at once too much and too little of an artist, over-elaborate in descriptive detail but artless in construction and indeed in all the more important aspects of poetic creation. Yet the older responses, inadequate though they were, are subsumed under the new, for we do not surrender the ways 'so exceeding spacious and wyde/And sprinckled with such sweet variety', or even the stroll through the Spenserian picture gallery. Indeed, it is through such things, properly experienced, that we know the sage and serious artist. The difference is that now they mean more, for they are part of a structure which for all its effortless ease is massive in its scope and exactly functional in its detail. The ease is the ease of certain power, and the luxuriance the controlled flow of an imagination which can afford to be generous, indeed must be generous, for *The Faerie Queene* depends for its meaning upon that very luxuriance, the giving of more than at first seems necessary. It is a poem which creates its own world, its own references, and as we read on, and are able to move more readily in that world, so relationships are perceived, richer meanings develop, and from a multitude of details, at first incompletely grasped, a comprehensive order arises.

But the Spenserian world is not, of course, created ex nihilo, the irresponsible product of fancy. The Renaissance poet, it is true, ranges 'within the Zodiack of his owne wit', and is responsible to no man. The shepherd poet must be his own master, for independence is a necessary condition of service to peerless poetry whose home is above kings' palaces. Piers, admonishing the dispirited and insufficiently high-souled Cuddie in the *October* eclogue of *The Shepheardes Calender*, calls on poetry

> Then make thee winges of thine aspyring wit,
> And, whence thou camst, flye backe to heaven apace.
>
> (ll. 83–4)

Cuddie sees himself only as the summer singer, the time-passing and time-wasting grasshopper who has but 'a sclender prise' in winter for all the delight he has given, and creative independence is not for him; but a Colin could make the ascent, the lofty flight like that of the singing swan. But it is a flight to truth, and the poet remains responsible, not to individual men or to the concerns or rewards of society, but to all humanity, and to the divine giver of his creative power, and perhaps most urgently to poetry itself, the imitation of nature which is held to no facts, but which yet must shape facts in the direction of truth. The poet is the autonomous creator, the zodiac of his wit alone circumscribes his universe. Yet Sidney's very phrase suggests by its cosmic image the relation between the poet's own universe and that of every day which he shares with all men. His is an imitation of the given, this world seen more clearly, its significances compressed and enriched. The poet's materials are given him in created things, and if from these he makes anew it is in a shape which is the essential shape of the world we know but do not understand until he reveals it.

The Renaissance poet is entirely free to invent, but only to invent purposefully. Hippogriffs and dragons there may be, and earthly paradises, but they must all reveal some otherwise inexpressible aspect of man's concerns. One does not go far along the winding paths of Spenser's narrative without recognizing that they are as orderly as a labyrinth, and that the traditional metaphors he uses for his task—purposeful metaphors of ploughing and steering a course—are as much in place as his other metaphor of wandering along spacious ways. Like all poems which attempt the imitation of nature in its most ambitious form, that of the investigation of man's life and nature in relation to the nature of the universe, *The Faerie Queene* must in some way reproduce both the apparent inconsequence and the felt significance of life; as Pope was to perceive, nature as imitated in a poem both traditional and ambitious must be a mighty maze, but not without a plan. The phrase has been dismissed as tautologous, but in fact it sums up the task of such poems, to present the poet's vision of ordered nature without doing violence to the moment by moment experience of living which is itself part of the nature to be ordered. It is a task in which Spenser pre-eminently succeeds. Faeryland is very close to what it feels like to be living in a world whose significance is only dimly and occasionally discernible. If we read without preconceptions and prejudgments, our impression is not at all of an inhuman world of abstract moral order but of a world of tentative movement in the half-dark of sublunary life, becoming more confident as events slowly take shape and the dusk resolves itself into the endless struggle between the light and the dark insidious power of chaos.

This effect, a poetic version of our familiar process of living and learning, is achieved through the handling of the romance narrative and of the chief characters, knights like Guyon and Britomart. We travel with them on their quests, and share (if we are willing to do so without prematurely deciding that Temperance here pursues Beauty or Chastity there overthrows Justice) their puzzled efforts to find and keep the path they should be on. Mr. Harry Berger has well demonstrated the dramatic quality of the second book,[1] and in much of the poem the characters' genuine involvement, and ours through them, in the events of the narrative is an important part of the effect. Guyon or Arthur or Britomart, trying to make sense of the persons and situations they encounter (for in this their quests consist) are our representatives, for they are not in themselves virtues but specialized versions of ourselves, acting out through their stories that

[1] *The Allegorical Temper* (New Haven, 1957).

aspect of the imitation of human nature with which their own area of the poem is concerned. Even for the strongest and best of them the quest is not easy and its meaning not plain. Looking back on the experiences we have shared with them, we can see what it all meant, but at the time it is a matter of doing what seems to be (but frequently is not) best, fighting unknown enemies and following unknown paths which as often as not end in the dark in a forest full of the lurking beasts of the passions. This is the lifelikeness of the poem, that in reading it is not abstract and schematic at all. The issues are known only by experiencing the poem, and even then they are not fully 'known' in the sense that they can be set down in another set of words than the poet's. So far as a poem can be lived through, and can be felt to have the inclusiveness and apparently infinite expansion of significance that life has, *The Faerie Queene* can be.

By this I do not of course intend to suggest that it is the best of all possible poems (or the worst according to the demands one makes of poetry) but to indicate by what can only be a meta-phoric statement the kind of poem it seems to me to be. It goes without saying that no poem is really more than the most approximate vehicle for whatever we mean by life, or can exhaust more than a little of it. The impression is an illusion of art, like any other, and we feel it as such as we read. This is the pleasure of it, that a work so highly wrought, so patterned, so improbable as to physical fact, should be so true to what we know. It is not life which delights us in the poem, but the likeness that the poet has by his art created. Our sense of expanding significance depends on the kind of poem Spenser has chosen to write. He has chosen a romance narrative, complete with knights and ladies, tournaments, monsters, and set it to work itself out in a universe of intelligible order; this relationship sets up the conditions which produce our sense of a living reality. Romance allows events to move against the questing knights in the apparently meaningless way that they do in real life, and situations and events do not, usually, make their significance immediately clear. In different degrees, according to the aspect of human life each knight explores, he must try to understand and order what he is going through, and incomprehension and wrong choice may and often do endanger his quest. Romance sounds, also, the note of inwardness and subjective truth, the dream world shared with fairytale where the submerged meanings of our lives take monstrous or enchanting shape, uncomprehended yet felt to be ominously important. Thus the romance element in *The Faerie Queene* ensures our involvement in the process conveyed in the poem, that by which the individual mind strives, moment by moment, to impose meaning on the flux of events.

But this alone would be for Spenser an incomplete effect, for what the modern mind, typically, knows as the imposing of a subjective order which grows as we grow, the Elizabethan, typically, would know as the gradual comprehending of an order which is already there, and this too must be part of the poem. God's order is broken and incomplete since Eden failed, but it was 'establisht first/In good estate', and though altered it still holds, to be recaptured and made to live again in poetry through man's aspiring wit. So the romance narrative is only apparently inconsequential, and all things have meaning even when the knights cannot see it. Digressive though it appears Spenser's poem is of an order as intricate and as triumphant as that of the Elizabethan—mediaeval physical world with its inter-enclosed spheres, its angelic ranks, its emblematic animals, all pointing towards the microcosm, man. The knights believe in the existence of order, and it is their belief in it, whether or not it happens to be visible in events, which carries them to the end of their quests. Thus Spenser's imitation of nature is of a very inclusive and, in one sense of the word, a very realistic kind. Indeed one is constantly surprised and impressed by the literalness with which Renaissance poets seem to have understood their task of creation, and by the confidence with which they approached it. Milton's vast universe rises at his word out of the chaos over which his mind sits brooding, the darkness is illumined, and all the huge fields of space and time are related with absolute precision to the point at their centre, the garden in Eden. On a smaller scale, *On the Morning of Christ's Nativity* marshals time and place, past and future, in eternal relation to the manger in Bethlehem. The poem's world is, ideally, all our world in little, with events shown in their essential meaning; and so in *Epithalamion* Spenser not only subsumes all marriages divine and human under the image of his own, he takes the place of the sun, the poets' god, and creates a wedding day hour by hour, with all the movements of time made to point towards it.[2] The sense in which the poet is free and the sense in which he is responsible to truth are particularly clear in such a poem. The poet masters the actualities of nature and compels them through his own re-creation to show what they were first created for, but he must have them to compel, to shape. Again, *The Shepheardes Calender* follows month by month the cycle of the year and so of all natural life,[3] and by pastoral analogy considers man's place in that natural course and his true home beyond it. It is a little year, an epitome of those aspects of human life which the pastoral is fitted to explore; but whereas the actual calendar can only repeat itself endlessly and has by definition no more than the permanence of mutability, Spenser's *Calender* arrests the process, translating the movement of the seasons into a circle of lasting significance circumscribed only by the poetic zodiac. In the terms of the *Mutability* cantos, the poet sees the world through the eyes not of Mutability but of Nature. So he has

> made a Calender for every yeare,
> That steele in strength, and time in durance, shall outweare:
> And if I marked well the starres revolution,
> It shall continewe till the worlds dissolution.

The claim is made not so much on behalf of the individual poet as on behalf of poetry; this is what Spenser considers to be the function of his art.

What we find in these excellent but relatively minor poems is the creation of a little world where time and space and life and death are seen in meaningful relation to a central point (marriage, or the right use of his powers) where the poet stands. It is only to be expected that the same kind of 'making' should be found again, more rich and full and finely organized, in Spenser's epic, the most ambitious and inclusive of his imitations. In *The Faerie Queene* there is much more, and much more difficult, material to be embraced, and several methods of organization interlock. One of them is allegory, which, as Professor Theodore Spencer has observed, itself implies order, and which here functions as a

[2] A. K. Hieatt, *Short Time's Endless Monument* (New York, 1960).
[3] A. C. Hamilton, 'The Argument of Spenser's *Shepheardes Calender*', ELH, XXIII, 1956; R. A. Durr, 'Spenser's Calendar of Christian Time', ELH, XXIV, 1957.

structural principle, working primarily towards the relating together of the various parts of the Spenserian poetic world rather than towards the attaching of that world to a series of abstract concepts outside it. For Spenser's allegorical poem cannot, of course, be satisfactorily treated as if it were what Professor Northrop Frye has called 'naïve allegory', the emblem-like or pageant-like presentation of abstractions in terms of sense experience. This kind of allegory does occur in *The Faerie Queene*, but for particular purposes and as part of a highly complex poetic whole which does not merely translate the abstract into the sensuous but holds a mirror up to nature, reflecting in more intelligible order the life we know. Like the glass sphere in which Britomart sees Artegall truly reflected, it is a little image of the world which shows all things in their true shapes.

> It vertue had to shew in perfect sight
> What ever thing was in the world contaynd,
> Betwixt the lowest earth and hevens hight,
> So that it to the looker appertaynd;
> What ever foe had wrought, or frend had faynd,
> Therein discovered was, ne ought mote pas,
> Ne ought in secret from the same remaynd;
> Forthy it round and hollow shaped was,
> Like to the world it selfe, and seemd a world of glas.
>
> (III, ii, 19)

Even in its unfinished state, *The Faerie Queene* is as self-sufficient and as self-consistent as Britomart's sphere, shaping within itself the multitudinous things that are 'in the world contaynd'.

Such an ordered richness can be achieved only through complex organization, through the allegorical narrative, the 'virtues' of the several books, the structural themes which work through several of the books, and the expanding net of images, all interlocking to form the microcosm of the poem. It is these structural relationships which it is the chief purpose of this book to investigate. My approach can be only a very partial treatment, but so can any approach; and it seems at least feasible that to examine the poem as an 'imitation of nature' in the sense I have suggested may furnish us with a useful standpoint. For all sympathetic readers of *The Faerie Queene* have responded to its self-completeness, whether as the child who follows breathlessly through the forest to see whether the lady is saved and the enchanter foiled, or as the adult who feels that here in this place of fantasy some of the deepest realities of our life are being shown us at once more profoundly and more clearly than we can normally experience them. Faeryland is a world we can enter, with its own values and truths, and this is the source of its attractive power. The romance element draws us in; generations have responded to and commented on the opening line of Red Crosse's adventures, 'A gentle knight was pricking on the plaine', in which is present all the promise of a story in which anything may happen. But romance alone could not keep us in, or draw us back again to a poem which reveals itself increasingly as rich in wisdom and reality. To hold us within it, a poetic world must have what romance as such generally lacks, intelligible order; and Spenser's has a great deal to be ordered. Man's experience of himself, of other men, and of inanimate things are brought together within a system of coherent laws, applicable at all levels of experience, psychological, moral, spiritual, social, political, cosmic. Faeryland is a place where, though human confusions are not glossed over, law is made more manifest through the poem's firmness of structure. A passage from Maritain's *Art and Scholasticism* is apposite:

> So, because it is subjected in the mind of a man, the law of imitation, of resemblance, remains constant for our art, but in a sense purified. It must transpose the secret rules of being in the manner of producing the work, and it must be as faithful and exact, in transforming reality according to the laws governing the work to be done, as science in conforming thereto.[4]

Such a poem can approximate to our experience of living because it can embody the 'secret rules of being' not only of the world outside us but of our minds which strive to comprehend it. The romance element, I have suggested, contributes to our sense of inwardness, of reality subjectively known, of facts which seem meaningless yet take shape within our minds as we live them. But as an element of structure it contributes also to the universe of law which the mind tries continually to know through its own efforts, and thus experience and the mind which experiences are kept in unbroken relationship; the secret rules are the same for each, and come together in a beautifully integrated structure.

[4] Jacques Maritain, *Art and Scholasticism* (London, 1930), p. 96.

Similarly for the allegory. This too is an inward thing, evolved in its ancient beginnings to dramatize the battles of Mansoul.[5] But this in itself suggests an attempt to relate mental conflicts to an intelligible order presumed to exist, and in *The Faerie Queene* allegory's implication of order is exploited so that it too contributes to the universe of law and thus to the unity of the poem. Perhaps what comes first to mind when one thinks of *The Faerie Queene* as an allegorical poem is the scheme of the 'twelve morall virtues' which the projected twelve books are to follow, of Holiness, Temperance, Chastity. They are, it seems to me, vitally important, not as labels for knights or even primarily as guides to the reader, but as means of organization. What *The Faerie Queene* is about, or is made of, is not abstract virtues and vices but human experience as that is known to a mind whose imaginative scope is wide and deep but which naturally turns, in its task of understanding and shaping, to such helps as its age provides. Virtues and vices are a help as good as any, and in Spenser's poem they do function as a way of ordering the material. Each provides a fresh point of view, a fresh centre from which the vast subject may be contemplated. The virtues do not define the books which they name or the knights by whom they are defended; the books and the actions of the knights define the virtues, by working them out through the narrative in human terms. Thus each book contributes to the total order not through abstraction but through providing a particular view of human concerns, and the books of the virtues are inter-related by sustained themes which are themselves seen, in each case, from the point of view which the particular virtue provides. Spenser marshals all his organizing principles as one; the poem moves altogether, and moves unerringly towards unity, the unifying of the virtues in magnificence, of the narrative in the court of Gloriana, of the 'secret rules' in Nature, who speaks for God. That the poem breaks off like Merlin's prophecy to Britomart, and 'yet the end is not', does not prejudice that much of its order which it does reveal, since each aspect of the final unity is developed in itself.

As I have tried to suggest, the complex order of *The Faerie Queene* can be approached from several converging directions, and to do justice to all the interlocking organizing elements which may be operative at any given point would scarcely be possible.

[5] C. S. Lewis, *The Allegory of Love* (Oxford, 1936).

xix

But a survey of the poem, concentrating more particularly on certain passages where the structural principles are more readily extricable, may go a little way towards demonstrating its richness and precision; and this is the chief aim of the chapters which follow. Since my intention is to consider the poem as a whole to which each book contributes, I have not attempted to deal closely with every incident. Detailed treatment is concentrated on those passages which seem particularly relevant to the developing meaning of the total work. Again, where some aspect—theological, philosophical, or historical—of an episode has been exhaustively and authoritatively examined, I have thought it unnecessary to repeat discussions which are still readily available. A poem like *The Faerie Queene*, rich in itself and rich in the opportunities it offers for scholarly investigation, must raise many problems of inclusion and omission, and I have tried to solve these by the criterion of relevance to the particular approach adopted in this book.

Chapter One

THE WARRIOR SAINT

OF the several interlocking structural principles I have mentioned as being at work in *The Faerie Queene*, one at least must necessarily be present throughout: romance, to which Spenser is committed by his choice of the romance-epic form.[1] The choice was doubtless made with care; it has considerable potentialities in contributing to the effect he needs, and he gets the utmost out of it. Obviously such aspects of the romance tradition as the knightly quest or the battle with monster or paynim are peculiarly apt to the purpose of embodying the inner life in a narrative fiction, and moreover romance can reach comfortably and without incongruousness towards pastoral or ritual, the Odyssey or the Bible. But most important for my present purpose is its power to lead us into a subjective world and its usefulness as a structural principle. The first is immediately obvious. We meet at once not two abstractions but two romance characters, a knight and a lady, who give us a sense of general familiarity and of particular anticipation. The knight especially, with his peculiar armour dinted in battles he himself has not fought, and his air of taking himself too seriously, promises a story with enough of mystery in it, and with more of individual human interest than romance always offers. Enough is given, and enough held back, to catch our attention, and we follow willingly on that gentle stroll into the wandering wood which is also the way into Spenser's creation.

[1] Spenser's use of the romance form is examined in suggestive detail by John Arthos, *On the Poetry of Spenser and the Form of Romances* (London, 1956).

The leisurely opening is excellently contrived. Killing time until the storm passes, the two enter the wood,

> with pleasure forward led,
> Joying to heare the birdes sweete harmony,
>
> (I, i, 8)

looking about them to identify the trees, and remarking upon their differing nature and use,

> The eugh obedient to the benders will,
> The birch for shaftes, the sallow for the mill.
>
> (I, i, 9)

The traditional tree-list, which separated from its context can seem a mere set piece, within its context has remarkable immediacy and narrative relevance. The formal descriptions are felt as the appreciative comments of the travellers, as they 'praise the trees so straight and hy', led with delight and beguiling the way with desultory talk. 'Faire harbour that them seemes, so in they entered ar', to find suddenly that they have indeed entered 'in', in to the centre of a labyrinth (i, 11) and to the monster Error; their pleasant excursion reveals itself as a potentially dangerous dabbling in interests which are not properly their concern, their path is in both senses an erring one. Una's sudden awareness of 'the danger hid, the place unknowne and wilde' shocks us into alert attention, and we realize how deeply we too are 'in', drawn by easygoing pleasure into a whole new world. It is an opening as simple, and as effective, as that of any good adventure story, say as that of *Treasure Island*, where the homeliness of the Admiral Benbow is changed by the coming of Black Dog. The ordinary comfortable things of every day, where aspens are used for staves and elms for vineprops and woods are attractive places to wander in, become suddenly alarming, and from this point we are involved in the story of Red Crosse and move in the world he moves in. The meanings he finds there will be meanings for us too.

Thus along the winding path we advance into a metaphor which we accept easily because of the poet's narrative skill. The transition from a pleasant, too relaxed ride to the involutions of Error's 'endlesse traine', from a world outside us to a world within, is affected without a jolt. When Red Crosse thrusts aside

Una's fears with his self-reliant confidence that virtue is its own light in darkness, and then finds that even his armour gives no more than 'a little glooming light, much like a shade' to fight by, we see that it is as we thought, this solemn sad young man does take himself too seriously, and if he had indeed had only himself to rely on things would be going hard with him. Meanings make themselves felt by the ordinary process of reading once our interest has been engaged to compel us to read well; and the old techniques of romance narrative ensure that we do so.

Romance, then, leads us into a world at once familiar and strange, but it also helps to order that world. This second (though of course not strictly separable) function, by which romance tradition operates as a structural principle, is not fully developed in the first book, for reasons which later become clear. The *Proem* to this book, with its elaborate invocation to Venus and Mars, the great opposites of love and war, is effectually an introduction to the whole poem, and not until the succeeding books do we see quite how much structural use Spenser will make of the basic situation of romance, the relation of man to woman, war to love. Yet some use is made of it even here. Red Crosse like many a knight before him stands between two ladies, the faithful Una and the faithless Duessa who presents herself to him as precisely what she is not, Fidessa. His own faith shifts disastrously, and a continuing play upon the word explores the ironies of a situation in which faith itself, once misplaced, becomes demoralizing. The manly force of the romantic hero, even his loyalty, is worse than useless if the loyalty is to the wrong thing; the chivalric code of love and war intimates the spiritual insufficiency of the self. Red Crosse cannot stand alone, and is not even strong enough to remain alone, and the romance convention by which each knight has a lady to serve is here at the same time the weakness of the human spirit which, having lost the good, must replace it with something else. The chivalric terms hold, and our reaction to Red Crosse's behaviour is expressed in Spenser's grave stanza:

> Young knight what ever, that dost armes professe,
> And through long labours huntest after fame,
> Beware of fraud, beware of ficklenesse,
> In choice, and chaunge, of thy deare loved dame,
> Least thou of her believe too lightly blame,

3

And rash misweening doe thy hart remove:
For unto knight there is no greater shame,
Then lightnesse and inconstancie in love.

(iv, 1)

The self-regard which begins Red Crosse's failure as knight
and lover is also the self-sufficiency which begins his failure as
a Christian, but what we feel as we read is regret for lost and
misplaced loyalty, without further differentiation or definition.
Through 'knights and ladies gentle deeds' the meaning of the
Christian warfare and of Christian devotion is being unobtrusively shaped, and the poem's world is being given its first broad
and essential outlines. Whatever complexities are built up later,
in this first book we are given the clue to the maze; this is a God-
centred world, and a knight must keep his attention steadily
away from self and upon the quest he has been entrusted with,
if he is not to go astray. This is the only book of *The Faerie Queene*
which reveals glimpses of what is beyond the created world; Red
Crosse sees the New Jerusalem and hears the song of the angels,
rejoicing in their 'trinall triplicities' about the throne of God at
his marriage to Una. The poem, which interprets our world,
here sets that world into the context which gives it meaning, and
it does so with full recognition of the strains and tensions, as well
as the peace, which that meaning involves for man. These tensions also can be expressed through the loyalties of chivalry, and
nothing in this kind, perhaps, can touch us quite so deeply as
Lancelot's sorrow that his perfect loyalty to the best things he
knows in this world holds him back from a still greater good. But
the grief of Arthurian romance at the incompatibility of the
fellowship of the Round Table with the fellowship of the Grail is
present in Spenser's romance too. When Red Crosse sees the
New Jerusalem from the mount of Contemplation, he recognizes
that it is more brilliant than anything he has seen on earth, even
than Cleopolis the city of glory. But his first reaction to the news
of his impending sainthood is the natural human one, a mixed
feeling of unworthiness and of loss.

But deeds of armes must I at last be faine
And ladies love to leave, so dearely bought?

(x, 62)

The 'fierce warres and faithfull loves' that have occupied him and

4

must continue to occupy him have been necessary in the world, but tarnished by the world's condition. From the heights of Contemplation the victory is bloodstained and his hands are guilty, and 'As for loose loves, they are vaine, and vanish into nought'. The noblest tasks of man are yet, being human, sinful, and the greatest things done in the world are as nothing.

Thus Red Crosse, fighting in our world with his eyes fixed beyond it, draws for us a defining circle around it. The knights who follow him do not have his awareness of two worlds of experience and of the relation and tensions between them. Rather, they are sustained in this world by the angelic one which Red Crosse has known. Without his victory, their quests could not succeed, and similarly without the relationships which the first book lays down for us—between Cleopolis and the New Jerusalem, the churches militant and triumphant, the angelic praises and the festival music of marriage—no order would exist for the poem to imitate. But only in the first book is the source of the order made visible, showing the dimness of even the brightest earthly things.

> This saide, adowne he looked to the grownd,
> To have returnd, but dazed were his eyne,
> Through passing brightness, which did quite confound
> His feeble sence, and too exceeding shyne:
> So darke are earthly thinges compard to things divine.
>
> (x, 67)

It is not my purpose here to relate the first book to the two orders of nature and grace. Professor Woodhouse's insight into the nature of the contrast between the quest of Red Crosse, the future saint, and that of Sir Guyon, must colour all our views upon the first two books, whether we agree with, or qualify it.[2] My concern will be to suggest that the saint's story, different though it must

---

[2] A. S. P. Woodhouse, 'Nature and Grace in *The Faerie Queene*', ELH, XVI, 1949. For further discussion see T. M. Gang, 'Nature and Grace in *The Faerie Queene*: The Problem Reviewed', ELH, XXVI, 1959; Robert Hoopes, '"God Guide Thee, Guyon": Nature and Grace Reconciled in *The Faerie Queene*, Book II', RES, n.s. V, 1954. Also relevant are H. Berger, op. cit., and A. C. Hamilton, 'A Theological Reading of *The Faerie Queene*, Book II', ELH, XXV, 1958, and '"Like Race to Runne"': The Parallel Structure of *The Faerie Queene*, Books I and II', P.M.L.A., LXXIII, 1958.

be from any which succeeds it, is yet essential to those succeeding stories and to the poem's imitation of nature. Red Crosse, though he strives to live coram Deo, must also live, like all of us, coram hominibus. 'He has to do both with the created order and with the Creator Himself.'[3] His battle is conducted not in pure light but in the half dark of fallen creation, and it is complicated by the tensions which surround a man living in the world and committed to heaven. It is this doubleness which makes the story human and touching. Without it we would have another theological tract, a map of the way and not the way itself. Through the resources of romance the attaining of the theological virtue of faith is given actuality and poignancy, or the muddled efforts of a man struggling to reconcile divided loyalties are given shape and meaning. Either statement is a half truth, for the confusion and the clarity, the realities of earth and heaven are held together in the romance narrative.

Red Crosse's quest is the freeing of Una's parents in their lapsed Eden from the dragon, the old serpent, and for this his prowess as a fighter is necessary. But just as necessary as the fierce war is the faithful love, the other aspect of knightly excellence. He succeeds in the strength of his armour, and that is the gift of Una; without it, and her, he is powerless and disgraced. He needs faith in her and towards her, not the mere assent which can be shattered by appearances like those Archimago can conjure up, but the true and lively faith which endures despite appearances and is known by what it achieves. The general course of Red Crosse's story is the difficult winning of true faith, and nothing could be more apt for embodiment in the traditions of knighthood. 'Faith' is the dominating word in Red Crosse's first trial, the battle with Error in which we begin to see the issues arrange themselves within the developing story. Red Crosse, standing helplessly wrapped in 'Errours endlesse traine' is 'in great perplexitie' (the pun exactly conveys the impasse into which the knight's confident curiosity has led him) and is saved by Una's cry

Now, now, sir knight, shew what ye bee:
Add faith unto your force, and be not faint.

(i, 19)

[3] B. A. Gerrish, *Grace and Reason: A Study in the Theology of Luther* (Oxford, 1962), p. 25. The sentence refers, of course, not to Red Crosse but to man's situation, but it is relevant to the function of the first book.

As with 'perplexitie' or 'Errours endlesse traine', the implications of 'faith' make themselves known in a single response to a vivid situation: to say that the literal (the warrior, when action seems impossible, must still act) is an apt vehicle for the allegorical (the Christian, having done all, must stand) distorts the process of reading and reduces meaning to mere notation. Faith, we see from this first trial, is a word that as yet the knight does not well understand. He has a kind of faith, but it is in his own 'force', the strength and light of his own virtue, and this must bar the way to the faith to be attained before he can achieve his quest. It is only very late in his story that Red Crosse learns what the poet, at the right point in the narrative, is to remind us of, that

> If any strength we have, it is to ill,
> But all the good is Gods, both power and eke will.
>
> (x, 1)

His first adventure, though successful through Una's intervention, has revealed the weakness in faith which is to be exploited at once by Archimago, whose appearance of sober sadness and demonstrative repentance makes him an acceptably reliable figure to Red Crosse.

With Archimago the prevailing atmosphere of the book (already sharply impressed upon us by the contrast between the apparent pleasant harmlessness and the actual 'danger hid' of the wandering wood) begins to deepen and spread: it is an atmosphere of deliberate and malicious deceit. To the degree that it is present here, this quality is peculiar to the legend of Holiness. In the other books there is occasional deceit, but the predominating impression is, rather, of difficulty and complication. The knights find their quests hard because the way is hard to see, and things are so hard to distinguish: as in our own life, meanings are not readily discernible in events and so the right choice is difficult, or one is not aware of making a choice at all until the moment is past and we are committed to something we were scarcely conscious of. It is in the nature of the world to be difficult and confusing, but what Red Crosse has to deal with is something different, the purposeful treachery of evil. 'The world' which for the other knights is the sphere of their operations, often baffling but not usually actively hostile, is for Red Crosse the kingdom of this

7

world where the prince of darkness, in unalterable opposition to the heavenly kingdom, lays his traps.

Archimago, with the legions of spirits 'Fluttring about his ever damned head', with his air of great age and untiring evil, is a representative of Satan, engaged in perpetual though hidden war 'To aide his friendes, or fray his enimies', and as the story advances the others gather about him, Duessa, Orgoglio, the brothers Sansfoy, Sansloy, and Sansjoy, their ancestress Night. Red Crosse moves among the two great opposing forces, the Sons of Day and of Night; nowhere else in *The Faerie Queene* is there so distinct a separation of all creatures into their final, judgment day forms, good and evil, sheep and goats. Distinct, that is, to us. To Red Crosse it is not so until his final battle, since it is the whole endeavour of the forces of darkness to appear to belong to the opposing side. Their skill in disguise is formidable, of course, and is seen in such episodes as Archimago's imitation even of Red Crosse's Christian armour and, more vividly, in the charm of his lowly hermitage, built 'downe in a dale' and with a holy chapel and a sacred fountain near it. It is described as straightforwardly as if the holiness and sacredness of the place were genuine. Perhaps they are: evil has the power to turn good places and institutions to its own ends. But however convincing Archimago may be there is no doubt that Red Crosse is to blame for being deceived. If his faith had been firm—if he had known what faith really is—he would have doubted the evidence of his senses before he doubted Una. As it is, his eye 'of reason was with rage yblent', 'Will was his guide, and griefe led him astray', he has ceased to see with the eye of reason and sees with the eye of the senses, and so he betrays his faith, the evidence of things not seen.

Archimago's power is at its greatest at night, when even the Christian armour cannot help minds 'drownd in deadly sleep'. The account of his spells and of the drowsy house of Morpheus evokes an atmosphere of hushed menace, of darkness, sleep, death, and effortless drowning among the lulling sounds of the waves washing and the streams trickling. The 'sleepy mind' is evil's ally, and the efforts of Archimago and Duessa are, throughout, to blind the eye of reason, to induce Red Crosse to relax his constant guard against the deceit through which evil works, in fact to disarm him. 'Put on the whole armour of God', says St. Paul, 'that ye may be able to stand against the wiles of the devil'.

8

The wiles of this devil begin with erotic dreams in which Una seems to be brought to the Knight's bed by Venus and the Graces. The description has a fresh pastoral charm which is pleasant but inappropriate—there is no innocence in Red Crosse's world—and it is made shocking here by the incongruous presence of Venus, identifiable as the earthly Venus by her association with Flora. As both dea and meretrix Flora was an ambiguously expressive figure in the Renaissance and later,[4] and her most famous mention in Spenser's poetry, glossed by E.K. in his comments on the *March* eclogue, is in a context of light-minded spring love-making. The flowers which are associated with her are an equally expressive symbol, suggesting as they do both chaste beauty and desire, and later in the poem Spenser makes extensive use of flower symbolism in relation to human love. Red Crosse's bewildered disillusionment is vividly present in the picture of Una, whom he had regarded as 'the chastest flowre that aye did spring/On earthly braunch', now being crowned by Flora with lascivious ivy, and seeming in such company herself a 'loose leman'. He wakes in the frame of mind one might expect of his character, feeling 'unwonted lust' and 'wonted feare of doing ought amis'. Because he thinks everything depends upon him, he is in constant fear of his own inadequacy, and in self-distrust he forces himself to assertive action. The apparent strength is a real weakness; again he shows his need to add faith unto his force, to know that 'If any strength we have, it is to ill', to recognize that he must, in himself, fail. His anger at the shamelessness of the false Una is angry fear of his own weakness, revealed to him in his dreams. Una, who had roused his feeble faith in the battle with Error, seems now to depend upon his faith, though she uses the word so differently that his belief in Archimago's false spirit only further underlines his faithlessness. When he hurries from the house at dawn he is 'flying from his thoughts and gealous feare' (ii, 12), flying indeed from himself, and the will which guides him may have the contemporary meaning of sensuality as well as of self-will.

He flies, of course, straight to Duessa, and this too is only to

---

[4] Julius S. Held, 'Flora, Goddess and Courtesan', *Essays in Honor of Erwin Panofsky*, De Artibus Opuscula XI (New York, 1961), Vol. I, pp. 201–18; E. Wind, *Pagan Mysteries in the Renaissance* (London, 1958), pp. 102 f.

be expected. Una, once revered for her unworldly purity, now seems to be all too much a creature of this world, and Red Crosse has been horrified not only by her behaviour but by his own first response to it. He is in precisely the state to succumb, in his need for what he thinks to be faith, to the meretricious, the whore of Babylon who really is what Una has been made to seem. Duessa can appeal to his baser nature while seeming to appeal to the higher, and he hurries to take part in the satisfying and soothing deceit. He can defeat Sansfoy because he still believes in the cross his shield bears,[5] but the victory is a doubtful one which sends him further on the rapid descent to Orgoglio's dungeon. With the blood of Sansfoy, he buys 'the wanton loves of false Fidessa fayre' (vii, 26). He is not without faith, but it is a faith never deeply rooted or fully understood, and it has too much of self in it. The evidence of his senses, which detached his faith from Una, now persuades him to attach it to Duessa, and he follows her eagerly, judging by his 'quick eyes' while his 'dull eares' scarcely hear the words upon which, if she is to be accepted as Fidessa, his reason should have been busy. He is to be blamed, for he believes because he wants to believe; yet Duessa's story is well enough calculated, though to our instructed ears it has all the marks of the world in its claim to greatness. By presenting herself as a truer Una, Duessa offers Red Crosse all that he wants in this moment of desolate disillusionment both with his lady and with himself. Una is a deprived king's daughter, Duessa is the daughter of the great emperor of the west. She makes claims that Una never made, for her account of her betrothal to a great prince cruelly slain is a version of the death and resurrection of Christ:

> His blessed body, spoild of lively breath,
> Was afterward, I know not how, convaid
> And fro me hid.

(ii, 24)

Evil is using truth for its own purposes, but it reveals to the reader (though not to the eager Red Crosse) its real relation to the truth it blasphemes. If she were the child of light she pretends to be, Duessa would know the living Christ; it is from the sons of darkness that the resurrected body was hidden. The story is

---

[5] The shield of faith (Ephesians vi, 16).

touching if one does not listen too closely to what it must mean, but in accepting it Red Crosse is hanging his belief upon the facile appeal to sentimentality and upon the easy gratification of the senses. These are what had both fascinated and horrified him in Archimago's house, but now he does not, or will not, even recognize them. In accepting Duessa's insidious distortion of the gospel story he accepts the earthly kingdom of appearances, its self-indulgence and its tinsel trappings of power.

How blind the eye of reason has become we see in Red Crosse's fatuity when he meets the tree which was once Fradubio. Fradubio has fallen deep into the world of sense and illusion through the same process as Red Crosse. He too has been betrayed by his own feeble faith and sensuous sight to the point of believing one woman foul who is really fair, and accepting the really foul, Duessa herself, as the fair. The incident is a last warning, but Red Crosse does not see any possible parallel between Fradubio's knightly shame of fickleness and his own. He goes blindly on to the fate in Orgoglio's castle that is already foreshadowed in Fradubio's imprisonment, held like a 'damned ghost from Limbo lake' in a life in death from which only the living well of a baptized faith can save him. Red Crosse has roused Fradubio through a thoughtless and infatuated act, the plucking of green branches to make a garland for Duessa's head. In another context this would be a harmless courtesy and an expression of human affection; in this book it is felt at once to be a tasteless frivolity. If Duessa were what she claims to be, such a gesture should never have occurred to him, a garland should be as incongruous as the false Una's ivy wreath. The very triviality of the action is shocking, for every action here is a move in the battle of light and darkness, and when the ripped branch bleeds, and the tree cries out, the effect is grave and horrifying but not altogether surprising. In Red Crosse's world even the slightest act or word may be indicative of spiritual conditions and may lead to grave spiritual consequences. The blood that his guilty hands draw from the tree shows how closely he is involved in Fradubio's sin and how much in danger of a like imprisonment. Faced with a truth expressed in complex action, or with a truth distorted in order to deceive, as in Duessa's account of herself, Red Crosse is unable to perceive it because, being now committed to faith in falsity, he does not wish to perceive it. His devotion to Duessa is

11

sensuous and worldly, depending upon an aura of jewelled beauty, distress, high birth, and imperial power—'Borne the sole daughter of an Emperour'. The dazzling power of the unveiled Una, attended by the lion's 'yielded pryde and proud submission' is lost to him, and it is only to be expected that his next adventure should take him further into the earthly realm. In Lucifera's house the kind of power he has been following declares itself, and even wilful infatuation cannot quite blind him to the fact that something is wrong.

The glory and richness of Lucifera's palace, brilliant on its foundation of sand, is of course altogether worldly, a sumptuous show passing the pomps of Persia. It is a place of ambition, where Duessa often comes; the alliance between the world and the Roman church, and perhaps also certain proud prelates of Spenser's own church, a recurrent theme in *The Shepheardes Calender*, is doubtless touched on here. But more importantly Lucifera herself embodies the primary sin of which worldly ambition is only an aspect, the pride of Lucifer which seeks to put itself in place of God. The physical pomp of gold and precious stone is dimmed by her own feverish brilliance, the 'bright blazing beauty' whose intensity is that of passionate aspiration not towards God but towards a selfhood which to her is the highest good. Worldly though her followers are, Lucifera looks to heaven, but in the wrong way and for the wrong reason. Heaven, to her, is her natural habitat, her rightful possession not as a child of God but as herself the highest of gods in virtue of the worth she feels:

> So proud she shyned in her princely state,
> Looking to heaven, for earth she did disdayne
>
> (iv, 10)

> Of griesly Pluto she the daughter was,
> And sad Proserpina, the queene of hell;
> Yet did she think her pearelesse worth to pas
> That parentage, with pride so did she swell,
> And thundring Jove, that high in heaven doth dwell,
> And wield the world, she claymed for her syre,
> Of if that any else did Jove excell:
> For to the highest she did still aspyre,
> Or, if ought higher were then that, did it desyre.
>
> (iv, 11)

Yet her origins are hellish and sorrowful,[6] and though her palace towers are 'high lifted up' towards heaven the dial high on the gilded walls ticks away the hours to destruction; she is a child of night who refuses to recognize her lineage. The damned pride implied in her name is emphasized by the comparison to Phaeton, who made a similar claim to absolute power over earth and sky and turned the lifegiving heat of the sun to the destructive fire of hell, to fall headlong from a sky flaming 'With fire not made to burne, but fayrely for to shyne'. Phaeton, who presumed to drive his father's great horses, and Lucifer who likewise fell in flames through his presumption, are unmistakably akin: in *Apelles Symbolicus* the fall from the sun chariot is confidently glossed 'In Luciferum aliosque rebelles Angelos e coelo dejectos'.[7] Lucifera's excessive brightness is heavily stressed by the grave repetition of a phrase across two stanzas:

> As envying her selfe, that too exceeding shone:
>
> Exceeding shone, like Phoebus fayrest childe
>
> (iv, 8–9)

The phrase, almost unchanged, occurs again when Red Crosse stumbles back into the world half blinded by the radiance of the eternal city:

> dazed were his eyne,
> Through passing brightnes, which did quite confound
> His feeble sence, and too exceeding shyne:
> So darke are earthly thinges compard to things divine.
>
> (x, 67)

Perhaps it is too much to suggest that this repetition is consciously intended; the phrase is ordinary enough. But the solemn handling of it in the fourth canto gives it such weight and importance that it echoes in the mind; only in the heavenly city can excessive light exist without blame. Lucifera's palace is, like Milton's hell, an imitation of heaven, its excess of glory is a sin of extreme gravity,

---

[6] She is the daughter of Pluto and 'sad Proserpina, the queene of hell', but she claims as her father Jove, 'Or if that any else did Jove excell'. In Marlowe Pride tells Doctor Faustus 'I am Pride. I disdain to have any parents.'

[7] Joannes Michael van der Kelten, *Apelles Symbolicus* (Amsterdam, 1699), Caput XLVII, p. 374.

13

only the New Jerusalem should be so bright. Similarly her coach 'strove to match' Juno's chair, as Satan's bad eminence strives to match the throne of God. This is the chair drawn by the six other sins appropriately mounted, whereas Juno's chair is drawn by 'fayre pecocks, that excell in pryde'. The peacocks would be suitable for Lucifera's coach too; the substitution of the miserable and grossly repulsive sins for their triumphant beauty is an effective reminder of what pride really is. Perhaps there is present also the peacock's other traditional meaning as the bird of real triumph, of immortality, replaced in Lucifera's triumphal car by the sick and deadly sins.

Lucifera, then, is something much worse than mere vanity, love of jewelled display, social arrogance. She is pride in its fullest Christian sense, the Satanic exaltation of self to the place of God. Spenser's imagery generates a curious heady excitement through its stress on Lucifera's restless mounting energy and her intensity of brightness; it is easy to feel the dangerous attractiveness of such aspiration as this, so like the nobility of the ancient world. Among the wretched captives in Lucifera's dungeon are 'High Caesar', Pompey, Romulus, Sylla, Marius, 'High Minded Cleopatra', as well as others like Alexander, Nebuchadnezzar and Antiochus who more openly acted the 'onely God'. The appeal of Lucifera's passionate glory is not that of worldly advancement merely, it is a more insidious and more deadly reliance on, and so glorification of, self which can masquerade as high minded virtue crying for other worlds to conquer.

The house of Lucifera is described with a richness and solemnity which mark it as of profound importance in Red Crosse's story. It is one of the finer passages in the first book, complex but exact in every detail, and as full an imaginative presentation of a particular state of mind as is the similarly precise and complex Bower of Bliss. Lucifera's power is genuine and exciting, for her greatest followers are those by whom the pursuit of power is felt as a spiritual aspiration. Red Crosse does not succumb, but he is touched by it, and his responses are muddled and inadequate. He keeps his armour and will have nothing to do with the macabre outing that Lucifera and Duessa take in the company of the sins because they are beneath him as a 'warlike swaine'. But he does stay a while in 'that sad House of Pryde', and makes present of his services to Lucifera, for he is tainted by a tendency to self-reliance (which must in this context be also self-aggrandisement) which was the downfall of some of the greatest of the pagans. It is here that he wins the second of his Pyrrhic victories, another battle that should never have had to be fought, and though he escapes it is only to fall at once into a captivity like that of Lucifera's prisoners.

In the House of Pride, Red Crosse meets the second of the three sarazin brothers, Sansjoy, who attacks him as a direct consequence of his earlier defeat of Sansfoy. In killing Sansfoy, he had saved his faith only to lose it in giving it to Duessa. The error is so fundamental that it leads inevitably to mounting disaster, his own unrecognized treachery leaves him at the mercy of Duessa's. The three brothers, all of them lacking the Christian faith as the first brother's name implies, live by a kind of non-Christian ethic, of which the necessity of vengeance is an important part. Thus both surviving brothers pursue Red Crosse to avenge Sansfoy's death. Sansloy, who attacks Archimago in his disguise as Red Crosse, is not simply lawless; he lacks the new law of the gospels, the law of mercy, and lives by his own mistaken and cruel law of wrath. His fury is stressed in every line as he hurtles upon Archimago behind the shield which bears his name in letters of blood. Standing over the defeated magician, he delivers a proud speech which sets out the ancient law of revenge:[8]

> Lo there the worthie meed
> Of him that slew Sansfoy with bloody knife!
> Henceforth his ghost, freed from repining strife,
> In peace may passen over Lethe lake,
> When mourning altars, purgd with enimies life,
> The black infernall Furies doen aslake:
> Life from Sansfoy thou tookst, Sansloy shall from thee take.
>
> (iii, 36)

A life for a life; and the different ethic with which Una appeals to him is brushed aside.

> Enough is, that thy foe doth vanquisht stand
> Now at thy mercy: mercy not withstand.
>
> (iii, 37)

---

[8] There is a sense in which pagan and Mosaic justice (as practical applications of natural law) can be taken as one in their joint contrast to Christian forgiveness.

15

Sansjoy encounters the real Red Crosse with the same furious urge for vengeance, and he and Duessa speak of Sansfoy's ghost in the same desolate pagan terms as Sansloy had done. The ghost wanders pathetically on the Stygian shores, unable to cross until the furies are placated by the blood of his killer. In Sansjoy, all the hopeless sadness of his brothers' faith and law becomes manifest; the sadness, too, of the sad House of Pride. For the brothers live to themselves, taking upon themselves as a solemn duty even that vengeance which is the Lord's, and Lucifera's unhappy palace, where pleasure coaches are drawn by images of sickness and death, is a fitting place for Red Crosse to encounter the profound sadness of those who depend upon self and not upon the mercy and grace of God. Red Crosse defeats both the brothers whom he meets, but in each case the struggle leaves its mark in a twisted faith, a deep uneasiness, an unacknowledged sense of guilt. His sober sad reliance on himself, so alien to what Spenser (or Luther, Aquinas, or Calvin in their different ways) means by faith, leads him not indeed into full Satanic pride or into paganism but into grave spiritual danger. He who relies on himself will fear punishment when he fails, as he must, to achieve the standards he has set for himself.

Red Crosse is moving towards the sorrow and fear of the law of guilt and vengeance, away from the true faith of salvation in Christ. All the ambiguity of Christian chivalry, the fighting which is yet sinful, comes into play as in the vision of the New Jerusalem to suggest that these are enemies whom Red Crosse should never have had to face. He has to fight them and to incur blood guiltiness because he has been unfaithful to Una. Thus the battles with Sansfoy and Sansjoy mark Red Crosse's increasing 'feare of doing ought amis', the dread of punishment and of the sad cycle of assertion, failure, and revenge. In fighting Sansjoy he still 'strives for right', but the words 'praise and honour' (v, 7) may —in this book—suggest that it is a too self-reliant right: and the dubious 'quickening faith' that saves him is aroused not by Una as in the battle with Error but by the faithless Duessa. Duessa is able to snatch Sansfoy away just at the moment when Red Crosse's words seem to show how close he is to acceptance of the brothers' ethic: to Sansjoy's taunt that he is to be sent with a message of release to the Stygian lake where Sansfoy sits wailing, he replies

16

Goe now, proud miscreant,
Thy selfe thy message do to german deare;
Alone he, wandring, thee too long doth want;
Goe say, his foe thy shield with his doth beare.

(v, 13)

His own thinking has become joyless, and he cannot kill Sansjoy. His own world is now too like that to which Duessa carries his wounded enemy, the place of Ixion and Tantalus where perpetual punishment fits a sin momentary in the doing but eternalized in hell. Here the law of guilt and revenge is once more enunciated, solemnly and emphatically, by Night:

Yet shall they not escape so freely all;
For some shall pay the price of others guilt:
And he, the man that made Sansfoy to fall,
Shall with his owne blood price that he hath spilt.

(v, 26)

The episode, magnificent in its evocation of the endless sadness of evil tied to its own immoral morality, shows us the grief which lies in wait for Red Crosse; his own fault has led him too close to the sorrows of the children of night.

To this shadowy pagan hell with its wailing ghosts Sansjoy is brought to be healed by 'sad Aesculapius'. It has been pointed out that the descent is a version of that of Aeneas; perhaps, too, it was in part suggested by whatever form of the St. George plays may have been current in Spenser's time. The plays and references which survive, now of course very garbled, indicate that one or both participants in the battle, St. George and the Turkish Knight, underwent death and a subsequent revival at the hands of the Doctor or some similar figure. A writer so sensitive to the meanings of old rituals and legends might well be struck by such a survival as this, and his habitually syncretic habit of mind would, if he knew such plays, have related them to Christianity and to those proud and pathetic attempts of paganism to attain eternal life through the efforts of the self of which Aesculapius is an example particularly 'sad'. It is sadness which is the dominant impression of the hell that the children of night have made for themselves under the old law, binding themselves to an endless cycle of vengeance, punishment which they must endure as well as inflict. In one stanza we move from the

17

hopelessness of Aesculapius—'Why fearest thou, that canst not hope for thing'—to the dungeon of Lucifera's palace, for the two are akin although in hell the issues are clearer. Red Crosse escapes the dungeon, but his own sadness is lingering now with Sansjoy among the failed attempts to escape from vengeance into eternal life. In guilt and sorrow and fear of punishment now that the light of his own virtue has failed him, he is ready for a prison of his own making. When he is safe away, he performs of his own volition the action towards which his enemies have been working: he takes off his armour. He has not been defeated in battle, nor could he readily be while protected by the armour of God. But saddened by failure, frightened by the danger so narrowly avoi ¹ed, he seeks escape in forgetfulness. Like the nymph whose wateɪ₃ he drinks, he has 'Satt downe to rest in middest of the race', forgetting the solemn warning which accompanies the gift of the armour:

> Wherefore take unto you the whole armour of God, that ye may be able to withstand in the evil day, and having done all, to stand.

The battle never stops, since 'we wrestle not against flesh and blood, but against principalities, against powers, against the rulers of the darkness of this world, against spiritual wickedness in high places'. And when his enemy comes upon him, the shame of the knight who has betrayed his trust and is found in the evil day unarmed and 'Pourd out in loosnesse on the grassy grownd' deprives him of all strength.

The state of mind in which Red Crosse is captured by Orgoglio is made clear enough. He is faint, powerless, hopeless, sad, and above all disgraced, like the nymph punished by Diana.

> Who haplesse, and eke hopelesse, all in vaine
> Did to him pace, sad battaile to darrayne,
> Disarmd, disgraste, and inwardly dismayde.
>
> (vii, 11)

Una later repeats the words when she tells Arthur how Orgoglio

> him disarmed, dissolute, dismaid,
> Unwares surprised.
>
> (vii, 51)

The meaning of the Orgoglio episode is conveyed not by such labels as the giant's name—which must certainly have some connection with pride—but by the nature of Red Crosse's experience as a shamed and disarmed knight. And what is conveyed, very vividly, is utter hopelessness, dull dispirited grief, the atmosphere of the hell of Night and Aesculapius realized in Red Crosse's consciousness. Now he sees where his life has been leading, and the battle with Orgoglio is lost before it begins. As so often in this first book, where to relax even for a moment is to invite disaster, the coming of Orgoglio is a sudden eruption of horror into a scene of carelessness. Before he is even within sight, he is preceded by the numbing terror which is his chief attribute and effect. The knight

> heard a dreadfull sownd,
> Which through the wood loud bellowing did rebownd,
> That all the earth for terror seemd to shake,
> And trees did tremble.
>
> (vii, 7)

'Astownd' by the atmosphere of dread he tries to buckle on his armour, but the weapons are 'unready'. There is scarcely time to snatch the abandoned 'sword of the spirit, which is the word of God', none to get his shield of faith, before Orgoglio is upon him.

No creature in *The Faerie Queene* is more overwhelmingly strong, or brings with him such demoralizing terror. He fills the whole place, his height seeming to threat the sky, the ground groaning for fear beneath his tread. His club, though it misses Red Crosse, stuns him with the mere wind of its passing, like the hell-made explosive engines of war. Orgoglio's power is enormous, yet it depends less upon his own strength than upon the paralysing fear which accompanies him; he is unconquerable— until the coming of Arthur—because he is able to make people believe that he is so, that there is nothing however terrible that he can not or will not do. In fact his huge size is empty of all but wind, like the hollow womb of his mother earth; he is a

> monstrous masse of earthly slyme,
> Puft up with emptie wynd, and fild with sinfull cryme.
>
> (vii, 9)

But since he is felt to be overwhelming he is so, and against such 'huge force and insupportable mayne' Red Crosse has no inner resources left. His sense of unbearable isolation is felt through the picture of the giant before whom even trees tremble, and

19

whose very weapon is an oak unnaturally torn from his mother's bowels, advancing upon the small unarmed figure. To Red Crosse, the great sword he holds now seems only a 'bootlesse single blade', he is alone, without hope, and worst of all 'inwardly dismayde', felled like a 'slombred sencelesse corse' by the wind of Orgoglio's weapon. The grace of God, not his own feeble efforts, saves him from death, but he knows nothing of this; to himself, he is abandoned, 'this man forlorne', man who sees too late the lonely consequences of trusting to his own force. Duessa begs for his life, for her power over the world depends upon the enslavement, not the annihilation, of those she has betrayed into a false faith, but he is thrown into the living death of Orgoglio's dungeon.

Red Crosse's pathetically unequal fight is clearly against something within himself; outward persecution alone would not reduce him to what has been rightly called the spiritual death of his imprisonment.[9] He has failed through inward dismay, and bound in the dungeon as in hell his sense of his own nothingness makes him long for the annihilation he has escaped. He is not yet one of the holy martyrs who cry on God for vengeance beneath the altar stone but who have been victorious in death; at this point in his story he seems utterly to have failed. Yet the failure is the beginning of his success, for at least he knows now that if any strength he has it is to ill. Orgoglio is, in some sense, 'the knight's fallen state',[10] and the encounter is Red Crosse's horrified realization of the results of his turning to self, his pride. Without Una and without his Christian armour, his selfhood finds itself alone with the monstrous consequence of empty pride, which he has no hope of withstanding. This, I take it, is why Orgoglio has such marked associations with pride as well as with overwhelming horror. His pride appears in his seeming 'to threat the skye' like the rebel giants who threatened the gods, in his stalking steps, his power grown great

> Through arrogant delight
> Of th' high descent whereof he was yborne,
> And through presumption of his matchlesse might.

(vii, 10)

[9] Even when we were dead in sins, hath quickened us together with Christ (Ephesians ii, 5).

[10] A. C. Hamilton, *The Structure of Allegory in The Faerie Queene* (Oxford, 1961), p. 75.

He has something in common with Lucifera, who similarly challenges heaven and who takes delight in an ancestry which she persuades herself is greater than it is. If Red Crosse had never done service to Lucifera he need not have fallen to Orgoglio, for in relation to the dismayed knight the giant's castle is the reverse side of Lucifera's palace, the sudden apprehension of the results of a fancied self-sufficiency.

As an endeavouring Christian, Red Crosse has escaped the fate of Alexander and Caesar to fall into a worse one, for the pagans after all were acting by the highest standards they knew. The horror of Orgoglio's dungeon is made much more real to us than the captivity of the ancients in the House of Pride, for it is the recognition of spiritual nothingness, an experience one may suppose closed to the pre-Christian world and more terrible, more truly deathlike, than any desolation known to it. But of course the central paradox of Spenser's faith is present; the greater depths may lead to a greater height, and Red Crosse's fall is the fortunate beginning of his rise. He now knows himself, but the knowledge of self has overwhelmed him because as yet he does not know God, he is not seeing with the eye of faith. Thus Orgoglio comes to him under the aspect of punishment, and he does not fight, he is flung down by the terror of a stroke of super-human power. He falls before the recognition that his force is weakness and his efforts are pride, and he scarcely resists the vengeance which he expects as the inevitable result of his failure. Already touched by the joyless law of the sarazin brothers, he sinks beneath the weight of sin and its expected punishment. The meeting with Orgoglio is a complex experience of numbing fear, dismay, and shame; and vengeance, or the hopeless expectation of vengeance, is a great part of it and a great part of Orgoglio's power. He is a bogy created by the guilt of man. This aspect of his nature is further stressed when Arthur comes to the rescue of the imprisoned knight. The imagery of earthquakes and of Jove's lightning, signs of divine wrath, reinforces the earlier simile of the 'devilish yron engin, wrought/In deepest hell'.[11] Against Arthur's diamond shield of clear spiritual knowledge Orgoglio's false power cannot survive, and he reads his end 'in that bright

[11] See, for the theme of vengeance as part of the Orgoglio incident, S. K. Heninger, Jr., 'The Orgoglio Episode in *The Faerie Queene*', ELH, XXVI, 1959.

shield', falling with 'no powre to hurt, nor to defend'. When he is killed, his huge windfilled body goes down like an empty bladder.

The coming of Arthur is another in that sequence of sharp and sudden contrasts through which the dramatic tensions of the Christian life are so vividly expressed in this book. Into the atmosphere of deathly hopelessness and grief rides a figure of vitality and victorious power, with chinkless armour and jewelled baldric, glittering in glancing light and shining far away. The contrast with the wretched disarmed knight makes itself felt immediately, and one begins to notice such details as the tamed dragon which spreads its golden wings over Arthur's helmet: Arthur's dragon is now a part of his strength, Red Crosse's is still to fight. But the contrast consists not so much in these particular details as in the air of easy triumph, gay irresistible power, which surrounds Arthur and has always been so lacking in Red Crosse. Most heartlifting of all is the stanza (vii, 32) which describes the bunch of hair at the very top of Arthur's crest, sprinkled with pearl and gold and seeming to shake and dance for jollity

> Like to an almond tree ymounted hye
> On top of greene Selinis all alone,
> With blossoms brave bedecked daintily;
> Whose tender locks do tremble every one
> At everie little breath, that under heaven is blowne.

The almond is a symbol of divine approval, because of Aaron's budding rod which yielded almonds and so marked him as the chosen priest of the Lord; but far more important than the traditional symbolism is the effect inherent in the image, the lightness and life and untroubled joy, the responsiveness to each breath of wind under heaven, each motion of the spirit: the sense of something high, remote, and untouchable which is at the same time sensitive and alive and delightedly aware.

Against this free and joyous power Orgoglio, depending for his strength on human distortions of the truth which Arthur knows, cannot exist for long, and we feel at once that this is so. But Arthur's words to Una have a direct bearing on our understanding of this easy mastery, and of Red Crosse's struggle:

> 'Despaire breeds not', quoth he, 'where faith is staid.'
> 'No faith so fast,' quoth she, 'but flesh does paire.'
> 'Flesh may empaire,' quoth he, 'but reason can repaire.'
>
> (vii, 41)

22

Red Crosse's eye of flesh sees the punishment which is the law of the flesh, and it leads him to despair; Arthur's eye of reason, a stayed faith, sees the true law of mercy. This law he at once puts into execution, redeeming Red Crosse from his bands (ix, 1), the hell he believes himself doomed to. Arthur's descent into the dungeon has been shown to be a parallel to the harrowing of hell: it is so because Christ's death, descent, and resurrection have cancelled the old debt of sin. Red Crosse has to experience this truth if he is to realize that he is wasting all 'his better dayes' in a prison of his own making. The opening stanza of the eighth canto—the canto which describes the redeeming of Red Crosse— functions as a more abstract statement of the acted meaning:

> Ay me! how many perils doe enfold
> The righteous man, to make him daily fall,
> Were not that Heavenly Grace doth him uphold,
> And stedfast Truth acquite him out of all!
> Her love is firme, her care continuall,
> So oft as he, through his own foolish pride
> Or weaknes, is to sinfull bands made thrall:
> Els should this Redcrosse Knight in bands have dyde,
> For whose deliverance she this Prince doth thether guyd.

Grace has already saved the knight from annihilation, supporting him in the weakness his pride has brought him to; now gospel truth is to show him that through grace he can be free of hell and victorious in Christ.

It is this inner meaning of the incident which is surely the most important, but to it is attached the consideration of what to Spenser was the outer, physical manifestation of Orgoglio's power, a power battening on man's conviction of sin and building upon this foundation of human suffering an edifice of pride and persecution. The false expectation of vengeance produces the false claim to be the distributor of vengeance, and so Orgoglio's castle is a place of persecution where from beneath the altar the blessed spirits of Christian martyrs cry to God for punishment upon the unjust avenger. Similarly John Bale's *Ymage of Bothe Churches* relates 'the souls of them that were slain for the word of God' (Revelation vi, 9) and were laid under the altar, to the persecutions of the Papal Antichrist, who came to persecute and judge, and if any gainsay him, 'they carye to slee bothe soule and bodye'.[12] As in Dante, the association of the harlot of Revelation with the giant becomes an image of the Papacy 'committing fornication with the kings of the earth', and Orgoglio's vengeance falls not upon the unrighteous but on those who, in Bishop Bale's words, held to 'the undefyled worde of God' and 'the syncere testymony of Jesu which they had by the gift of his onelye sprete'. The old man Ignaro is the keeper of Orgoglio's castle because the Papacy depends upon widespread ignorance of the true doctrine, as Blenerhasset's Alecto tells the ruler of hell:

> The worlde thou knowest, I all the worlde was thine,
> Thy caves were cramd, when heaven all emptie was,
> Blinde ignorance that mighty mother mine
> Shee ruld, shee rainde, she brought it so to passe
> That all was thine, even shee maintained the masse,
> And shee it was which gave the triple crowne
> To him of Rome.[13]

The connections which could exist for Protestants of the sixteenth century between pride, the old law, ignorance, and Popery are suggested in William Perkins's *Commentarie upon the Epistle to the Galatians*:

> In this preface, first Paul meetes with the pride of mans nature, whereby the Galatians went about to establish their own righteousnes by the lawe, when he saith, *ye that will be under the law, &c.* With this pride were the Iewes tainted, Rom. x, 3, and the young Prince that came to Christ and said, *Good master what must I doe to be saved?* And the Papists of our time, who will not be subiect to the iustice of God, but set up their owne iustice in the keeping of the law. The like doe the ignorant people among us, who hold that they are able to fulfill the lawe, and that they are to be saved thereby.

---

[12] Bale's play *King John*, in which 'The Pope' and 'Usurped Power' are two names for the same character, is a good example of the way in which actual historical persons or institutions could be readily seen as making 'actual the preordained patterns of vice and virtue'. [G. K. Hunter, 'English Folly and Italian Vice', *Jacobean Theatre*, Stratford-upon-Avon Studies, I (London, 1960), p. 103.] Spenser's way of relating his invented characters both to moral concepts and to real persons is quite the ordinary fluent mental habit of his time.

[13] Thomas Blenerhasset, *A Revelation of the True Minerva* (1582), ed. J. W. Bennett (New York, 1941), C2. For a discussion of resemblances between Blenerhasset's verses and *The Faerie Queene* see the Introduction, pp. xi–xiii.

And when they say, they look to be saved by their faith, they understand thereby their fidelitie, that is, their good dealing. . . . This
ignorance was to the Iewes as a vaile before their eies in the reading
of the lawe, 2 Cor. iii, 14. And this ignorance has blinded the Papist
at this day: for he supposeth that the Gospell is nothing els but the
law of Moses, and that Christ indeed is but an instrument to make
us keepers of the lawe, and consequently saviours of selves.[14]

Equally, therefore, ignorance of the true faith is what enables
Orgoglio to hold Red Crosse imprisoned, and as Arthur descends
to rescue him the emphasis moves once more to the inner drama
of faith. Orgoglio can take the shape of physical persecution
because ignorant fear has allowed him to do so,[15] but it is that
fear and inward dismay which is the book's chief concern.[16]
When Red Crosse emerges from his spiritual death it is not
through any victory of his own but through Christ's, of which
revealed truth has reminded him, and the effects of his sin and
his incomprehension are still upon him. He no longer feels abandoned, the 'man forlorne', but he is still profoundly sad, 'The
chearelesse man, whom sorow did dismay' (viii, 43) suffering
from a long famine of that food of the spirit of which Duessa's
treachery has deprived him. Una sees his weakness, but she is
unable to keep him from the encounter with Despair, the morbid
introspection which

[14] Cambridge, 1609, p. 344.
[15] The keys which Ignaro carries but cannot use (he is blind and the
keys are rusted) may lend support to such an interpretation. 'In Protestant
symbolism the word of God is both a *key* and a *sword*: the word of God is
the only means of salvation and the only instrument of damnation.'
[G. W. Whiting, *Milton and This Pendant World* (Austin, Texas, 1958),
p. 35.] The power residing in God's word is falsely usurped to himself by
the Pope. Mr. Whiting discusses this symbolism and its variants and cites
Tyndale, Bullinger, Bale, and others. In Spenser Ignaro holds, but is
powerless to use, the keys, but Arthur can do so. It is noticeable however
that there is no key to the locked dungeon Red Crosse is in, and the door
has to be broken. This does enforce more dramatically Arthur's Christ-
like power as the harrower of hell and as grace.
[16] Disdaine in Book VI, cantos vii and viii, who is 'sib to great Orgoglio'
and who like him stalks proudly and carries a club as deadly as lightning,
is another figure who combines 'inner' and 'outer' significance. He can
punish Mirabella because she believes her punishment to be just, and his
power depends upon her assent. She prevents Arthur from killing him
because his death will involve hers; he is the result of her own past and
repented disdain.

like dropping honny, mealt'h
Into the heart, and searcheth every vaine.

(ix, 31)

This meeting is the last struggle with the concept of vengeance. The fleeing knight is staring-eyed with terror, 'as one that had aspyde/Infernall furies' (ix, 24), and Despair's long yearning speech is an insidiously beautiful presentation of the theme of inescapable punishment for sin.[17] In Despair's soft cadences, it becomes a temptation to Red Crosse to repeat in more fatal form his earlier lapse of disarming, to give up the unending watchfulness which has already proved almost too much even for this potential saint. Again and again comes the flesh's false doctrine, 'For life must life, and blood must blood repay', which because it is based on the partial truth of God's inexorable justice can make suicide seem not only attractive but right, an act of acceptance of the divine will, an avoidance of the sins which God abhors. God is good, therefore just, therefore avenging: the theme proceeds through repeated lines and phrases. 'Who then can strive with strong necessitie . . . If in true ballaunce thou wilt weigh thy state . . . Against the day of wrath . . . Is not He just . . . Is not His lawe, Let every sinner die:/Die shall all flesh?' (ix, 42–7) With visions of hell and wrath and the 'righteous sentence of th'Almighties law' before his eyes, Red Crosse lifts the knife, but now Una is with him to save him from Despair, as from Error, with a ringing call to the true faith.

In heavenly mercies hast thou not a part?
Why shouldst thou then despeire, that chosen art?
Where justice growes, there grows eke greter grace.

(ix, 53)

---

[17] It seems to a modern reader entirely proper that Despair's grave-like dwelling should be the haunt of the owl, bird of night and ill-omened shriek. But we inherit in vaguer form more precise connotations which Spenser excellently exploits in his picture of 'the ghastly owl, /Shrieking his balefull note, which ever drave /Far from that haunt all other chearefull fowle'. In medieval tradition the smaller soaring birds of day, driven from Despair's cave by the owl, connote spiritual values, the dark owl the conscious denial of these values. See J. Rosenberg, 'On the Meaning of a Bosch Drawing', *Essays in Honor of Erwin Panofsky* (New York, 1961), p. 424. The more general connotations (Satan, solitude, wisdom—Despair *seems* wise) are also relevant.

It is the narrowest of escapes, for the knight's faith is still not sufficiently firm and enlightened to overcome his acute sense of personal sin. Knowing very well now that he has no strength except to ill, he has not grasped the rest—'all the good is Gods'. Judged by the carnal reason Despair's argument is sound enough: the man who sins is damned and his life is an offence to God. Only a baptized reason can really accept that salvation depends not on our goodness but on God's. The conviction of sin, which the old law produces, is a necessary part of Red Crosse's development, but alone it is negative and destructive, 'accusat et praeterrefacit conscientiam, iram Dei annuntiat et in desperationem adigit'.[18] Red Crosse's lack of knightliness is, throughout his story, the lack of a true and saving faith, and without this he will lose the dragon fight as so many before him have lost it 'for want of faith'. 'Fie, fie, faint hearted knight', cries Una, enraged at last by such feebleness,

[18] Luther, quoted by B. A. Gerrish, op. cit., p. 108, n. 5. Henry Smith, in a sermon on the text 'Rejoice evermore', tells us that we must sorrow and rejoice, fear and hope, together: 'That is, have one eye to the law, to keep us from presumption, and another eye to the gospel, to keep us from despair.' And again: 'But when you forget to rejoice in the Lord, then you begin to muse, and after to fear, and after to distrust, and at last to despair, and then every thought seems to be a sin against the Holy Ghost.' Also: 'Every care which is not of God, is of Satan, and we may not bear that which God commandeth us to cast upon him. Should I hang my joy, my faith, and my hope, because I have sinned, as Judas hanged himself?' [*Works* (London, 1866), Vol. I, pp. 394, 322.] In referring to Luther, I do not mean to place Spenser as a follower of Luther in theology; nor do references to Calvinistic or Puritan thinkers suggest that he was a Calvinist. *The Faerie Queene* is a Christian poem; for all its antipathy to the Papal power, it is more concerned with those attitudes which all the churches have in common than with those in which they differ. If it is necessary to define it further, Professor Whitaker's conclusion, that it is the poem of a conservative Anglican, seems clearly right. And as Professor Whitaker says, 'the Anglican position was a compromise, in which theology was largely Protestant while ritual was largely Catholic, and theology, in turn, was a blend of elements from Lutheranism and Calvinism with indigenous ideas'. [Virgil K. Whitaker, *The Religious Basis of Spenser's Thought* (Stanford, 1950), p. 31.] Marlowe's Faustus, in the opening scene of the play, finds the Bible message as forbidding as does Despair:

Why then belike
We must sin, and so consequently die.

What meanest thou by this reprochfull strife?
Is this the battaile, which thou vauntst to fight
With that fire-mouthed dragon, horrible and bright?
(ix, 52)

Again he has almost withdrawn from the only battle it is his business to fight, and she hurries him off to be disciplined out of his spinelessness in Dame Caelia's house.

The House of Holiness is by no means a piece of slick machinery. If it stood alone it would seem over schematic, but coming as it does after nine cantos of very human frailties and agonies it illuminates the nature of Red Crosse's failure, while on the other hand the failure gives reality and significance to the emblematic figures. Fidelia especially, exemplifying the virtue Red Crosse finds so hard to achieve, is moving because in her is summed up so much that we have seen of the darkness and difficulty of faith to the well-intentioned man whose carnal reason naturally draws him back to the sadness and fear of the old law. She is not gay, or easily victorious; she holds the chalice of faith, and in it a serpent 'That horrour made to all that did behold'. The cup with the serpent, the poisoned chalice that will not harm the man of faith, is an attribute of St. John the Evangelist, and it reminds us too of the Grail romances and the perilous quest; it is both life-giving and dangerous,[19] like the dread of sin which Red Crosse has felt so deeply and must learn to make a part of his faith. Fidelia is constant in spite of, or perhaps it is because of, the serpent; so must he be. In her other hand she holds

> A booke that was both signd and seald with blood,
> Wherin darke things were writt, hard to be understood.
> (x, 13)

This is the Testament, which Red Crosse has given to Arthur, but his volume

> Was writt with golden letters rich and brave;
> A worke of wondrous grace, and hable soules to save.
> (ix, 19)

So it is, but it has to be understood first, and under Fidelia's

---

[19] The serpent can signify both danger, or warning, and renewal of life. It is associated with the healing god Aesculapius and, in Christian symbolism, with Christ upon the cross.

tutelage as she opens his dull eyes to the light[20] the golden letters
are seen to be written in blood, and to speak of the death and
the salvation which that blood brought: there is justice in it, but
there is also grace, it can kill, but it rouses to new life.

> And that her sacred Booke, with blood ywritt,
> That none could reade, except she did them teach,
> She unto him disclosed every whitt,
> And heavenly documents thereout did preach,
> That weaker witt of man could never reach,
> Of God, of grace, of justice, of free will,
> That wonder was to heare her goodly speach:
> For she was hable with her wordes to kill,
> And rayse againe to life the hart that she did thrill.
>
> (x, 19)

Similarly Speranza is no facilely optimistic figure, she is steadfast
despite the dread and anguish in her heart; these are emblems
made out of human fear and indomitable courage.

So in the House of Holiness Red Crosse, having been admitted
by the true Humility and Zeal of which his self-abasement and
earlier self-reliance have been only wrong (because self-centred)
versions, learns fully at last that the 'witt of man', 'fleshly might,/
And vaine assurance of mortality' will not prevail against spiritual
foes. Here for the first time the knight takes off his armour guilt-
lessly, not to give up the Christian warfare but the better to wage
it through the discipline of obedience. He relives his past experiences, within himself and in new knowledge and understanding,
fasting 'in a darksome lowly place far in' as he had fasted in
Orgoglio's dungeon, but now purposefully, to heal inward corruption. The 'paines of hell' now lead not to despair but to repentance, and when he is brought back, cured, to Una, she touches
at once on his weakness, begging him

> Himselfe to cherish, and consuming thought
> To put away out of his carefull brest.
>
> (x, 29)

His failure in faith has involved a failure in love, but his new
understanding of God's love for man will produce a new sort of
kindness to himself (he will demand less of his own efforts) and

[20] The eyes of your understanding being enlightened; that ye may know
what is the hope of his calling (Ephesians i, 18).

to others. Faith will issue in a knowledge of the divine love, but also in the works of love. In all this he is now instructed as the 'unacquainted guest' of Charissa, traditionally surrounded by her children, and Mercy helps him to show to others the mercy he has received from God. The fourth beadman, one of his teachers, redeems prisoners because God has redeemed us:

> God to us forgiveth every howre
> Much more then that, why they in bands were layd,[21]
> And He, that harrowd hell with heavie stowre,
> The faulty soules from thence brought to his heavenly bowre.

(x, 40)

Among the seven beadmen Red Crosse learns to do 'godly thing', 'godly works of almes and charitee', turning his attention away from self to others who are 'images of God in earthly clay', and thus his mortal life is perfectly framed in holy righteousness.

From this point the knight's quest rises swiftly to its climax. He ascends the mount of Contemplation, whose likeness both to Sinai where Moses received

> writt in stone
> With bloody letters by the hand of God,
> The bitter doome of death and balefull mone

(x, 53)

and to the Mount of Olives, proclaims that he now fully comprehends the truths of the old law and of the new, and then comes the three day fight with the dragon. In this, and in the marriage celebrations which follow, we are in the realm of high ritual, for Red Crosse is now no longer the touchingly frail and human knight but the warrior saint, perfect enough to re-enact Christ's victory over sin and death as Arthur has re-enacted the harrowing of hell. The battle is moving, but impersonally so; there can be no intimacy with the new Red Crosse, 'this man of God'. Yet its details still refer us back to the old failures now redeemed and surpassed, and the dragon aims as Duessa had done to divest the knight of his armour, and above all of the shield. On the first day it breathes a flame which makes the burning armour a torment to him, so that he 'thought his armes to leave, and helmet to unlace'. But it is impossible now that the knight should abandon

---

[21] Compare canto viii, 38 and canto ix, 1.

his 'godly armes', though the Christian armour can become an agony under the assault of evil. His baptism in the spirit has supplied him with reserves of strength, and he arises newborn like the eagle[22] from the Well of Life. On the second day the dragon tries to wrest the shield from his hand, but again power is renewed from the Tree of Life, and the battle is finished on the third day with the slow ritual fall of the enemy. Red Crosse has fought to the end with no further loss of the armour of God, but he has done so in the strength of the victory of Christ. The paradisiacal Tree of Life, whose balm refreshes him on the second night, is richly symbolical, being a type of the cross, the lignum vitae;[23] it is the sacrifice of Christ which enables him to conquer on the third day. When he does so, he becomes through Christ a second Adam, restoring Paradise; and so the Tree of Life is (again traditionally) set alongside the first Adam's tree, of the knowledge of good and evil, and there is pastoral imagery of trees and fountain and dancing maidens fresh as flowers, and Una's green garland linked not now with Flora but with Diana. For Red Crosse, Eden is restored, and of this particular quest no more remains but the marriage festival whose music blends with the heavenly noise of the angels' song.

The book closes with hieratic praise of the victorious saint: Red Crosse's struggle against the rulers of the darkness of this world has been stark and austere, and it ends in the exalted bliss of sainthood. This could have been a remote and even unsympathetic book, committed as it is to the soul's journey towards the heavenly kingdom, for there is one aspect of the chivalric tradition

[22] The eagle, which periodically renewed its youth by flying towards the sun and then plunging into water, was a symbol of resurrection but also of the new life of baptism and the strengthening by grace of the Christian soul. William Perkins describes the heartening effect, in times of difficulty, of recalling one's baptism. 'Baptisme is of great force, to releeve the heart in distresse. For when any child of God, feeles himselfe loden with the burden of his sinnes; the consideration and remembrance thereof, that God hath pardoned them all, and given him a speciall, and certaine pledge of his pardon in baptism; will serve to stay and support his soule.' [*The Whole Treatise of the Cases of Conscience* (Cambridge, 1609), p. 92.]

[23] For further meanings see J. M. Steadman, 'The "Tree of Life" Symbolism in Paradise Regain'd', R.E.S., n.s. XI, 1960, pp. 384–91. The well and the tree are both figures of Christ in Bale's *Ymage of Bothe Churches*, the well being the refreshing spirit of Christ and the tree Christ as the Church.

that the knight has not lived out, the succouring of the weak and distressed. His battles, necessarily, have been in, and for, his own soul or for the release of Adam who is himself. For Red Crosse there is only a narrow way, in a sense a narrow view too, since all is danger—'all that is in the world, the lust of the flesh, and the lust of the eyes, and the pride of life'—except the constancy of faith and the upward gaze of hope. Yet it is, none the less, a moving and intimate book, because the immense difficulty of the way and the danger of distraction is made so real through the faults and fears of the very human hero, and also because the active charity which Red Crosse cannot exercise on his quest is present in the humble and loving service of the beadmen to 'the wondrous workmanship of Gods own mould'. The knight's relationship to God has been set right, now he can return among his fellows, and the earthly kingdom is changed from a place of spiritual danger to one of spiritual opportunity. Among the beadmen we meet for the first time the gentler virtues, humility, loving kindness, the courtesy of complete simplicity, which are to be further explored in Spenser's sixth legend. The second beadman is described in the accents of the good old shepherd Meliboe:[24]

> The grace of God he layd up still in store,
> Which as a stocke he left into his seede:
> He had enough: what need him care for more?
> And had he lesse, yet some he would give to the pore.
>
> (x, 38)

The ritual act of the slaying of the dragon is preceded by those works of love which are the necessary product of a true and lively faith.

For Red Crosse's God is known to us, after all, in his 'images ... in earthly clay', and Spenser is very much the poet of humanity and of human relationships. It is typical of him, and of his feeling for God's human images, that he should dwell on compassion and kindness, as the perfection of 'mortall life', before the final battle; and it begins the movement downwards and outwards to the mortal concerns of Faeryland continued in the second book. Guyon's story of Temperance enacts Red Crosse's battle in another way; his endeavours are all in the earthly king-

[24] Compare VI, ix, 21.

dom, yet it is the same battle, and without what Red Crosse has done in Christ it could not be won. The legend of Holiness apart, the whole poem moves among specifically mundane, though not necessarily worldly, concerns. The knights are good men (and woman, for Britomart is one of the greatest and best) but they are not saints. Guyon, the loneliest of all of them except Red Crosse, plods on foot along most of his path to self-control and complete humility, hearing no angels sing, never seeing the cherub who guards him. Britomart and Calidore ride in full knightly chivalry among thronging fellow humans who need to be helped or, sometimes, disciplined: Artegall must deal justice among individuals and states. Red Crosse stands behind them all, and often in their quests we are reminded of his; but perhaps we are recalled most often and most touchingly to the beadmen's holy hospital. The quest of Red Crosse in his godly arms is centred upon St. Paul's image in sixth Ephesians, but the whole of that fine and theologically influential epistle has relevance to the legend of Holiness, and not least the apostle's exhortation to the charity and compassion which are as necessary as the Christian combat in a world where we are members one of another:

> And be ye kind one to another, tenderhearted, forgiving one another, even as God for Christ's sake hath forgiven you.

In this sense also the story of the warrior saint is moralized by fierce wars and faithful loves.

Chapter Two

THE IMAGE OF MORTALITY

IN the legend of Temperance we find ourselves labouring with Guyon among the detailed difficulties of that world whose biggest issues have been mapped out for us by the victorious saint. The adjustment in tone, the different point of view which Temperance is to give, is lightly suggested in the proem, where we are told that Faeryland is a mirror of that most ordinary of places, the poet's and the reader's own country. It is a reminder, in effect, of the poem's sober truth. Faeryland exists, for it is built out of the concerns of every day, its invisibility no more prejudices its existence than the invisibility of Virginia or Peru does theirs. Such places have simply been hidden from sight until now. The parallel between what is unseen but concrete and actual—'Who ever heard of th' Indian Peru?'—and what is unseen because it exists within and between the poet's mind and ours—

> Why then should witlesse man so much misweene,
> That nothing is, but that which he hath seene?

—is a claim for, rather an assumption of, the truth of poetry, but it is a claim put in exactly the right matter-of-fact terms for its context. It suggests that if we see it rightly Faeryland is a place of as hard reality as the Amazons' huge river, or as Elizabethan England. The hardness, the solid material imperviousness of things, is very much a part of the second book and succeeding books of *The Faerie Queene*.

The transition from Red Crosse's spiritual sphere of transcendence to the moral and temporal sphere of balance, control, and

34

reconciliation in which temperance must be achieved, is made with great skill and great emphasis in the first canto. We have been prepared for such a transition, of course, in the later part of the first book, where Red Crosse is reminded of the duties which still await him among men in 'the world, whose joyes so fruitlesse are', but the contrast remains, and to place Temperance next in order to Holiness is to stress both contrast and transition very sharply, for temperance is especially a virtue of this world and especially a way of controlling our own internal discord. By its very name it was connected with the golden mean, 'in medio virtus', the tempering of contraries at the mean quality and of extremes at the point of balance, and the term temperantia was often used indifferently with concordia and harmonia.[1] The connection of Guyon's Temperance with Red Crosse's Holiness may be elucidated by a comment of Professor Wind.[2] Discussing the two juxtaposed mottoes in the July eclogue of *The Shepheardes Calender*, 'in medio virtus: in summo felicitas', he suggests that they express the relation, made explicit in Florentine neoplatonism, between balance and transcendence. Man must live his mundane life by the mean, the uniting of opposites and the balancing of extremes, but he can attain the mean only by looking beyond the temporal to the divine, from the difficult management of the opposites to their source and end. Some such relation certainly exists between the quest of Holiness and those which follow it. Red Crosse looks towards God, the source and final coincidence of all the contraries with which his earth-bound successors must struggle. But even as Guyon sets out on his quest Spenser's narrative ensures that the transition, though marked, will be smooth, and that we will recognize from the outset the relevance of the saint's victory to all that is to come.

[1] Leo F. Spitzer, 'Classical and Christian Ideas of World Harmony', Traditio, II, 1944, pp. 409–64 and III, 1945, pp. 307–64. Giordano Bruno's *Gli Eroici Furori* develops in detail the Aristotelian connection of the strong soul's temperance with the mean point where the opposites are held in balance. The perfection of a thing, says Bruno's Tansillo, 'consists in unity, and there where the opposites meet, its composition and virtue exist'. And Cicada says of the nobly vicious 'heroic enthusiast', 'because he is not in the temperance of mediocrity, but in the excess of contradictions, his soul is discordant'. [*The Heroic Enthusiasts*, translated by L. Williams (London, 1887), Part I, pp. 61, 59.]

[2] *Pagan Mysteries in the Renaissance* (London, 1958).

Canto One looks both forward and back. Archimago, still doggedly pursuing Red Crosse with all his subtle engines, persuades Guyon that a knight with a crossed shield has ravished an innocent lady (impersonated by Duessa) and Guyon is as easily roused to hasty anger as Red Crosse had earlier been by Archimago's apparent proofs. But Red Crosse is now the impeccable knight, Guyon the hasty one; the saint is discovered with helm unlaced, austerely quenching his thirst at a cold little river and ready to take arms at a moment's notice. The controlled and astringent atmosphere contrasts sharply with that of the enervating fountain at which Orgoglio overcame him. He is now of course as temperate as he is holy, and Archimago's attempts to draw good knights 'To slug in slouth and sensuall delights' will be useless so far as he is concerned. But sloth and sensuality are Guyon's enemies too, and Acrasia is of the same deathly provenance as the more obviously devilish Archimago and Duessa. The fellowship between the knights is made clear: Guyon will not turn his spear against 'The sacred badge of my Redeemers death' or Red Crosse his against the image of Gloriana. 'So beene they both at one', each recognizing that the other fights, in his own way, what is essentially the same battle, and they part 'With right hands plighted, pledges of good will'. In their speeches and the palmer's the likeness and the difference between their quests is treated with grave emphasis. Red Crosse 'a saint with saints [his] seat [has] wonne',

> But wretched we, where ye have left your marke,
> Must now anew begin like race to ronne.
> God guide thee, Guyon, well to end thy warke,
> And to the wished haven bring thy weary barke.

(i, 32)

From sainthood registered above the sun we turn to a like race—the parallels between the two books have been demonstrated[3]—and one in its own fashion as important, but a race in which God's guidance is less recognizably present. But present none the less, as the palmer knows, and Guyon goes on his way with the lesson Red Crosse has so laboriously learned sounding in his ears:

[3] A. C. Hamilton, 'The Parallel Structure of *The Faerie Queene*, Books I and II', P.M.L.A., LXXIII, 1958.

His be the praise, that this atchiev'ment wrought,
Who made my hand the organ of His might:
More then goodwill to me attribute nought;
For all I did, I did but as I ought.

(i, 33)

Guyon himself presents at his first appearance a contrast-within-likeness to Red Crosse. He appears upright, temperate, but terrible, and he rides a great trampling steed. Horse and rider are led by the prudent and reasonable palmer, that repository of moral saws and of traditional wisdom, who enforces upon them an equal tread and does not suffer the knight's hasty steps to stray in wrath. Guyon's horse, named later as Brigador, and described much more fully and frequently than any of the anonymous and colourless mounts belonging to other people, appears to be that in him which is at once a help and a potential hindrance to his quest, a proud and passionate knightliness. At the first encounter, with Archimago, horse and rider take over responsibility from the palmer who remains silent, and it is the sight of the cross, not the voice of reason, that checks Guyon in full career and so foils the devil once more. The horse, so hard to hold with the bridle which is an attribute of Temperance, has been since the Greeks a familiar symbol of passion,[4] and Ariosto's steeds, from one of whom (Brigliadoro, Golden Bridle) Guyon's Brigador derives, were often interpreted as appetitive desire. Brigador, no doubt, contains in him whatever of passionate strength could prove fatal to temperance, but for Guyon he would seem to be chiefly the desire to trample baseness, a proud impetuous aspiration. There is no horse of spirit that does not look like an embodiment of this kind of nobility,[5] and the armed and panoplied horse of chivalry, trampling and rearing, as much a warrior as its rider, scarcely needs the emblem tradition to establish its

[4] Among many renderings of this rather hackneyed figure (which is of course 'ex Platone') that in Petri Costalii Pegma, cum narrationibus philosophicis (Lyons, 1555), p. 157, is one of the more spirited; the rider, who could not control his mount, lies almost under the horse's hooves. Guyon's superb mastery of the difficult Brigador, and Braggadocchio's swaggering incompetence to ride, both obviously relate to this figure.

[5] The horse is to be met with in the emblem books signifying noble pride, etc. Sometimes the dangerous ease with which noble aspiration can become ignoble ambition is hinted at; e.g. in Apelles Symbolicus horses can convey such meanings as 'gloriosus animus'.

highmindedness. This great horse Brigador, a 'loftie steed with golden sell/And goodly gorgeous barbes', has much in common with his master. Where Red Crosse had to learn to be a Christian knight, fighting the battle to the end but remembering that it is not he who conquers but Christ in him, Guyon must train himself to the avoidance of glory and high honour, the subduing of all in him that responds to Brigador's speed and impatience of restraint.

The horse so vividly and appreciatively described soon vanishes from Guyon's story to be found much later, but his first function has been to show us what kind of person this new knight is, what power he has and delights in, what aspiration to high and honourable action, how much that is finest in him may lead him to destruction in quest of temperance. Above all Guyon is a warrior, a knight in the tradition of Huon of Bordeaux, a man of the lists and tourneys riding a horse whose powerful tread seems only the heavier for its compelled incongruous slowness and measure. Archimago, subtle as ever, appeals at once to the warrior in him:

> Fayre sonne of Mars, that seeke with warlike spoyle,
> And great atchiev'ments, great your selfe to make . . .
>
> (i, 8)

'Fayre sonne of Mars'—yet the force of Mars is one of the things that temperance has to temper. Again romance and the values of chivalry suggest their own limitations. The temperate man is not a man of war, not Mars's man or Venus's, though he may have something in him of both these great forces. Frequently in Guyon's story this negative signification is used to positive effect. Even at the end, this most knightly of heroes has no battle to fight. Red Crosse's long drawn out struggle with the dragon is replaced by the walk through Acrasia's parkland, sword and spear by the palmer's net. Yet as we read we feel the likeness in the quests and know that Guyon's chief moral danger is akin to Red Crosse's spiritual one, a danger to which the term 'pride' might in each case be applied accurately though with different connotations because of the different spheres in which the two operate. The motive of personal aspiration can in some cases be good, but to holiness it is potential pride and to temperance potential unbalance. To seek with 'great atchiev'ments, great your selfe to make' will not produce temperance (as temperance defines itself in the narrative) any more than it will produce holiness.

When Guyon leaves Red Crosse he travels under the palmer's firm control for what we are told is a long way but which is covered here in less than two stanzas. Thus it is still with the atmosphere of Christian struggle around us and around Guyon, still remembering the humble utterance of the saint who has conquered not in himself but in Christ, that we enter on the first stage of the journey to the Bower. As Red Crosse had heard the voice of the tree Fradubio adumbrating his future fate, so does Guyon hear the lament of his enemy's victim Amavia. The two episodes are similar in their tone of menace and desolation and in the sense they give of the sheer difficulty involved in being human. What is true of Mortdant is true of us all, 'For he was flesh (all flesh doth frayltie breed)' (i, 52). Hearing a woman cry out, Guyon hurries into the pathless forest where so much of the ensuing action is to take place, and finds there the dead Mortdant and the dying suicide Amavia, thick blood gushing from her wound and a baby dabbling in the blood upon her lap. 'Pitifull spectacle, as ever eie did vew', says the poet, and indeed no sight could more painfully convey the heritage of man than this pathetic and horrible one of the child playing with the blood which signifies its parents' destruction and its own inherited taint.

Thus Guyon moves into the scene in which his quest must be achieved, that of blind and sinful humanity, well-meaning often (for Amavia was loving and Mortdant was brave) but easily at the mercy of the warring forces in its own chaotic nature. The dead knight and lady are jointly victims of the unbalance which gives Acrasia her power, and together they are, as Guyon says, 'the ymage of mortalitie', of failed human nature in which a precarious order is overthrown by the passions and a balance of forces deteriorates into confusion.

> Behold the ymage of mortalitie,
> And feeble nature cloth'd with fleshly tyre.
> When raging passion with fierce tyranny
> Robs reason of her dew regalitie,
> And makes it servaunt to her basest part,
> The strong it weakens with infirmitie,
> And with bold furie armes the weakest hart:
> The strong through pleasure soonest falles, the weake
>   through smart.

(i, 57)

Here is the beginning of that use of 'knights and ladies', their deeds, wars, and loves, which is to serve as a principle of structure (and hence of meaning) in this book and still more in the two which follow it. Man is a creature of tensions, of opposites held in creative balance at best but chaotic at worst, and health of mind and of body depends upon the balance being kept. This is a guiding principle of the old moral, psychological, and medical lore which survived into the Renaissance. The right tempering of our elements is what temperance is, and Acrasia is the lack of it. The union of male and female in proper relationship is an obvious and ancient figure for such right tempering, the necessary balance of opposing qualities, and similarly a faulty union can figure an imperfect balance. We are perhaps most familiar with such a use of man and woman from Milton, whose Adam and Eve after the fall present the image of mortality—man now doomed, in his own unredeemed nature, to failure and death—in something the same terms as do Amavia and Mortdant. In either case, there is a displacement of power and function: the masculine principle of strength has become yielding and sentimental, the feminine principle assertive and masterful. Guyon's detailed comment on the dead pair shows his understanding of them as an image of humanity's fatal failure to reconcile its contraries, producing the same chaotic alternations and displacements in the microcosm as would a corresponding failure among the elements which form the macrocosm. The warrior Mortdant, the fine knight who 'pricked forth, his puissant force to prove', has been reduced to sensual weakness and has become the giver of death to himself and his wife. She, on the other hand ('her that loves to live') is armed with the bold fury of self-murder, they have displaced and destroyed themselves and each other.

Their unbalance is embodied in Acrasia, who first depraved Mortdant and whose magic causes his death after, and although, he appears to be cured 'to a better will,/Purged from drugs of fowle intemperance'. She gives him a charmed cup to drink before he leaves, with the prophecy that death will come to the death-dealing Mortdant and loss of love to Amavia whose love is (too much) her life when the wine is mingled with 'the Nymphe', and when he drinks of the pure well in the forest he falls dead. To a contemporary reader the reversal of a familiar emblem must have been striking. Among the commonest attributes of personified Temperance was a flask and cup, or two flasks, in which she mingles wine and water.[6] Here the tempering comes too late, the damage is done and is permanent. Something of Acrasia's charm of 'lust and lewde desyres' still lingers in Mortdant and the sudden mixing of her wine with the cold pure water of Diana's nymph can only destroy him. The shock inherent in such deliberately twisted symbolism gives a harsh conviction to the story. This, we feel, is what would and does happen, and it is entirely characteristic of Spenser's unsentimental realism both psychological and moral. The dead pair, only too typically representative of humanity, are accorded a dignified if stark burial, and a lament from Guyon and the palmer which at once expresses pity and tolerance for the dead and draws general moral conclusions from their destruction. 'After death', says Guyon, 'the tryall is to come.' Even in this book where the world sometimes closes in upon us like a prison we must remember that judgment lies beyond it and that it is not for us to condemn one another.

Thus the unbalanced union of Mortdant and Amavia ends in death, and their issue is discord and disproportion, the ill-starred blood-covered child. The knights and ladies of the world of romance embody right and wrong relationships within the inner world of man.[7] Guyon makes over the child as over its parents one of those speeches of exalted commonplace which are so curiously moving when they have behind them the individual pathos of the 'particular example'; in it the child is placed as

[6] Cesare Ripa has a lengthy explication in *Iconologia* of the various attributes of temperance, in which the virtue is, as usually, associated with the mean. The two liquids denote the bringing together of extremes. This reference is noted also by A. D. S. Fowler, 'Emblems of Temperance in *The Faerie Queene*, Book II', RES, n.s. XI, 1960, p. 148. When Temperance holds a bridle in one hand and a golden cup in the other, the cup is presumably taken to contain a mixture of wine and water, as in Peacham's *Minerva Britannica*: 'I'th'other hand, that golden cup doth show,/Unto excesse I am a deadly foe'.

[7] 'The union of male and female in marriage was endlessly likened to unions of might and passivity, mind and imagination, spirit and flesh in the individual personality'. (M.A.N. Radzinowicz, 'Eve and Dalila: Renovation and the Hardening of the Heart', in *Reason and the Imagination, Studies in the History of Ideas 1600–1800*, ed. J. A. Mazzeo (New York, 1962), p. 163.

representative of all men in its personal haplessness and its inherited stain of disproportioned sin.[8]

> Ah! lucklesse babe, borne under cruell starre,
> And in dead parents balefull ashes bred,
> Full little weenest thou, what sorrowes are
> Left thee for porcion of thy livelyhed:
> Poore orphane! in the wide world scattered,
> As budding braunch rent from the native tree,
> And throwen forth, till it be withered!
> Such is the state of men! Thus enter we
> Into this life with woe, and end with miseree!
>
> (ii, 2)

Even the phoenix image brings a painful comfort here, for the child rises from its parents' ashes only to perpetuate their distress in the series of human sorrows. But one cannot but be aware of the underlying hope of the new life although it is bred from the old.

It is strange that Guyon has so often been described as an unsympathetic hero, detached, superior, even a little smug. Looked at in another way he is, on the contrary, peculiarly and touchingly sympathetic in his readiness to identify himself, victorious Elfin knight though he is, with the image of mortality, the pitiful failures in whose cause he must conquer. The bodies are buried tenderly and a sacred vow is taken over their grave, ritually enforcing his identification with them and the child by the mingling of 'all their heare' with the blood and earth. Then he takes the child, now his own unquestioned responsibility, and tries to wash away the blood. Being what it is—the sign of blood-guiltiness with which High God has overprinted the child's personal innocence—it will not be cleaned, and the palmer's explanation of the stream's nature is no pretty digression but part of the progressive definition of those themes which in this book are to be explored under the aspect of temperance. The stream, the palmer says, took its origin from a virgin nymph of Diana,

---

[8] A. C. Hamilton, 'A Theological Reading of *The Faerie Queene*, Book II', ELH, XXV, 1958, sees the child as the effects of original sin. See also an equally important article by A. D. S. Fowler, 'The Image of Mortality: *The Faerie Queene*, II, i–ii', Huntington Library Quarterly, XXIV, 2, February 1961, pp. 91–110, which elaborates the identification of the child and interprets the fountain as one of baptismal regeneration.

who when pursued by Faunus prayed weeping to the goddess to let her die a maid. In response Diana turned her to a stone and her tears to a stream 'Yet colde through feare and old conceived dreads', its absolute purity recoiling in fear and horror from the blood, the human stain of sin. This is the stream of which the child's father had drunk and died. The palmer's account serves to differentiate *this* fountain from the lifegiving well of baptism with which at first sight we might associate it; it will not wash away sin, it will not forgive, it simply dissociates itself. Thus far and no further will natural purity go, and it is Guyon's distinction that he goes, knowingly, a good deal further. The stream, virtuous, cold, and repellent, shows him and us that this particular quest can be achieved only by humbly entering into the human situation, not by rejecting it. Temperance is the proper ordering of our chaos of contraries, not their denial, and what may be admirable in Diana and her nymphs can only be inhuman and inhumane in us.

Guyon's compassion for, and participation in, the fate of the dead pair and their child is marked throughout, and when the water will not wash the blood away he accepts the palmer's view which stresses not the parents' guilt but the goodwill and the curious blamelessness which surrounds them despite their faults. They tried to do well, but life and human nature were too much for them; they erred chiefly in their lack of comprehension. The blood is a sacred symbol not only of our propensity to sin but of the suffering which that propensity brings. So Guyon burdens himself and the palmer with the child and with its father's blood-stained armour, the weight of human failure, sorrow, and precarious hope, and since Brigador has vanished he must go on foot. For the reader, the laborious journey is the way into an area of experience where Red Crosse's conquest of the old dragon, prototype of all knightly quests, gives way to its humbler parallels, the steady unspectacular effort towards a right balance in ourselves and a balanced relationship with our fellow men which is seen in Britomart and in Artegall but first, and perhaps most movingly, in the difficult humility of Guyon. For Guyon is, Arthur excepted, as spirited and aspiring by nature, as clearly a son of Mars and a follower of Gloriana, as anyone in the poem, and yet of all the heroes he is the one who must avoid the heroic itself, abjuring all transcendence for the mean. As the palmer reminds him so often, he must move slowly and with 'equall steps' along the middle way between the extremes which Amavia and Mortdant fell victim to, and his first task is to make sure that the child, the representative of 'the state of men' will go along that way too.

It is a hard way. As Professor C. S. Lewis pointed out in *The Allegory of Love*, Spenser remarks more than once upon the weariness of it and the temptation to rest. And what is most arduous about it is the necessity to subdue oneself always to the dull and humble, in one sense the unheroic, thing. The really hard part of the quest is not the final overthrow of unbalance in Acrasia's Bower. That, it is true, Guyon accomplishes with ease. The difficulty is in understanding fully, and sticking to, what such a quest involves, stooping to the point at which this perhaps lowliest of the virtues can be achieved, continually and patiently keeping the balance true. What has to be done is made plainer to him when he brings the baby to Medina, the golden mean whose 'sisters, two Extremities,/Strive her to banish cleane'. Here again it is arduousness and persistence in a wearisome effort which is stressed. The extremes are always seeking their opportunity to master Medina and each other, her work is always to do again. If temperance is heroic—and in a way of course it is—it is so in virtue of its ability to take up day after day a task which (it seems at this point in the poem) can never be lightened. Medina's balance is precarious and difficult to maintain, and one has to keep working at it; no wonder that Mortdant and Amavia failed. But the child will learn, and is left with Medina to be trained in virtue and thus to overcome what has destroyed his parents.

The visit to Medina's castle is not, like the Amavia episode, presented in depth. The thickness of texture characteristic of Spenser at his best is absent, but the castle sketches out the difficult but achievable nature of the mean as a moral aim with considerable allegorical precision. Doubtless this is all it is meant to do, for much of the verse has a brisk, snip-snap, prosaic quality which can only be deliberate.

> Therein three sisters dwelt of sundry sort,
> The children of one syre by mothers three;
> Who dying whylome did divide this fort
> To them by equall shares in equall fee:
> But stryfull mind and diverse qualitee
> Drew them in partes, and each made others foe;

Still did they strive, and daily disagree;
The eldest did against the youngest goe,
And both against the middest meant to worken woe.

(ii, 13)

The description is interesting (as is the related one of Concord, holding together the half brothers Love and Hate, in the fourth book) in its relation to that long tradition of the 'extremities' and the 'opposites' which, though it now merged various conceptions originally separate, had gained in analogical inclusiveness as much as it had lost in Greek clarity. At this particular point in the poem, it is true, neatness rather than richness prevails; one supposes that Spenser's poetic strategy demands that at this early stage the principle of the mean and the hardness of keeping it should be pressed home as a basis for later variations. For example, in the stanza quoted, the birth of Medina and her sisters is exactly arranged to suggest the traditional assumption that whatever things are to be held together must have some common quality; 'extremes' and 'opposites' or 'contraries' can be held at the mean, things which are flatly contradictory cannot. In its dry way the Medina episode brings together a number of details which perform very well the office of a signpost, if they do no more.

The castle's age and solidity vouch for it as a well-established moral tradition; it is

an auncient worke of antique fame,
And wondrous strong by nature, and by skilfull frame.

(ii, 12)

Medina is in charge of it, but not of right, except the right of manifest superiority; she has to exercise unceasing and tactful control over her sisters, the 'too much' and 'too little' who encourage the stern melancholy of Huddibras and the lawless lust of Sansloy. Medina's task is the one which dominates the central books of the poem in one shape or another, the imposing of concord among those who left to themselves would be in a state of purposeless, directionless hostility. Sansloy and Huddibras are fighting when Guyon arrives and promptly turn upon him, and the double effort he is forced to make is described with the balanced tidiness suited to the occasion. Guyon is carefully fighting the only kind of battle that concerns him, not for glory and not to kill but to defend his own position by wearing down his

45

attackers. He balances his way between them, yielding temporarily when he must and pushing forward when he can.

> Attonce he wards and strikes, he takes and paies,
> Now forst to yield, now forcing to invade,
> Before, behind, and round about him laies.
>
> (ii, 25)

His method, working 'Betweene them both, by conduct of his blade', conveys very well not only the steadfastness but the flexible intelligence necessary for the restraining tactics of the temperate man. But to have to fight at all is regrettable, since the state of war exemplifies the jangling of the discordant and muddled soul, as the next stanza suggests:

> Straunge sort of fight, three valiaunt knights to see
> Three combates joine in one, and to darraine
> A triple warre with triple enmitee,
> All for their ladies froward love to gaine,
> Which gotten was but hate. So Love does raine
> In stoutest minds, and maketh monstrous warre;
> He maketh warre, he maketh peace againe,
> And yet his peace is but continuall jarre:
> O miserable men, that to him subject arre!

on love

Through generalization from the particular occasion, the schematic battle, in itself no more than neat, takes its place as part of the warring state of man, whose passions in opposing one another become horribly confused with one another until love is hate and peace is but continual jar. The twin themes of love and war set before us in the proem to Book One and touched on here are to grow more dominant as the poem proceeds. Seeming so different, they yet merge very queerly into each other, and by means of them the paradoxes of human nature can be thoroughly explored. Love is hate, love is war, love co-exists with force, the 'stoutest minds'. What we call peace or concord—inner peace or peace between persons or states—is often but continual jar, the peace of mutual hostility in deadlock, what Blake calls mutual fear. Such is our condition that aggressive fear is implicit even in affection.

Sansloy and Huddibras are urged on by Elissa and Perissa in the name of love, and it takes all Medina's persuasive eloquence to stop the fight. Her middle way consists not in attacking *them*, but in persuading them not to attack her and each other; she tries always to moderate the extremes and their knights 'with equall measure', to 'attemper' one to another, and so to attain the nearest approximation she can to 'lovely concord, and most sacred peace'. Guyon has more to learn than the castle of the mean can teach him, but what he sees here is an essential first step, underlying in simpler form the lesson of Amavia and Mortdant. For Guyon there must be no extremes, even the extreme of noble aspiration, only the steady and difficult exercise of control. Both through the schematism in which it begins and ends, and through the comparative allusiveness of Medina's speech, which opens upon wider issues to come, the episode fulfils its explanatory and generalizing function well enough (though no more than well enough). It perhaps refers also to what has been called 'the typical Anglican claim of avoiding both excess and defect',[9] and though this can be only a subsidiary meaning it helps to establish the mean as a necessary part of every human effort towards the right.

Guyon's next encounter, in the fourth canto, is with Occasion, Furor, and Pyrochles, and it is of the same subdued kind as that of the battle at Medina's house. Some of the point of these early adventures is their very unadventurousness; they have to press home that the task of temperance is less to conquer than to control. It is fair, I think, to remark that a certain stodginess at this point does contribute to the effectiveness of the book as a whole. Temperance goes far beyond stodginess in the end, but to achieve it one has to be ready to perform inglorious tasks and be sneered at for unknightliness by such as Pyrochles. The effect seems plainly deliberate. The palmer reiterates his moral lesson, Guyon has to struggle with the ungentlemanly methods of the kicking and biting Furor and then, as Atin scornfully tells him, to fight with an old woman. And it is further emphasized by the presence, between the dour efforts at Medina's castle and against Furor, of Belphoebe, her charm and swiftness forming the most absolute of foils to Guyon's armoured heaviness. For sheer pleasure, a light uplifting quality of imagery and movement, the third canto is unsurpassed in the poem. Belphoebe, described at length and with a sparkling brilliancy of detail, is clearly of importance. Yet she and Guyon do not meet, instead she meets Braggadocchio

[9] The phrase is taken from the Introduction to Helen Gardner's edition of Donne, *The Divine Poems* (Oxford, 1952).

who has stolen Guyon's horse and spear; and she appears in all her dazzling radiance of victorious aspiration in between two of the least glorious but most necessary incidents of Guyon's plodding quest. She contributes to the definition of temperance by being absent from the pursuit of it, for she embodies a kind of honour, akin to Brigador and to that in Guyon which must for the time be avoided. Braggadocchio is there, with Brigador, to complete the meaning of this interlude of comic action. He behaves in a way which constitutes a foolish parody of Guyon's native love of honour.[10] Being 'of kestrell kynd', of 'baser brest', he substitutes for real honour, the aspiration to great deeds, what Spenser calls a pleasing vein of glory—the appearance and the talk of honour without the reality of it which is desert of gentle deed. Thus he does encounter Belphoebe, as Guyon may not do, but since his conception of honour is summed up in his injured remark to Trompart,

> What fowle blott
> Is this to knight, that lady should agayne
> Depart to woods untoucht, and leave so proud disdayne!

(iii, 43)

she vanishes, and is seen no more in this book.

Spenser's description of Belphoebe gives her, through its sensuous and very allusive use of language, an exactly ambiguous blend of sophistication and innocence, ideality and reality. She is described partly in a highly literary style, 'sonneteer's language, the kind of hyperbolic imagery identified with "Petrarchism" ',[11] interwoven with memories of the sensuous cadences of the Song

---

[10] The relation of honour to temperance, and also the nature of true and false honour, are interestingly treated by Robert Ashley, *Of Honour*, ed. Virgil B. Heltzel (San Marino, 1947). For him, honour must follow 'some mediocritie or meane' (p. 41), and again 'true honour consisteth not in vaine boasting of swelling tytles, but in the moderacion of the minde' (p. 47). Honour, which 'cometh out of the angry part of the mind' and is found in men of 'high spirite' (p. 40) is especially a quality which the knight Guyon would find it necessary to moderate. Leone Ebreo also considers the question, and handles it characteristically: 'Spurious honour is that which flatters power: true honour is that which rewards virtue.' [*The Philosophy of Love*, by Leone Ebreo, translated by F. Friedeberg-Seeley and Jean H. Barnes (London, 1937), p. 29.]

[11] H. Berger, op. cit., p. 137. Mr. Berger makes a detailed and valuable analysis of the treatment of Belphoebe.

of Songs. Her appeal to the senses is very strong and is expressed with a certain earthiness:

> Like roses in a bed of lillies shed,
> The which ambrosiall odours from them threw,
> And gazers sence *with double pleasure fed*.[12]
>
> (iii, 22)
>
> Her daintie paps; which, like young fruit in May,
> Now little gan to swell, and being tide,
> Through her thin weed their places only signifide.
>
> (iii, 29)

Heavenly as she is, she attracts desire—though only to quench it at least in its base form—and her forehead is like an ivory tablet

> For Love his loftie triumphes to engrave,
> And write the battailes of his great godhed:
> All good and honour might therein be red.
>
> (iii, 24)

The graces sit on her eyelids, 'Working belgardes and amorous retrates'. In fact her ambiguous relation to Cupid and Venus, which is to be more fully exploited later in the poem, exists already here. Her manner of dress clinches this doubleness of impression. She is dressed as a hunting nymph, and as far as the basic necessities of the chase are concerned she is furnished in an unmistakably workmanlike way with a boar spear and a bow and quiver. But the quiver's baldric serves to show off her figure, it lies 'Athwart her snowy brest, and did divide/Her daintie paps'. Her skirt is girded up as of course it should be, and her buskins are the proper wear, but both are gilded, and the golden fringe trailing a little below her thigh serves to set off the straight legs to whose description a whole stanza is devoted. Her hair flows around her shoulders and is blown by the wind and tangled with flowers; again a huntress may be expected to be a little dishevelled, but flowing golden locks are in *The Faerie Queene* (and outside it) the mark of feminine attractive power.[13] Belphoebe is

---

[12] My italics. The rose and the lily are often enough mingled in the face of the sonneteer's lady, but the stress on their double, over-sweet scent here gives them more actuality, so that the heady mingling of the red rose of passion and the lily of purity contributes to what Mr. Berger calls, I think rightly, 'a shade of the sinister' in Belphoebe's ambiguity.

[13] Compare Florimell's flowing hair, and Britomart's when she loosens it from her helmet, in Book III.

engaged in the chase of honour and glory, and sincerely engaged; the description is too glorious and too exhilarating to suggest any doubleness of conscious intention. But there is a doubleness of effect, and her pursuit of the wounded hind leads her straight to Braggodocchio, whom she almost shoots in mistake for it.

Belphoebe's appearance here is of course modelled on the appearance of Venus, in the guise of a hunting nymph, to Aeneas in Virgil's first book, though Spenser's description is noticeably more elaborate and intricate and emphasizes more fully the implications both of the Venus aspect and the Diana aspect of this dazzling figure. Her opening inquiry to Trompart, and his reply to her as a goddess, are close enough to the Aeneid to make the reference unmistakable, and the analogy with Virgil's Venus/Diana is usually seen as relating to the allegorical meanings which were attributed to the Virgilian passage by neoplatonist commentators. Venus, they suggested, was Venus Urania manifesting herself in active life, the beauty of moral ideals. Some such meaning is certainly applicable to Belphoebe, but the imagery surrounding her and the part she plays in relation to Braggadocchio (and in a negative way to Guyon) indicate that Spenser is here, as frequently, using a familiar reference to contribute, through the narrative, to new and often complex effects. Belphoebe is in herself admirable and fine, but the ideal she represents, the high chivalric aspiration where love and battle are both ways to honour, is a tricky one to follow. Human beings are only too likely to get it wrong. The knightly modes of love and war blend in the chase—which is one of the oldest of metaphors for the pursuit of honour and the pursuit of love—and in this Petrarchan hunting nymph. Spenser never sneers at this or any ideal, but he knows how easily they can turn into something else, and the confusing or the debasing of love and war and honour is from this point on one of his major organizing themes. What is in itself an excellent creation of the human mind can at the same time be a danger to that mind's health. One of Spenser's greatest assets as a poet of the human struggle towards virtue is his recognition of those queer movements of the psyche which the formal psychology of his time could not compass but which poets had explored since the Greeks first showed them how. Belphoebe is an ambiguous figure because she is an ideal creation of the ambiguous mind of man, whose loftiest aspiration is not free from his deepest self-indulgence, the pretence that we can both eat our cake and have it.

Braggadocchio is base, but he is only isolating and distorting an element that is really present in Belphoebe, and cannot help being present in the ideals we create for ourselves to worship. His comic inadequacy, and Belphoebe's comically hurried departure, place the ideal perfectly in Spenser's scheme; the whole scene blends affection, admiration, amusement. It does not do to be too solemn or too singleminded about Belphoebe. She is a great deal too good for Braggadocchio, but she is rather too good for anybody. Even before we know of her innocent birth the Petrarchan description, the basically simple clothes made brilliant and attractive, the spontaneity elaborated by a traditional literary art, establish her as a creature of man's idealizing imagination, something he can adore but not achieve. It is not for humanity to be so sure of itself, so demanding, or so simply triumphant. Belphoebe quells the savage beasts of the forest of the passions with such ease for honour's sake that it is all play to her, 'victorious play', 'great triumphant joy'. In every line of the description we recognize the delighted exercise of an effortless power, untrammelled by the inherited human troubles 'ingenerate in fleshly slime' and so pathetically represented in this book by the babe with bloody hands. So the horse Brigador carries to Belphoebe not the knight of temperance dedicated to the avoidance of extremes but 'glory Vaine', unable to control his stolen mount 'to tread in dew degree'.

At its simplest level one may say that the effect of the Belphoebe episode is to emphasize by a sharp contrast in tone the kind of effort it is necessary for Guyon to make. But of course from this central effect related ones circle out. The sight of all that Guyon has to renounce in his championship of the image of mortality underlines his steadiness in subduing his knightly nature but it also makes that steadiness more touching. It is as it were the poet's recognition that temperance, though it is our first step to virtue, is not the whole of human potentiality. Belphoebe's radiance and glory, and her doubleness too, appeal to something in us as deep as the palmer's wisdom and as necessary to our completeness. As the poem goes deeper and deeper into the forest of passion and instinct and all unreasonable things these dangerous but life-giving potentialities of man, standing on

51

the border between the ideal and the instinctual, spring up everywhere in an inner world more and more uncharted. Temperance, called the guardian of the threshold, is so in more senses than one, for the consideration of it takes us down into the complexities of human behaviour. Belphoebe is no help to temperance, but she is a creation of those needs which temperance has to take into account. The moral certainties of the palmer and the schematism of Furor and Occasion do not contain all the truth about the temperate or the intemperate man, and the episode, genuinely noble and exciting and at the same time rather endearingly absurd, adds a richly comic dimension to the image of mortality.

We return to the schematism in Canto IV with a heightened sense of our possibilities for good and evil and for every mixed quality between, for in us is the origin of the strange Belphoebe as well as the desperate Amavia and the patient Medina. Guyon, held back by the palmer, is still making his careful way between strong passion and weak fleshliness, taking as his task 'the weak to strengthen, and the strong suppresse' (iv, 2) and so to set right the primal failure of Amavia and Mortdant. Like that earlier failure, Phedon's is regarded with commiseration as part of human frailty, for 'all flesh doth frayltie breed'. Phedon sees himself as the victim of misfortune, blameable only through weakness, and the others do not disagree although the palmer explains that he must be wary, as Guyon always is, and that his trouble is not so much unavoidable weakness as a failure to bridle what *should* be weak, so that it gains unnatural strength. Guyon, fighting 'wary wise' and with 'faire sleight', pales in this encounter before the huge fury of Pyrochles, wilfully seeking occasion for the wrath which makes him feel more fully alive, and even before the dissolute luxury of Cymochles. But it is part of Guyon's function to seem dull in some of these earlier scenes, and to put up with seeming so. Pyrochles and Cymochles are more exciting, but they are obviously burning themselves out. With them the themes of love and war are taken a stage further as expressions of inner conflict and chaos.

Pyrochles, as both Guyon and the poet point out, is in a state of troublous war, deliberately self-inflamed. His victories over others are vain since he is continually overthrown by himself. His brother, equally fierce, equally in conflict with himself, slides from one kind of war to another which has, as their ready alterna-

tion suggests, a kinship with it. Cymochles is the first of those
'womanish weake knights' through whom so much and such
varied meaning is expressed in the poem, a simpler version of such
as Artegall and Marinell. Atin, seeking to rouse him to anger,
finds him in the Bower of Bliss, where having relaxed from the
extreme of wrathful activity he flows 'in pleasures and vaine
pleasing toyes'. His warlike weapons are cast aside, and the only
armour in the glade where he lies is the punning 'prickling armes'
of the eglantine, reddened only by entangling roses. Near him
grows the aspiring tree of the besotted hero Hercules, one of his
traditional prototypes, but now it gives shade to singing birds and
to Cymochles's pleasure.

> And on the other syde a pleasaunt grove
> Was shott up high, full of the stately tree
> That dedicated is t'Olympick Jove,
> And to his sonne Alcides, whenas hee
> Gaynd in Nemea goodly victoree:
> Therein the mery birdes of every sorte
> Chaunted alowd their chearefull harmonee,
> And made emongst them selves a sweete consort,
> That quickned the dull spright with musicall comfort.
>
> (v, 31)

He rides away in anger, but soon lapses into womanish weakness
again when he meets Phaedria, who persuades him to show his
sovereign lordship of nature by the dubious but attractive method
of yielding to nature's idleness.

To the same island Phaedria brings Guyon, separated for the
first time from the palmer but still 'wise, and wary of her will',
and there the knights join battle, for Cymochles's sensuality
turns as readily into wrath as his wrath does into sensuality.
Phaedria takes note of this kinship in her efforts to appease him,
addressing him and Guyon in a parody of Medina's earlier appeal
for peace. What Phaedria wants is no true concord; she wishes
merely to replace one kind of war by another in the service of her
mistress Acrasia, and she speaks in the familiar convention of
many an Elizabethan poem.

> Such cruell game my scarmoges disarmes:
> Another warre, and other weapons, I
> Doe love, where Love does give his sweet alarmes,

53

Without bloodshed, and where the enimy
Does yield unto his foe a pleasaunt victory.

Debatefull strife, and cruell enmity,
The famous name of knighthood fowly shend;
But lovely peace, and gentle amity,
And in amours the passing howres to spend,
The mightie martiall handes doe most commend;
Of love they ever greater glory bore,
Then of their armes: Mars is Cupidoes frend,
And is for Venus loves renowmed more,
Then all his wars and spoiles, the which he did of yore.

(vi, 34–5)

Thus Phaedria, whose demoralizing of Cymochles parallels that of Verdant by Acrasia, is given a speech which suggests those aspects of ambiguity and unbalance which are to become particularly important later; again to consider temperance is to point the way to many complications of our life. What Phaedria aims at is not the concord to be achieved through the mean but an extremism which confuses concord and discord, love and war, and debases them both.[14] So Mars and Venus, the great symbols of discordia concors, can be wrongly interpreted in terms not only of sterile sensuality but of unbalance itself, the unproductive chaos which Acrasia lives by and which contradicts all that they properly stand for. Phaedria is a lightweight, but her words look back to the fate of Mortdant and forward to Verdant and Acrasia.

To Guyon of course Phaedria is no real danger. She is so silly, and her views are so frankly and frivolously wrongheaded, that she merely embarrasses a mind as naturally serious as his. He is ill at ease and bored on the Idle Lake where everything is weightless and meaningless, and he does not need the palmer's help to get away with obvious relief (shared, it has been pointed out, by poor Phaedria who finds him equally dull). He has moved now, it is true, into places where the palmer must be left behind, but we are not made to feel that this is altogether a fault in him. Rather, we feel that if temperance is to be worth anything it must know

[14] Lyly makes a similar use of the battles of Mars and Venus in *Campaspe* (II, ii, 57 f.), though as usual his wordplay operates on a level of joking triviality. Alexander is advised to 'fall not from the armour of Mars to the arms of Venus, from the fiery assaults of war to the maidenly skirmishes of love'.

54

about things that the palmer would have hurried him away from.
A man is sometimes compelled to be idle, and a temperance sustained only by constant busyness is on no very secure foundation.
It is the foundation that Guyon is now to strengthen in the greatest
test he has to encounter. Always a lonely figure, he is now completely alone. The opening lines of the seventh canto emphasize
his isolation.

> As pilot well expert in perilous wave,
> That to a stedfast starre his course hath bent,
> When foggy mistes or cloudy tempests have
> The faithfull light of that faire lampe yblent,
> And cover'd heaven with hideous dreriment,
> Upon his card and compas firmes his eye,
> The maysters of his long experiment,
> And to them does the steddy helme apply,
> Bidding his winged vessell fairely forward fly:
>
> So Guyon, having lost his trustie guyde,
> Late left beyond that Ydle Lake, proceedes
> Yet on his way, of none accompanyde;
> And evermore himselfe with comfort feedes
> Of his owne vertues and praise-worthie deedes.
>
> (vii, 1–2)

In situations where the palmer, voicing a traditional moral wisdom of prudence, could have nothing to say except 'keep out',
Guyon's native virtue comes into its own. It is all he has to rely
on and (by the grace of God) it is enough; as Milton's Raphael
tells Adam,

> Oft times nothing profits more
> Then self-esteem, grounded on just and right
> Well manag'd.

The knightly aspiration after, and consciousness of, 'praise-
worthie deedes', subdued to the bare necessity to keep up his
spirits and not disgrace himself in the unfamiliar territory he has
to get through, proves useful and good. He takes comfort in the
certainty of past achievement, in the habit of virtue that long
temperance, long submission to the palmer's wisdom, has bred
in him. This is his card and compass, 'The maysters of his long
experiment'; if temperance cannot stand in these regions beyond
the reach of the palmer's moral saws it is a surface virtue scarcely

worth the having or the writing. So Guyon goes on alone, as usual meeting with no high adventure and no shrill trumpet of fame, until he comes to the experience which must make or break him, the descent into the depths through Mammon's cave, next door to hell. As Red Crosse had to fall into Orgoglio's dungeon so does Guyon have to endure the darkness of Mammon for three days to arise newmade. But his descent is made in full awareness; this is a temptation deliberately undergone in the effort to see, and know, and yet abstain, to see more than the palmer's wise avoidance of danger can show him.

The descent is so plainly vital in some way to the making of Guyon that it has been the subject of much detailed investigation.[15] Errors, including that of curiositas, have been suggested as the cause of the temptation, but in reading we do not feel it as an error but as a necessity of growth, as, in Upton's words, 'a kind of initiation' and, in Professor Kermode's, 'a purgatorial experience'. It has often been pointed out that it has likenesses to the descent of Aeneas and a more basic likeness to the temptation of Christ in the wilderness (to get to Mammon's cave Guyon goes through a place of desolation described as 'wide, wastfull ground' and 'desert wilderness') of which Aeneas's journey was an adumbration. Both these exemplars underwent their experience by their own necessary choice before their work could be done, and Guyon's decision to accept Mammon's challenge is to be seen in relation to these choices rather than as an act of wilful and dangerous curiosity. His first exchanges with Mammon take place above ground, and neither here nor later does he show any inclination to weaken. Mammon offers him the world, not riches only but the 'renowme, and principality,/Honour, estate' which in the world's eye riches can get. He is the god of the world, opposed to and imitating God, generous (like God) in pouring out plenty and envying his graces to none, throwing down the mighty and raising the low at his will. Guyon rejects him because he knows what honour really is, he bends his knightly pride to his task of negative heroism, the refusal to serve Mammon. The god sees well enough that he is saved by his 'noble hart' and his understanding of honour not as renown but as virtue—that he is sus-

---

[15] See, in addition to the critical works cited in Chapter I, note 2 above, F. Kermode, 'The Cave of Mammon', *Elizabethan Poetry* (Stratford-upon-Avon Studies, 2, 1960), pp. 151–74.

tained, in fact, by a sense of what is due to one's self. 'Vaine glorious Elfe', he calls him, rash, heedless, hardy.

But there is more to Guyon than this. Pressed further, he appeals to the measure of the mean as an act of duty not to one's self only, but to what is greater than one's self. To be content and humble is to show gratitude to the one God who is greater even than Mammon, and in Guyon's second answer as in the words of Red Crosse's beadman and Calidore's old shepherd the 'antique world' of the Golden Age has its accepted connotations of Christian humility.

> The antique world, in his first flowring youth,
> Fownd no defect in his Creators grace,
> But with glad thankes, and unreproved truth,
> The guifts of soveraine bounty did embrace:
> Like angels life was then mens happy cace:
> But later ages pride, like corn-fed steed,
> Abusd her plenty and fat swolne encrease
> To all licentious lust, and gan exceed
> The measure of her meane, and naturall first need.
>
> (vii, 16)

The choice for Guyon becomes more and more clearly one between Mammon and God, between 'pompous pride' and humble duty. Temperance, modest preliminary effort towards goodness though it seems, opens not only upon the queer dualities in the depths of our being but upon the terrible simplicities of Red Crosse's world. The everyday effort against greed and avarice is shown for what it is, not expediency and propriety of behaviour but resistance to the values of hell, and in that resistance Guyon's knowledge that he has proved himself praiseworthy—as we might put it, his self-respect—is a steady help. But it must be free from all touch of pride; Guyon's heroism like Christ's must show itself in the avoidance of the conventionally heroic, he is great in refusing greatness. Thus the terms of his debate with Mammon, with its exact definitions, are important in stating the two attitudes which can so readily merge and be confused but which are really so differently aligned.

Debate, however, is not enough. Guyon, though dismayed and doubtful at the sight of Mammon and his dreary hoard and aware of the dread and horror of the way down, accepts the god's simple 'Come then, and see'. And he comes back safely along this oblique passage to hell because he resists temptation completely. Spenser makes a fluent use here of the old tradition of folklore and of Pluto's hell, that if you sit, or eat or take anything, you cannot get out. A fiend follows Guyon, ready to seize him

> If ever covetous hand, or lustfull eye,
> Or lips he layd on thing that likte him best,
> Or ever sleepe his eiestrings did untye.
>
> (vii, 27)

To rest among these things, or to touch or even desire them, would be to assent to them, and they are all part of the devil's trap; among them the spider, emblem of the devil, spins her cunning web. But Guyon goes through unscathed, gazing at everything with the greatest interest but with no spark of desire. Instead of greedily seizing them he uses them as food for the mind, he learns from them and about them:

> But th'Elfin knight with wonder all the way
> Did feed his eyes, and fild his inner thought.
>
> (vii, 24)

His resistance continues to be made in terms of the true honour, and the true lordship and control, but with an increasingly subtle knowledge of what that spiritual lordship is;

> And to be lord of those that riches have,
> Then them to have my selfe, and be their servile sclave.[16]
>
> (vii, 33)

Indeed as Guyon goes on the gulf widens between God and Mammon, 'greatest god below the skye', while the word 'grace', ironically echoed by Guyon (vii, 32, 33, 50) and the appeal to eternal God (34) simultaneously enforce the parallel. When we come to Philotime, and recognize her as the exact counterpart in Guyon's experience of Red Crosse's Lucifera, we know that we are dealing not with impropriety but with deadly sin.

> Nath'lesse most hevenly faire in deed and vew
> She by creation was, till she did fall . . .

---

[16] In the apocryphal Acts of John Mammon is called a devil who is set over carnal gains, and the master of them that love the world. But the lovers of the world 'do not possess riches, but are possessed by them'.

> There as in glistring glory she did sitt,
> She held a great gold chaine ylincked well,
> Whose upper end to highest heven was knitt,
> And lower part did reach to lowest hell.
>
> (vii, 45, 46)

Mammon's version of her fall is that it was unfair, she was too good for the gods and they envied her glory and beauty; Philotime like Lucifera has not got her rights:

> Worthie of heven and hye felicitie,
> From whence the gods have her for envy thrust.

Love of honour can (though it need not) become Satanic pride, and Guyon must know to the very limits of knowledge what his own nobleness could lead to if he does not go on making the right distinctions. He must be aware of the abyss of excess over which the mean carries him. His reply to Mammon indicates how precise that knowledge has become:

> 'Gramercy, Mammon', said the gentle knight,
> 'For so great grace and offred high estate,
> But I, that am fraile flesh and earthly wight,
> Unworthy match for such immortall mate
> My selfe well wote, and mine unequall fate:
> And were I not, yet is my trouth yplight,
> And love avowd to other lady late.'
>
> (vii, 50)

Guyon's elegant irony expresses an exact truth. Such a superhuman claim is not for frail flesh and is of all things what would disqualify him for the task he is subdued to. His loyalty is to Gloriana, the other lady who has the true glory of virtue and who demands of him now the refusal of power. True honour for him is *not* to aspire.

In the Garden of Proserpina Guyon sees further representatives of those who reach beyond what is proper to frail flesh and earthly wight, and sees them in a setting of profound sadness. The Garden is the other side of honour, and its deadly sorrow is like that of the sad House of Pride. It makes its first effect visually; it is full of dark and death-giving plants, among them the herb which killed the wise and temperate Socrates. The air is thick with the leaves of the fatal tree which dominates this

59

garden as the tree of knowledge did Eden,[17] and casts its shade everywhere. It is laden with golden apples, here (as traditionally in Eden) malum, the evil fruit of death, and it is from this tree that all the golden apples of legend came, even those which Hercules, another of Guyon's predecessors in the descent to hell, took from the dragon guarded tree of the Hesperides. Lovely as are the stories of the gardens of the west or of Paris's judgment on Ida, here is their origin and meaning. Spenser lists more of them: Atalanta's apples, Acontius's, and 'most famous' and most fatal the apple that Ate threw among the assembled gods and so caused the mounting evils of the Trojan war. They are treacherous apples, bringing discord;[18] they have appealed to all that is greedy, ambitious, and intemperate in man, and they hang into the waters of Cocytus where Tantalus, familiar emblem of greed, tries to snatch them in a symbolic punishment for reaching beyond man's grasp when alive. Tantalus's greed was aspiring ambition like Philotime's. Though mortal, he used to mix with the gods until he served to them his blasphemous and inhuman meal and in his efforts to rise above humanity fell below it to the bestial. All his ambition has ended in this vain labour among the fruits and waters of hell. In this place the greed of Tantalus is the insatiable desire to know the gods and be their equal. He must 'ensample be of mind intemperate', and like Philotime (or Milton's Satan) he will not accept his guilt. Intemperance, in its most total form, is a sin against the first giver, 'blaspheming heaven bitterly,/As author of injustice'. Next to Tantalus, and like him losing in death as in life 'his labour vaine and ydle industrie', is Pilate whose desire to make good in Mammon's

[17] Ralegh regards the dragon-guarded apples of the Hesperides as a version of the tree and serpent which tempted Eve; a natural and common interpretation. Spenser here exploits both the paradisal associations of the golden fruit and their connection with greedy desire.

[18] The golden apple of discord which caused all the wrong of sad Ilion hangs as a memorial in the dwelling of Ate (IV, i, 22). As for Atalanta's apples, Alexander Ross later interprets them as 'the golden apples of worldly pleasure and profit, which Hippomenes the Devil flings in our way'. The three apples which Hercules himself took from the Hesperides are supposed by Ripa to signify the hero's power to moderate anger, avarice, and pleasure; a similar interpretation occurs in Achillis Bocchii *Symbolicarum Quaestionum* . . . (1555). If such moralizing versions were at all in Spenser's mind, one might perhaps take it that what Hercules was strong enough to master may prove a fatal temptation to lesser men.

world led him to the ultimate in ambitious blasphemy, the judging and condemning to death of the just and living God.

> I Pilate am, the falsest judge, alas!
> And most unjust; that, by unrighteous
> And wicked doome, to Jewes despiteous
> Delivered up the Lord of Life to dye. (vii, 62)

Here in the Garden Guyon is finally challenged to take Proserpina's silver seat, the throne of power set in a world of death:

> Thou fearefull foole,
> Why takest not of that same fruite of gold,
> Ne sittest downe on that same silver stoole,
> To rest thy weary person in the shadow coole?

Like the devil who tempted Christ, Mammon offers a short cut, a simplification fatal to the precariously balanced virtue of man: power and glory attained at the cost of abandoning the specifically human and with death always at the end of its extremism. Pride, even pride in well-doing, is enemy to temperance as it is to holiness, but in a different way. The places of Lucifera and Philotime show how it is that while Guyon has 'like race to ronne' it is not the same race.

Guyon is untouched by the imputation of cowardice—after all, he is getting used to this sort of challenge—and does not even incline towards the offered temptation, and Mammon has to let him go after 'three dayes of men' spent in timeless darkness. His collapse when he reaches the vital air again is a sign not of failure but of the magnitude of his success, what he has taken upon himself is the limit of what frail flesh can stand.[19] He faints because he has conquered at the necessary cost of going without the food[20]

[19] This is a much discussed crux and has been interpreted in sharply diverging ways. See, in addition to the works cited in Chapter I, note 2, and Chapter II, note 15, Maurice Evans, 'The Fall of Guyon', ELH, 28, 1961, pp. 215–24.

[20] There is a reminiscence also, in Guyon's refusal to eat, of Christ's reply to the tempter, 'It is written, Man shall not live by bread alone.' D. W. Robertson, *A Preface to Chaucer, Studies in Medieval Perspectives* (Princeton, 1963), pp. 382 ff., has an interesting reference to a homily of St. Gregory, quoted by Lombard, in which the three basic sins to which the devil appealed in his temptation both of our first parents and of Christ, are given as gluttony, vainglory, and avarice. The temptations of both the first and the second Adam are relevant to Guyon's resistance in Mammon's cave and Proserpina's garden.

61

and sleep which would have committed him to Mammon, a risk taken in order to learn the utmost man can know and see the utmost man can have from Mammon and to reject it. He did not eat, but he 'all the way/Did feed his eyes, and fild his inner thought'. When he rises he does so a new and completer man for having gone into the depths of his and all men's experience. But while he lies in apparent death friends and enemies gather round him and there takes place that strange battle, ritual-like as Red Crosse's dragon fight, between Arthur and the passionate brothers Pyrochles and Cymochles.

The canto opens with the remarkably beautiful and wondering lines which prepare us for the coming scene where the lowliest of the knights is accorded the rarest of honours just *because* he has subdued himself to the way of humility.

> And is there care in heaven? And is there love
> In heavenly spirits to these creatures bace,
> That may compassion of their evilles move?
> There is: else much more wretched were the cace
> Of men then beasts. But O th'exceeding grace
> Of Highest God, that loves his creatures so,
> And all his workes with mercy doth embrace,
> That blessed angels he sends to and fro,
> To serve to wicked man, to serve his wicked foe!

The palmer is guided back to his charge by the call of one of these same angels, the 'young man' of the Gospels and the Apocryphal stories who watches at tombs and over the virtuous dead who are to be brought from sleep back into life. Winged, divinely bright, Cupid-like, he is divine love itself, the direct emissary of God.[21] His words hold the Gospel promise:

> Yet will I not forgoe, ne yet forgett,
> The care thereof my selfe unto the end,
> But evermore him succour, and defend
> Against his foe and mine: watch thou. . . .
>
> (viii, 8)

Guyon has tried and proved himself to the utmost, and what he cannot now do will be done for him. During his swoon he suffers

[21] Professor Kermode's reference to Matthew iv, 2 seems to be the right one. At the close of Christ's temptation 'the devil leaveth him, and, behold, angels came and ministered unto him'.

the basest indignities—though the palmer and Arthur prevent them from being more than verbal ones—from the brothers, who have always thought him inglorious and to whom he is now an 'outcast carcas', a 'dead dog'. Their notion of knightly honour is so inaccurate that it has led them, as Arthur and the palmer try to show them, to bestiality and sacrilege.

The meanings contained in the battle which Arthur fights as Guyon's 'dayes-man' against Pyrochles and his brother are more readily felt than explicated. Arthur comes, clearly, under God and as the 'flowre of grace and noblesse'. But he fights without his own sword, which Pyrochles attempts to use, and he is hampered by Pyrochles's possession of Guyon's shield with its picture of Gloriana. Pyrochles has usurped and misused the attributes of the seeker after glory, and the true glory even of Arthur is disarmed—both literally and, figuratively, by his unwillingness to strike at the portrait of the Faery Queene. He kills the brothers at last with Guyon's own sword, which the palmer gives him.[22] It is as if the battle which goes on around the sleeping Guyon is fought within him and on his behalf, and with the weapon that he has proved by doing all that unaided humanity can. Of course he is guilty, like everyone else, and his identifying of himself with mankind, emphasized early in the book, means that he is 'wicked man', God's 'wicked foe'. Sin descends to all man's seed, as Arthur says; but equally it is true that, as wicked man goes, Guyon has deserved the care of heaven and the protection of grace. His virtue is feeble, and so is all human virtue, but heaven will stoop to it; and Guyon wakes refreshed when the brothers are killed for him and with his sword. The affects which they embodied are now dead in him, and cannot distort his natural nobility into a caricature of honour. After his descent and the humility of his helplessness as a 'slumbred corse' who can do no more for himself, he fully knows his own humanity, in its limitation but also in its true powers. His temperance and his knightly

[22] Maurice Evans, 'The Fall of Guyon', sees this as part of the symbolism of Christ the Redeemer, which here resides in Arthur: 'it is with man's weapons that Arthur triumphs and it was as a man that Christ redeemed mankind'. I would by no means disagree with this insight—the term 'dayes-man' and the discussion of guilt and vengeance support it—but I would prefer here to stress that Arthur, a parallel to Christ and an instrument of grace, yet does conquer with Guyon's own weapon and that it is that human weapon (with grace to wield it) which matters at this point.

passion for glory are at one, and he rides with Arthur 'in fayre accord', each with his own proper weapons restored.

What Guyon has now attained is, certainly, a recognition of human weakness, but at the same time it is a recognition of human strength in resistance and suffering. Both aspects of the knowledge of man are essential to his particular quest as they were to the task of Christ for which the temptation in the wilderness was a preparation. Only now does he proceed to the Bower of Bliss by way of the Castle of Alma the temperate soul, where humanity is seen in another aspect than that which Amavia and Mortdant showed. What first strikes us about the castle, though, is how different it is from Medina's. There the mean is held with difficulty and continuing effort and is abstractly, even pedantically, presented as a principle of action. In Alma's house we see the result of that continuing action, and we see it in the warmly human and even humorous terms now proper to Guyon. Warmly human may seem a misnomer, for no incident in *The Faerie Queene* has been oftener condescended to as 'quaint', and quaint perhaps it is: the human body is an odd thing. It is also an impressive and admirably managed thing created by the cleverest maker of all, and Spenser's honest admiration for 'goodly workemanship' is the source of much that seems quaint to a modern reader. The temperate body as an excellent dwelling-place is presented with particularity and physical impact, and the first emphasis is on this excellence of 'mans body both for powre and forme,/Whiles it is kept in sober government'. Alma keeps it so well that the queer residents of the psyche, playing with straws or gnawing rushes, frowning or fawning, express their queerness quite harmlessly and stand up politely as soon as she appears. Habitual control has produced the perfect balance of differing forces which is displayed in the very frame of the human body and the nature which it symbolizes—at least, when these are as they should be.

> The frame thereof seemd partly circulare,
> And part triangulare: O worke divine!
> Those two the first and last proportions are;
> The one imperfect, mortall, foeminine,
> Th'other immortall, perfect, masculine:
> And twixt them both a quadrate was the base,
> Proportioned equally by seven and nine;

Nine was the circle sett in heavens place:
All which compacted made a goodly diapase.

(ix, 22)

In this symbolic geometry[23] is the ancient concept of man's
duality, so vivid in its Christianized form to the Renaissance mind
and seen in its positive aspect. The opposites in us can pull us
apart or they can produce the concord of which this stanza with
its basic contraries—mortal, immortal; feminine, masculine—is
so harmonious an evocation. Feminine triangle and masculine
circle have as their common base the firmly set quadrate, and the
calmly balanced movement of the verse expresses that fruitful
harmony which is potentially present in our dual nature. Alma
has succeeded where Mortdant and Amavia as the image of
mortality have failed. Her castle is subject to no disorder from
within, only to assaults from outside upon the gates of the senses.

If the Castle of Alma extends our understanding of what temperance is through evoking the healthy mind and body, it does so
also, less directly, through defining further the relation between
Guyon and Arthur in two of the small social events which take
place. Among the various qualities who pass their time in Alma's
parlour are the two—very different but each tending towards
good behaviour—who correspond to what activates conduct in
either knight. Arthur meets 'Prays-desire,/That by well doing
sought to honour to aspyre', dressed in purple and gold, holding
a branch of the restless and aspiring poplar (Hercules's tree
according to Cartari and others), and chafing with 'great desire of
glory and of fame'. He remarks upon her pensiveness with what
is for him a rather heavy-handed authority, and is sharply told
that although he does not know it he is very much the same himself, as his long search for Gloriana proves. Guyon meanwhile
approaches Shamefastnes, silent, blushing, 'straungely pas-
sioned'. The two encounters (in which, naturally enough, neither
of the knights recognizes the thing he lives by) serve to define
what Guyon has become. By nature, his earliest appearances suggest, he has much in him of Arthur's Prays-desire. He is a son of
Mars seeking to make himself great by great achievements, fittingly mounted on the proud Brigador and quick to act in scorn

[23] For the details of the symbolism Upton's account, given in the
Variorum Spenser, seems as helpful as any. The *Variorum* collects together
many possible meanings.

of baseness but that the palmer 'suffred not in wrath his hasty steps to stray'. But now, with his weary journey drawing to its end, he is characterized by a modest acceptance of limitation. His aspiration is subdued to his task and can sustain him even where the prudent counsel of the palmer can no longer help; so that Arthur can fight for him and with his sword. The two can work together and to the same end, but the requirements of Guyon's quest have imposed upon him a high degree of differentiation, and during their stay in the castle he and Arthur follow their separate courses even to the books they read.

Arthur's chronicle of Briton kings is necessarily more detailed and precise than Guyon's rolls of Elfin emperors, since British history is more fully documented than that of the builders of Cleopolis, but Spenser has more in mind than to cater for his countrymen's historical interest or national pride. Certainly there is much achievement among the British rulers, but at the same time the danger of the aspiring mind is emphasized. Many of these legendary kings are great in conquest or invention or the giving of laws, they are 'roiall', 'bold', 'noble', but too often they end in overweening pride or the more crass kinds of ambition, especially the greed for an earthly crown. Phrases accumulate: 'his ambitious sonnes', 'But O! the greedy thirst of royall crowne', 'envious of uncles soveraintie', 'O hideous hunger of dominion!' Aspiration brings greatness, but it can also bring Philotime's values, and with them discord, treachery, tyranny. King Locrine, after great battles won, came back proud of victory and in his insolence fell to vain voluptuousness, but even those who continue to exercise themselves in high and useful action may fall through aiming too loftily, like King Bladud who 'in artes/ Excelled at Athens all the learned preace' and to whose science we owe the Bath waters.

> Yet he at last, contending to excell
> The reach of men, through flight into fond mischief fell.
>
> (x, 26)

A kind of Icarus, Bladud ends as a warning against a too soaring ambition. The Renaissance knew more than most ages about aspiration, and they knew it as a fine but a perilous thing, in a noble mind perhaps the chief danger to temperance because its intentions are so good. The knights of *The Faerie Queene* owe much to Arthur, but perhaps he learns something also from them, not least when he fights with Guyon's sword and reads in the castle of the temperate body the story of Bladud who contended to excel the reach of men.

Guyon meanwhile is reading the history not of a particular country or race but of humanity itself, as it exists within the zodiac of Spenser's world and wit. Elfe is related to the progenitor of mankind by his Promethean creation. The myth is fittingly used for the origin of Spenser's people of Faeryland since it could be taken as a tentative pagan effort towards Bible truth; moreover it enables him to suggest the mixed nature of man which makes Guyon's controlled effort towards the mean so necessary:

> It told, how first Prometheus did create
> A man, of many parts from beasts deryv'd,
> And then stole fire from heven, to animate
> His worke, for which he was by Jove depryv'd
> Of life him self, and hart-strings of an aegle ryv'd.
>
> (x, 70)

Eden has a counterpart in the gardens of Adonis,[24] which we are to enter later in the poem and where the man Elfe, the ancestor of the Elfin race, meets the creature like a sprite or an angel, 'th'authour of all woman kynd'. The inconspicuous movement between elf and man, Adonis and Eden, Prometheus and God,[25] like that between Guyon and the British Arthur, quietly establishes the identity of Guyon's people as mankind as 'what may be, and should be', and as they are in Spenser's imitation. The two races, British and Faerie, man and man as he is potentially and as art creates him, merge throughout the poem and especially here where their relationship is so important to our understanding of the necessity for temperance. Guyon, Gloriana's knight, shoulders the burden of mortality which is his as well as St. George's of England; Arthur of Britain travels into Faeryland to seek and serve that queen whose forbears have succeeded so much better than his own. The monarchs of the Elfin history are great in martial and in civil rule, but without pride, luxuriousness, or

---

[24] An etymological connection was thought to exist.

[25] Prometheus as creator suggests God's creative providence both to Arthur Golding and to Bacon. Alexander Ross (Mystagogus Poeticus [1647]) draws on Tertullian to say that God is the true Prometheus.

envy, and their line extends unbroken through seven hundred princes in peaceful power and glory. The two chronicles are alike and yet very different: the histories of Faeryland and Britain merge in the figure of Gloriana in whom Elizabeth is shadowed as Guyon and Arthur, Elfin and Briton, merge in their glory and in their temperance.

Our sense of the knights as different and yet related is strengthened in the eleventh canto, where Arthur again undertakes a task we might have expected in theory to fall to Guyon. In theory; but in practice the narrative has so thoroughly established the kinship and interpenetration of the two that we accept it as a natural thing. Arthur's battle in Canto VIII, so striking and strange yet made to seem so right through the change of weapons, through Guyon's swoon in which his life seems less suspended than submerged, and through Arthur's immediate acceptance of his role as dayes-man, has accustomed us to a situation in which, when Guyon can not or must not do more of his own conscious will, Arthur will be there to act. If the lowliest virtue is followed to the end as a given task much beyond it will be done in you, and for you; this, after all, is in part what Red Crosse's quest has shown. Maleger is perhaps original sin, the body of this death; he is certainly the diseased source of those assaults on the senses which Alma's castle has to sustain. That Maleger's troops renew their attack only after Guyon's departure is to be expected in view of the nature of temperance, and implies no particular fault in it; Guyon kills nobody on all his quest, not so much because he is incapable of it as because he ought not to. His function is to reach through ceaseless control a state so finely balanced that attacks are not even made, or not perceived. Alma's castle is 'a body which doth freely yield/His partes to reasons rule obedient', and in it all is 'Attempred goodly well for health and for delight' (xi, 2). But even such a body must endure the siege of strong affections, fiercer 'through infirmity/Of the fraile flesh' —frail, like Mortdant, both physically and morally.

Maleger, the infirmity of the frail flesh, presents in himself the chaos of strength and weakness in Mortdant and Amavia, for his strength is, as critics have pointed out, in his weakness, the diseased impulses which give power to strong affections. He is strong yet quaking, broad but of unsound substance, alive but dead, mounted on a swift tiger which serves him to avoid cap-

ture, he flees but shoots behind him as he goes. Arthur sees that
the only course with such an enemy is to stand firm and wait until
the shower of arrows is exhausted, but Impotence keeps renewing
the supply, and far from standing firm he is unbalanced and held
on the ground at Maleger's mercy, by Impotence and Impatience.
Arthur is the 'prowest' and noblest born of knights, 'greatest and
most glorious thing on ground', but the great and glorious are the
likeliest to be mastered by impatience as they feel their powerless-
ness against an attack of this kind. Arthur himself this time needs
the help of grace, whose instrument is the weaker hand of his
squire, subduing the two hags. Arthur's failure is only temporary
but it is considerable, and it is shame at his inglorious situation
which unites his powers and sends him mounting from the ground
like flame to his natural place.

> The whiles the Prince, prickt with reprochful shame,
> As one awakte out of long slombring shade,
> Revivyng thought of glory and of fame,
> United all his powres to purge him selfe from blame.
>
> (xi, 31)

But even death is only more power to Maleger, 'most strong in
most infirmitee', since he is revived by contact with earth, our
'earthly slime'. His arrows have to be withstood passively, for to
fight him only strengthens him and weakens his attacker. The
weapons of Prays-desire keep Arthur in the fight, but they are no
final use against a lifeless shadow of such persistence, and Maleger
is only disposed of in the lake where the earth his mother cannot
help him.

The Antaeus legend, Spenser's obvious source, was already
heavily moralized. Fulgentius and Boccaccio regard it as an allegory of the conquest of appetite, born of the flesh, while Ripa
has a more elaborate version of this meaning, in which Hercules
kills bodily appetite by holding it against his breast, the seat of
wisdom, thus raising it above the earthly things which nourish
it.[26] But for Hercules it was sufficient to lift Antaeus from the

[26] Thus the dominant allegorization of Antaeus supports the interpretation of Maleger as the flesh, the body of our death, though there are others:
Alexander Ross compares Antaeus with Satan, overcome by inexorable
justice, and Milton in *Paradise Regained* compares Christ's defeat of the
tempter with Hercules's defeat of Antaeus.

69

ground; Arthur finds it necessary to throw Maleger's corpse into water. As an addition to the original legend the lake draws attention to itself, and presumably one has to take it as a reference to baptismal grace as the critics say; but it is an oddly cursory reference. The difference between the guiding subjects of Holiness and Temperance makes inevitable some corresponding difference in tone between Arthur's matter-of-fact 'standing lake' and Red Crosse's Well of Life, but even so it seems curiously understated. The baptismal interpretation is inescapable, and yet it is a logical conclusion coming from outside the poem rather than a meaning that the poem itself enforces as profoundly relevant;[27] for this reason one wonders how much stress ought to be laid on it. The lake is given no origin, and no attribute save that of standing; as the narrative presents it, it happens to be three furlongs off from the battle ground where Arthur has his brainwave about water as a means of separating Maleger from earth. In itself, it reads like an intensification of Hercules's wisdom in lifting appetite above earthly things, it suggests—rather flatly—removal, total extinction, rather than baptism as a means of extinction. It is more like the engulfing of Artegall's enemies the giant and the pagan at Munera's castle than it is like a sacramental symbol. Arthur's sensible and workmanlike behaviour similarly suggests a wise prudence by which fleshly influence can be swamped when 'thought of glory and of fame' has failed to extirpate it, rather than any special virtue in the lake itself. Since the poetry lays so little stress on the water's virtue and so much on Arthur's good sense in thinking of it and his patient and determined conduct of the fight (which becomes as unknightly a struggle as any of Guyon's own) perhaps this is where our main stress also should lie. By grace of God knights who help themselves in the weakness of 'mans state, and life unsound' (xi, 30) will be helped; Guyon by the Prince's magnanimity and the Prince himself by the devoted persistence of his own squire and the existence of the lake. In this later part of the book it is the knights' own harmonious blending of aspiration and controlled wisdom that is the important thing; Arthur is so close to Guyon as to seem his other self, a relationship he does not have with any

[27] There may be iconographical or other considerations which would put a different complexion on the matter without distorting the tone the narrative seems to me to have, but I do not know of them.

other knight in the poem.[28] By their joint effort temperance
begins to rise from its humble foundations to show how high and
praiseworthy a thing it really is.

> Now ginnes this goodly frame of Temperaunce
> Fayrely to rise, and her adorned hed
> To pricke of highest prayse forth to advaunce,
> Formerly grounded and fast setteled
> On firme foundation of true bountyhed:
> And that brave knight, that for this vertue fightes,
> Now comes to point of that same perilous sted,
> Where Pleasure dwelles in sensuall delights,
> Mongst thousand dangers, and ten thousand magick mights.
>
> (xii, 1)

Guyon is ready, and on his way direct to the Bower of Bliss.
He has set out in the bright armour of his perfected strength,
though with the palmer in contrasting and necessary 'habit sad'
alongside him. The way, too, is brighter at last. Guyon no longer
trudges but is carried buoyantly over the mind's sea, watching
with that wary intelligence which characterizes him the phenomena of the depths. He is embarked now on a journey well
charted in allegorized myth, joining the select number of those
who have exemplified the steady wisdom of temperate virtue and
of whom Ulysses is the type. This is one of the oldest of the
mind's paths, well known to the good pagans and embodied in
the archetypal figures of myth; the way where monsters are en-
countered, and sirens, and Circe with her beasts. The middle
course that Guyon learned in Medina's castle is no longer an

---

[28] Eugene M. Waith, *The Herculean Hero* (London, 1962) has an
interesting and relevant discussion of the implications of Hercules, whom
Arthur copies here, in his aspect as 'a pattern of self-control' who at the
same time reaches 'a kind of excess which can be called heroic or divine
virtue'. The author compares this heroic virtue to Aristotle's megalo-
psychia or magnanimity and remarks 'Only in a very special sense is this
virtue a mean. It is justifiable pride, and hence, from a Christian point of
view, closely related to the most dangerous of all excesses. The meaning
of Hercules in the Renaissance approaches a paradox when it includes both
justifiable pride and reason subduing passion' (p. 40). The close relationship of Guyon and Arthur seems to illustrate this paradox. The relationship itself is treated by William Nelson, *The Poetry of Edmund Spenser*
(New York, 1963), and it is matter for regret that my own writing was
done before I could profit from Professor Nelson's excellent study.

abstract lesson difficult to master, it is Scylla and Charybdis, natural and proverbial part of the journey of life and part of that distillation of human experience which for Spenser's age as still for ours lingers in the old story of the canny and steadfast Ulysses. Guyon has less difficulty than his exemplar: it has been remarked that his voyage is like an interesting pleasure trip. But he has learned and is not now learning from experience as Ulysses was. It is as if he were reading rather than acting out the Odyssey, and the delusive horrors of our inner ocean, the sea-satyr and the greedy rosmarine, are at the palmer's command.

The Bower of Bliss itself has been much documented, and it deserves all the attention that it has had. Nowhere does Spenser use the ancient themes with more precise expressiveness of detailed imagery. The way in through the fragile wall is by the dream gate of ivory (the Idle Lake, we remember, was an earlier stage of the route) showing the outcome, all blood and flame and sadistic horror, of Medea's obsessive sensuality. Near it sits the false Genius, working like Acrasia and the other enchantress Medea through 'guilefull semblants' to procure our fall. Inside the gate, the place is lovely. We are warned that it is meretricious, wanton like Flora who seems an innocent goddess of natural growth but whose naturalness is achieved by art; nature is not really like this,

> goodly beautifide
> With all the ornaments of Floraes pride,
> Wherewith her mother Art, as halfe in scorne
> Of niggard Nature, like a pompous bride
> Did decke her, and too lavishly adorne,
> When forth from virgin bowre she comes in th'early morne.
>
> (xii, 50)

But whatever art is behind it, it succeeds in appearing not only beautiful but natural and healthy. Spenser even uses for it terms that are key words for this book of mental and moral health, 'attempred', 'temperate', 'holesom', 'moderate';

> Thereto the heavens alwayes joviall,
> Lookte on them lovely, still in stedfast state,
> Ne suffred storme nor frost on them to fall,
> Their tender buds or leaves to violate,
> Nor scorching heat, nor cold intemperate,

T'afflict the creatures which therein did dwell,
But the milde ayre with season moderate
Gently attempred, and disposd so well,
That still it breathed forth sweet spirit and
  holesom smell.

(xii, 51)

To reach Acrasia one goes through a state of apparent krasis, and this is why there is so much stress on dreaminess and guile, on the Circe prototype and on Medea and Flora, and on the porter who calls himself Genius like the life-giving regulator of nature in Alanus's *Pleynte of Kynde* and in the Garden of Adonis but who is really the foe of life. There is a state of relaxed ease which can seem to be a state of perfect balance, wholesome and well tempered. But it is premature, extreme heat and cold have not been taken into account, no balance has really been made. It is easy to persuade ourselves that our inner conflict is only the result of unhealthy scrupulosity and that if we make less fuss we can live as harmoniously and harmlessly as the animals do. But in the end Acrasia's animals are not harmless or harmonious; they are furious, devouring, and monstrous wild beasts, because what is natural for the animal world is not natural for man. The poor hog Grylle[29] refers us, by way of Plutarch's *Gryllus* and Gelli's *Circe*, to the wide Renaissance context of the 'natural', as of course does the interweaving, throughout the description of the Bower itself, of the meanings of 'nature' and 'art'.

The nature of the way to the Bower is an infantile fantasy state, a refusal of the effort required to achieve a real human krasis; it is a false, premature or regressive Eden. None the less it does seem like an Eden, and the weight of Spenser's emphasis on the delusive healthiness of this sweet air can only be conveyed by quoting at length.

More sweet and holesome then the pleasaunt hill
Of Rhodope, on which the nimphe that bore
A gyaunt babe her selfe for griefe did kill;
Or the Thessalian Tempe, where of yore
Fayre Daphne Phaebus hart with love did gore;

---

[29] Grylle was well enough known to appear in the works of the allegorizers; e.g. *Pegma*, p. 175 ('Voluptatem immanissimus quisque sequitur lubens').

Or Ida, where the gods lov'd to repayre,
When ever they their heavenly bowres forlore;
Or sweet Parnasse, the haunt of Muses fayre;
Or Eden selfe, if ought with Eden mote compayre.

(xii, 52)

These beautiful places are associated with what is unnatural (for man) and monstrous, the giant babe, suicide, the vegetable metamorphosis of Daphne, the lusts and angers and conflict of Troy. Nature can be innocent for man only on Parnassus, in the paradises the poet has the right to create, for there is nothing in actuality now that with Eden may compare. Eden like the other paradises ended in disaster, and since the loss of the first there can be no other. Acrasia's is a fraudulent appearance of naturalness and temperateness, bought like all the false satisfactions of this book at the cost of part of our nature, since our temperance has to be worked for by Guyon's way of the mean. But Spenser insists on its convincing *appearance* of being naturally temperate and good; Acrasia's first insidious appeal is not to our impatience of what is sound, natural, and wholesome, but to our very wish for it. So, though more naïvely, her servant Phaedria had appealed to Cymochles to live like the lily of the field, who neither spins nor cards yet has silken curtains and gold coverlets and all simple elegant luxury, provided by her mother Nature. When once a false krasis is taken for a true one the descent from vitality to the passive flowerlike Verdant or the bestial Grylle is easy, and as Guyon walks further towards the centre of the place, where Acrasia waits in her Bower, the unbalance beneath the appearance of natural health reveals itself. Nature becomes more and more peculiar, with a queer twisted relationship both to humanity and to art. Nature and art do not co-operate but compete, straining after an effect proper to neither.

That Nature had for wantonesse ensude
Art, and that Art at Nature did repine;
So striving each th'other to undermine.

(xii, 59)

The second gate is not constructed and carved by man but made by the trees themselves, distorting their branches into sensual embraces, stretching 'Their clasping armes, in wanton wreathings intricate' (xii, 53). The vine, a symbol of faithful and devoted

love when it clings to its 'vine-propp elme', here offers itself to
anybody:

> an embracing vine
> Whose bounches, hanging downe, seemd to entice
> All passers by to taste their lushious wine,
> And did them selves into their hands incline,
> As freely offering to be gathered.[30]

(xii, 54)

Green and red and purple grapes are not enough, golden ones
made by art must add to the impression of the 'natural' as also
the good, because generous and life-giving. But it is beginning
to look a good deal less temperate; it is becoming 'overburdened'
like the richness of Comus's nature, as if a too obsessive natural
health and generosity is turning before our eyes into decadence
and disease.

As Spenser puts it, it is luscious; what first seemed temperate
turns out to belong to Excess, pressing the grapes straight into
a cup to offer passers-by and set off admirably by the implied
but inevitable contrast with the emblematic Temperance, carefully mixing water with her wine. The atmosphere becomes over-
heightened, discordant, and strained as we hear of the wanton
strivings by which art and nature have produced the beauty
of the place. At Acrasia's fountain, overwrought with 'curious
ymageree', embraced by the creeping lascivious arms of the
golden ivy whose moist flowers 'drops of christall seemd for
wantones to weep', the hectic endeavours by which the devotees
of the natural must eventually maintain their values become
plain. The supposedly natural must commit itself to the obviously unnatural in order to keep itself going. It is the same with
the music which emanates from the Bower's centre. Its melodious-
ness is exquisite, but though birds (the traditional musicians of
the world's harmonious praise of God) and waters make up much
of it it could not be more contrived and unnatural. It exists
nowhere save in this fraudulent paradise; it is a false impossible
harmony made up of 'all that pleasing is to living eare'. The

---

[30] The symbolism of Christ the true vine, and the Eucharistic associations of the cup of wine, are probably present also, both here and in the
figure of Excess which follows. The pollution of the sacrament (and at the
same time of the natural sacredness of God's gifts) is finely used later in
the 'mystery of wine' at Malbecco's table.

madrigal-like stanza in which Spenser imitates this highly artificial harmony of natural things—birdsong, water, warbling wind—and musical instruments appeals once more to the age-old tradition of harmony as concord or balance. 'The notes unto the voice attempred sweet . . . divine respondence . . . the base murmure of the waters fall'. Even the tuning of the Pythagorean cosmic lyre is present in this last phrase, as the silver treble of the instruments mingles with the base of the water—'The silver sounding instruments did meet/With the base murmure of the waters fall' (xii, 71). But Sebastian's words to the imprisoned Charlemont in Tourneur's *The Atheist's Tragedie* form an apt comment both on Acrasia's false music and on the viability in Spenser's time of the connection between music and concord and the mean:

> What, hast no musicke in thee? Th' hast trebles and bases enough.
> Treble injurie and base usage. But trebles and bases make Poore
> musick without meanes. Thou want'st Meanes, dost?

(III, iii)

At the Bower's centre, the contraries which temperance must temper appear again as male and female, activity and passiveness. Opening the book in the fatal unbalance of Amavia and Mortdant, they close it in Acrasia and Verdant. These two, caught by Guyon in a golden net like that in which Vulcan had trapped Venus and Mars for the gods to laugh at, enact a version of the union of contraries which is as false as the temperate air of the Eden-like garden. The young man Verdant, the inactive and degraded warrior reduced to a kind of suspended animation while his armour hangs forgotten upon a tree, and Acrasia leaning over him awake and dominant, 'greedily depasturing delight', are Spenser's most explicit version of a subject treated often and variously in contemporary art.[31] In paintings there may be an exquisite balance of the two figures, a gentle Venus exerting enough persuasiveness to temper martial power into the strength

[31] See especially Edgar Wind, op. cit. There are relevant observations also in Erwin Panofsky, *Studies in Iconology* (New York, 1939), 'The Neoplatonic Movement in Florence and North Italy'. When Book III and the Garden of Adonis are reached, we are able to see that Verdant is a false Adonis as well as a false Mars; he and Acrasia strive to perpetuate a single moment, while Adonis is part of the vitality of a mutable world, dying to live again 'eterne in mutabilitie'.

of perfect concord. Or there may be a crafty Venus, taking Mars's weapons for her own subtle purposes of power and subduing him to sleepy weakness, as Acrasia here subdues Verdant. One contrary force has been allowed to displace and tyrannize over the other; this is no true 'nature' and no true tempering. The two symbolize not only a surrender to sensuality but a state in which the active and passive elements, instead of balancing each other, have changed places. In resisting the charm of Acrasia's wanton maidens, who emulate Venus as they play in the fountain like 'the Cyprian goddesse, newly borne/Of th'oceans fruitfull froth' (xii, 65), and in breaking Acrasia's power and restoring Verdant to his proper strength, Guyon is performing the task which the narrative has kept constantly before us in the words and actions of character after character; the restoration of balance, 'the weak to strengthen, and the strong suppresse'. Acrasia and Verdant are the revealed centre of the ambiguous relationships which Spenser has played over throughout the book, and which are to become more complex in the books which follow: strength and weakness, aggression and submission, effort and pleasure, love and war. When we come to the last stanza we are able to respond to Guyon's final comment with a fullness which, if it stood alone, its brusqueness would seem scarcely to command. 'Saide Guyon', when Grylle preferred to stay a hog,

> See the mind of beastly man,
> That hath so soone forgot the excellence
> Of his creation, when he life began,
> That now he chooseth, with vile difference,
> To be a beast, and lacke intelligence.

We respond because we recognize that this is a summing-up, in general terms, of what the book has explored in sensitive detail. In defining temperance the narrative has defined our nature as we know it through our efforts to live well in the earthly realm. If man attains unity it is 'a dialectic unity, a coexistence of contraries',[32] this assumption, on which so much of the practical morality and the psychological insight of the Renaissance tradition was based, still has its element of truth. For Spenser it was a truth at the heart of the physical and moral universe; it applies

[32] The phrase, which I have taken out of its context, is Ernst Cassirer's in *An Essay on Man* (New Haven, 1944), p. 222.

to man and to the world he must adapt himself to. Unity, within himself and in relation to others and to the laws which govern the universe, is what man must achieve: if he does not, there is only discord, perhaps masquerading as natural peace, perhaps undisguised, but in either case deadly. Only the concord of the opposites can lead to a good and creative existence, and this is why Guyon's enemies like Acrasia and Genius are the foes of life: they oppose the structure upon which all life is based. Guyon's humble path along the mean is the way to an understanding of more than temperance, and in the next books the mythical embodiments of true and false concordia are dominating presences, organizing around themselves the complexities of experience.

Chapter Three

THE TERMS OF MORTAL STATE

THE central books of *The Faerie Queene* are commonly considered together, and with good reason. Not only do characters and their stories run from one to another, but the virtues which Spenser chooses to call chastity and friendship are aspects of one inclusive and complex subject. Either book could be called of Love, or of Concord. But this would be at some loss to organization and precision of meaning, for generally speaking Book III is concerned with 'chaste affection' and with the kind of emotional integrity and completeness which that term suggests, as well as with other and related kinds, while Book IV is concerned with the bonds of friendship, whether between persons of the same sex or not, and with the things which break such bonds. The distinction is by no means sharp; it could not be since for Spenser friendship is a kind of love and love a kind of friendship, and Britomart plays a major part in both books. The legends are linked also by the Temple of Venus in Book IV; the goddess is the creative Venus of generation, Venus genetrix, but her gardens have room not only for pairs of lovers but for such traditional pairs of friends as David and Jonathan, 'another sort/Of lovers lincked in true harts consent', and the gate to the temple is guarded by Concord.

Concord embodies the presiding idea of both these closely integrated books, but it is fitting that she should make her actual appearance in the second of them in which so many pains, confusions, and misunderstandings are resolved in friendship. Concord arises, if it arises at all, out of discord actual or potential; and at the Temple of Venus the personification of Concord holds on

79

either side of her Hate and Love, his younger half-brother, and forces them to join hands. Her responsibilities as Scudamour describes them are many, ranging from the sustaining of the whole universe through the concord of its parts to the subduing of human strife and the establishing of peace within the afflicted mind.

> For strength and wealth and happiness she lends,
> And strife and warre and anger does subdew;
> Of little much, of foes she maketh frends,
> And to afflicted minds sweet rest and quiet sends.
>
> By her the heaven is in his course contained,
> And all the world in state unmoved stands,
> As their Almightie Maker first ordained,
> And bound them with inviolable bands;
> Else would the waters overflow the lands,
> And fire devours the ayre, and hell them quight,
> But that she holds them with her blessed hands.
>
> (IV, x, 34–5)

All these aspects of Concord's work become visible in the third and fourth books, and to some degree also in the succeeding ones, for as Spenser builds up his world on the 'secret rules' of its being the virtues, as different aspects of experience, become less and less separable.

In the third book, however, we are conscious chiefly, though not only, of the discord out of which, if all goes well, concord will be made. It is a book of perplexities, in which the incomprehension of the characters and the inscrutability of the conditions in which they live combine to express the paradoxical quality of our apprehension of each other, ourselves, and the world around us. The poet's comment on Proteus's misleading prophecy, which not even the prophet himself appears to have understood, provides a comment also on the action of the book:

> So ticle be the termes of mortall state
> And full of subtile sophismes, which doe play
> With double sences, and with false debate,
> T'approve the unknowen purpose of eternall fate.
>
> (III, iv, 28)

Not everyone in the book has an oracular riddle to deal with, but the predicament of Cymoent and her son is a type of everyone else's. Life is full of 'double sences', ambiguities by which the purpose of fate is worked out through us and, sometimes, despite us. It is 'the *unknowen* purpose of eternall fate', the inscrutable doubleness of things, which is felt most strongly in this book. Things happen, and people try to puzzle out how and why; but they are so double-sensed, so subtle, that it is difficult to work out what they mean without simplifying them to the point of disaster, which is what Cymoent, Marinell, Amoret, and Scudamour do. Natural phenomena are instruments of eternal fate, but they are no more than that, and are therefore unfathomable: thus the sea plays a large part in these central books but it plays that part unconsciously and its representatives are moved to do they know not what. Proteus speaks what he is inspired to speak, and Cymoent in trying to avoid fate by interpreting the prophecy merely brings that fate about; great Neptune mourns for Cymoent's grief as she passes 'Yet wist not what their wailing ment', and her son Marinell moves blindly to his sacrificial fate with the confident mindless dignity of the sacred ox, gilded, garlanded, and 'Proud of his dying honor and deare bandes'.

As is usual in *The Faerie Queene*, the opening cantos define the atmosphere which is to prevail in the book. First there is a merging of the concerns of temperance and of chaste love; Guyon and Arthur, joined in a 'hunt for glory' in Gloriana's service, encounter the famous Britomart. But these two highly accomplished knights are not particularly competent in those regions of Faeryland where Britomart moves unconquered. Guyon, overthrown by her enchanted spear, gives way to 'disdainefull wrath', 'wrathfull will', 'angry corage', and has to be calmed down like a spoiled child by the palmer and by Arthur, who tactfully puts the fault for Guyon's disgrace on the page who had not properly saddled up his horse. Since they are all essentially sensible people with a good deal in common, peace is made and they are tied together with the 'golden chaine of concord', but the moment of ineptitude has suggested that this is Britomart's sphere of action rather than Guyon's or even Arthur's. Guyon's control, so exquisite and ironic in his own world, fails him here, and he is soon to ride out of the story. For they pass on together into the forest of the passions, a sad and frightening place where bears, bulls, and lions roam around them and no other living things are to be seen; and suddenly across their sight there flashes one of the most startling of Spenser's pictures, a white palfrey with an unnamed rider whose face is clear as crystal and bone-white with fear, and who is dressed all in gold. She bursts out of the thickest of the brush and is gone across their path so quickly that they scarcely see her pass, but she has upon them the same striking effect, of remote beauty and portentousness, and of speed frozen into permanence, as a comet might have. The logical point of contact in the simile is her yellow hair, flying behind her as she rides

> All as a blazing starre doth farre outcast
> His hearie beames, and flames lockes dispredd,

but it continues in terms of disaster:

> At sight whereof the people stand aghast:
> But the sage wisard telles, as he has redd,
> That it importunes death and dolefull dreryhedd.

(i, 16)

The lady's flowing hair, the symbol of her power to attract, merges into the 'hair' of the comet, the mysterious and alarming natural portent—all the more disturbing because of its startling beauty—which the wise man interprets as a sign that things are about to go wrong. And so they do; wisards may be no more accurate about the meaning of portents than Proteus and Cymoent are, but in this instance the traditionally disruptive quality of the comet's flaming locks does have a certain bearing on the situation. The knights gaze dazedly after the fleeting vision; and then, seeing that the lady is pursued by a lustful foster brandishing a boar spear, they all take off in pursuit and are scattered in different directions, lost and aimless in the forest. All, that is, except Britomart, 'whose constant mind/Would not so lightly follow beauties chace,/Ne reckt of ladies love'. She goes, as she is always to do, forward, 'As lay her journey, through that perlous pace,/With stedfast corage and stout hardiment' (i, 19).

The fleeing and fearful lady is, of course, Florimell, and I have omitted her name not with any hope of preparing a surprise but because Spenser omits it too. At this first appearance we know nothing about Florimell except that she is riding very fast through the dangerous passionate forest, pursued by the foster and then by everybody, except Britomart; and that she strikes us in the way a comet would, as being mysterious, beautiful, fleeting yet powerful and obscurely ominous. She is gone in a moment, but because of that very speed and brightness her image is fixed in our minds, and in Arthur's, as brilliantly as is that of the blazing star. Like the comet, she does not seem harmful in herself, or by intention, but she brings the portent of harm; she is as inscrutable and disturbing as Proteus and his sea. If we think of her in this appearance as the touching and suffering creature we know later, we will perhaps misunderstand her; we will certainly lose much of the atmosphere Spenser is building up at the book's opening, the atmosphere of 'subtile sophismes, which doe play/With double sences'.

The ambiguities begin promptly. Timias rides after the foster, to engage in the forest with lust; Arthur and Guyon ride after Florimell, and their motive is stated not as rescue but as capture.

> The Prince and Guyon equally bylive
> Her selfe persewd, in hope to win thereby
> Most goodly meede, the fairest dame alive.
>
> (i, 18)

The pursuit is frankly called 'beauties chace', they are engaged on a chase, a hunt, though no doubt their mixed motives are more perceptible to the poet than to themselves. For this is what is typical of the Faeryland of Book III, that one's own intentions and those of others, and the meaning of situations and actions, constitute a net of enigmatic possibilities. To ride after a distressed lady would seem to be the knightly thing, but in this area of experience its motives may turn out to be dubious enough. The obviously chivalric thing may not do, may serve only to conceal from one's self a trace of the predatory. At any rate, Britomart seems to be in the right in having nothing to do with the instinctive pursuit of beauty which leads the others away from their quests and their proper allies. She goes singlemindedly forward, with the poet's approval.

The first canto sets the tone, then: a forest of fierce creatures, where it is easy to lose one's way; a mysteriously dangerous fleeing beauty; proven knights somehow out of their element and course, and losing their former clarity of intention; a third knight with an enchanted and invincible spear who is known to us, but not to her companions, to be a woman. There is no ill-intentioned deceit, unless it be Archimago's; we are told later that he is pursuing Britomart's downfall 'Now that he had her singled from the crew/Of courteous knights, the Prince and Fary gent' (iv, 45), and this hint of deliberate evil adds, when it comes, to Florimell's ambiguity. She is the unwitting occasion, but still the occasion, of the separation Archimago aimed at. But this underlining of Florimell's unintentionally dangerous quality is perhaps all that the reference to Archimago is intended to do; at least we hear no more of him, and the book as a whole does not, like the books of Holiness and Temperance, suggest that the knights are being deliberately tempted by the forces of evil. Rather, they are encompassed by the problematical, and are likely to get into trouble with the best intentions in the world. So could the knights of the first two books, of course; it is a matter of emphasis. Red Crosse and Guyon were following well-tracked paths, however difficult; they had a precise end in view, the defeat of the dragon or the overthrow of Acrasia, and their successes and failures can be estimated in terms of virtue and sin.

Guyon's story is beautifully poised as a transition between Red Crosse's high holiness and the loving, just, and courteous dealings of the other knights among their fellow men and in the world; it opens upon 'the termes of mortall state'. But whereas to Guyon the issues are always fairly clear (as we can tell from the wise commentary which he and the palmer keep up through their adventures), in the area of human relationships into which the poem is now moving there are few rules that can be of much use. All that the palmer's 'mighty science' comes to here is the prudent advice to leave Britomart and her magic spear alone. He supports his advice with moral saws, as is his habit, but these, which in his own book were wise and touching commonplaces, here echo with a proverbial obviousness which points their limitation:

> Nothing on earth mote alwaies happy beene.
> Great hazard were it, and adventure fond,
> To loose long gotten honour with one evill hond.

(i, 10)

True, no doubt, and prudent: but these general rules will not take one far in Britomart's world of particulars.

Britomart's world, certainly, it is; not in the sense that she is the only actor in it, moving as Red Crosse and Guyon do through a background of possible sins and errors, but in the sense that among all the crowding figures around her she is the only one fully competent to deal with it. It is a truism that the third and fourth books are made up of interlocking stories with their own major characters, some of whom never meet at all, after the style of Ariosto's romance epic, while the books of Holiness and Temperance are firmly constructed along a clear narrative line, with a single hero. The second book, parallel in structure to the first but loosening it slightly in the larger role given to Arthur, perfectly manages the movement into 'the world', but the difference is still marked. It is so—and this is equally a truism—because human experience appears in a different shape when one looks at it from the viewpoint of love, and so requires a different structure. The books of Holiness and Temperance have behind them a traditional framework, theological and moral, and although the narrative humanizes and actualizes it out of all rigidity its firmness is felt. Moreover holiness and temperance are achieved within one's self, in Celia's house or Alma's. Love, chastity, concord are inner things too, but they involve not only one's own harmony but one's harmonious relations with others. Nor are they precisely matters of right and wrong; the black and white world of Red Crosse, already somewhat blurred in the practical efforts of Guyon, becomes far more shaded and shifting here. To become truly and fully loving is not to be achieved by resisting a series of temptations and overcoming one final enemy; it is something to be worked out by trial and error, and if it is to be presented with any adequacy the trial and the error must be shown as well as the success. There must be people who really love and are really loved, but whose affection is less wise than it is genuine. There must be Amoret and Florimell as well as Britomart, and even knights like Paridell and Claribell who can be called good knights although they are bad lovers.

So in the third and fourth books the straight narrative with a single hero is replaced by the arrangement that the subject requires: a number of stories proceeding side by side and relating by Spenser's favourite parallel and contrast to explore experience as it is revealed through the consideration of love. The structure is necessarily more complex, and since it depends less on narrative progression than on a pattern of relationships it is revealed gradually. Indeed this must be so if the trial and error, the difficult adjustments, the narrow line which separates success from

85

failure, are to be expressed, and these are of the essence of the subject. Thus it is apparent shapelessness which strikes us first, as I have tried to suggest in describing the action with which the third book opens: instead of a knight with a red cross and a lady with a lamb, or a clearly defined image of mortality, there is the brief undignified meeting of knights and their rapid dispersal in pursuit of a woman whose nature is no clearer to us than to them. Pattern, and the meaning which pattern unfolds, emerges by degrees as the book advances. There is no map of the passionate forest or the mysterious sea; a path must be made by going forward as Britomart does, with a mind firmly and honestly fixed on the objective. Then things will gradually fall into place, but to turn aside is to be quickly lost among trivialities or illusions or greater or lesser perversions.

It is easy for even a modern reader to recognize the variety and ambiguity subsumed under the word love. We are trained to detect the dangers inherent in emotion, the distortions and deceits that can grow up within ourselves and be reflected in our behaviour to others. Spenser was trained to similar perceptions, like generations of poets before him, but he was trained to others too. There is no need to claim modernity for him. He had available a more inclusive and flexible means of psychological expression than a modern can readily attain, and his poetry is supremely of the Renaissance. Insight into psychological and emotional states is likely to be the same in all ages, and we can recognize our own concerns in Spenser's, but love to him embraced a great deal more than the personal affections which circumscribe it for us. In the third book it is these affections, and the inner maturity on which their successful management depends, that are central, but a responsible poet relates them to their public consequences, as in Merlin's prophecy of the future of Britomart and Artegall as rulers, and of the concord which they are to realize not only in and between themselves but eventually in their country's peaceable blend of Celt and Saxon.

Again, love was analogically present in other spheres than the human; the universe was made and is sustained by it. As Spenser puts it in *Colin Clouts Come Home Againe*,

> For by his powre the world was made of yore,
> And all that therein wondrous doth appeare.
> For how should else things so far from attone,

And so great enemies as of them bee,
Be ever drawne together into one,
And taught in such accordance to agree?

(ll. 841-6)

In the *Hymne in Honour of Love*, too, there is the famous description of how Love created the world out of the contrary forces of the elements in their mutual hatred:

Ayre hated earth, and water hated fyre,
Till Love relented their rebellious yre.

He then them tooke, and tempering goodly well
Their contrary dislikes with loved meanes,
Did place them all in order, and compell
To keepe them selves within their sundrie raines,
Together linckt with adamantine chaines.

(ll. 83-9)

Concord, holding Love and Hate together, is another version of the same concept, for the theories of love, cosmic and human, philosophical and psychological, had a natural and traditional connection with the doctrine of the opposites. The connection can be seen, in one form, in the pseudo-Aristotelian *De Mundo*, one of the many channels along which the speculations of the ancient world passed, in generalized and popular form, to medieval and Renaissance Europe. Indeed this little treatise contrives to draw together, in its genial if not very logical way, many of those loosely related acceptances which underlie the Spenserian world picture. The uniting or the balancing of contrary principles is the core of the treatise, for it is seen as a universal law. Civic concord and the arts of painting, music, and writing are examples of it equally with the structure of the physical universe; it is the basis of order, harmony, justice, and its clearest analogy is that of generation.[1]

It may perhaps be that nature has a liking for contraries and evolves harmony out of them and not out of similarities (just as she joins the male and female together and not members of the same sex), and has devised the original harmony by means of contraries and not similarities.[2]

[1] Among many ancient dicta to the same effect Proclus's statement that if generation is to continue to exist there must be contraries, from which alone generation can arise, is an excellently concise example.

[2] Aristotle, *Works*, translated by W. D. Ross (Oxford, 1931), III, 396b.

As the basis of all existence the opposites are present in all creative activity, sometimes held, as the elements are, at their mean qualities, sometimes gaining strength in turn as the seasons do. The author of *De Mundo* goes on to see their workings in the balanced succession of summer and winter, day and night, and in the paradoxical permanence which earth maintains through perpetual birth and death, 'eterne in mutabilitie', to use Spenser's phrase. 'Some have wondered how it is that the Universe, if it be composed of contrary principles—namely, dry and moist, hot and cold—has not long ago perished and been destroyed', but

> Of individual things upon the earth some are coming into being, others are at their prime, others are decaying; and birth checks decay and decay lightens birth. Thus an unbroken permanence, which all things conspire to secure, counteracting one another—at one time dominating, at another being dominated—preserves the whole unimpaired through all eternity.[3]

All this, of course, is medieval and Renaissance commonplace,[4] and I restate it only to emphasize its inclusiveness and its value— which Spenser exploits to the full—as a structural principle in that part of the poem which is especially concerned to re-create the world in terms of love. Love, concord, friendship, became interchangeable terms for the binding together of things which also have between them discord or 'enmity' or 'hate'. Neoplatonism, which permeates (again, in a popularly general rather than in a philosophically exact form) Spenser's mind as it does that of the age, enlarged upon the relation of love to the doctrine of contraries, sometimes pursuing connections so far that the creative tension is slackened in a vague aura of universal harmony,[5] and

[3] Aristotle, op. cit., 396b and 397b.
[4] See for example R. Tuve, 'A Medieval Commonplace in Spenser's Cosmology', S.P., XXX, 1933. Miss Tuve demonstrates, with reference to Batman's rescension of Bartholomaeus Anglicus, the traditional nature of Spenser's cosmology.
[5] I am much indebted, for a precise and detailed historical account of the vicissitudes of the concept of discordia concors, to Brendan O'Hehir, 'Balanced Opposites in the Poetry of Pope, and the Historical Evolution of the Concept', an unpublished dissertation for the doctoral degree at the Johns Hopkins University. The use I make here of the concept, and its application to Spenser's poetry, is of course my own responsibility. In *The Faerie Queene* the tradition is used very flexibly, even loosely, and unphilosophically, except for such careful passages as the description of Concord, where exactitude is required.

the concept loses much of its precision and much of its usefulness. But the Heraclitean bow is never quite unstrung, and among that group of ancient and recent writers—often so different in aim and capacity and yet so comfortably homogeneous—on which the period drew for its authority there are many for whom the opposites are taut still, each retaining its proper nature although they join in love. Among such writers are Plutarch, Philo Judaeus, Alanus de Insulis; Ficino and Pico, and the painters who imaged their concepts; and Leone Ebreo, whose *Dialoghi d'Amore* is perhaps the handiest of compendia on the nature of love and a useful commentary, too, on Spenser's handling of the subject, for it touches on love divine and human, love in the inanimate world, love perfected, faulty, or merely travestied. And in all these treatments, whether in the high imaginations of the Florentine philosophers or in such practical volumes of instruction as Palingenius's *Zodiacus Vitae*, the opposites fight and unite, ebb and flow, to the sustaining of life.

What the philosophers and popularizers and pedagogues expound, Spenser incorporates into the structure of his poem. 'The union of contraries, a friendly enmity, a disagreeing concord', which is a principle of order in the created universe, orders Spenser's small universe also. The two central books build up the world of man's personal relations, his harmony with his surroundings, his concord within himself, and for all these meanings the relation of the sexes is a symbol. One aspect of the universal truth expresses other aspects as well as itself. The cosmic, political, and generative embodiments of the creative union of contraries are familiar, but one should perhaps recall also that the golden mean, and the internal concord which is treated in the book of Temperance, has its relation to strife and love, as Acrasia and Verdant and Phaedria suggest. Man, says Pico della Mirandola, is the chain that binds the world together, and is placed in the midst, 'and as all mediums participate of their extreams, his parts correspond with the whole worlde; thence called "Microcosmus" '. As microcosmus, man is the supreme example of the necessity for concord among the extremes which meet in him, and that necessity gains significance and resonance from the echoes which it stirs in all the parts of the analogical universe.

It is in such a universe that the pairs of lovers in the books of Chastity and Friendship exist. In the symbolic atmosphere of

Elizabethan literature human marriage stands for itself, but for more besides. Ben Jonson's *Hymenaei* is an obvious example, in which marriage, exemplifying concord, is related to the concord of qualities in man and in the universe, to what Spenser's admired Du Bartas calls 'le noeud du sacré mariage/Qui joint les elemens', and there are many more examples among marriage masques and epithalamia. The aura of the hieros gamos hung about any marriage, including Spenser's own, ready to be exactly invoked. The ancient commentators on cosmic myth, and their successors the Renaissance mythographers, made the symbolism of marriage easy and habitual, and with it related symbols like that of the hermaphrodite or the double-sexed or double-natured god. Thus there was available for Spenser a rich body of symbolic material, wide reaching and many layered, by which his books of concord could be organized into a pattern of meaning. Much of that material is mythological, for from classical times up to the Italian neoplatonists the great gods had provided both the suggestion for, and the means of expressing, speculation about the nature of things. Venus and Cupid, who with Mars were of particular interest to the Florentines, and who had as many aspects as life itself: Diana: the heroes of the Troy legend: all these had developed through the centuries into a complex of meanings which would have astonished Hesiod or Homer. Cupid, for example, is as much at home in *The Romaunt of the Rose* as in the commentaries on Plato. His connections, or his mother's, with Diana or Mars provided a natural means of expression for, say, a poet of the Pléiade discussing the nature of his mistress or for a philosopher discussing (like Ebreo) the nature of love itself.

In the proem to his first book Spenser had referred to Venus, Mars, and Cupid in terms which recall those ambiguously meaningful relationships expressed so often in Ficino and Pico, in epigrammatic verses, in paintings. In these and in other related figures is summed up much of the many-sided significance which the Renaissance saw in the discordia concors of love. Mars's strife and Venus's mildness can vary in proportion and in meaning; Cupid can be cruel, or when he lays his deadly bow aside, gentle, can inspire the lover to glory and creation or condemn him to a living death, for he may be, in Guillaume Alexis's typical phrase, not 'Dieu d'Amours, mais de mort'. Such ambivalent creatures are the focal point of several of those familiar themes by which experience was ordered in the mind of many a Renaissance poet and painter: the nature of love and the nature of its connection with enmity; the value of love according to Plato and of love according to Ovid; the meaning of the hunt or chase of love, the hunt of honour, the hunt of death; and the ways in which all these relate to each other and to the great opposites for which god and goddess, or man and woman, can be symbols. In this part of the poem, therefore, the union of contraries, or their failure properly to unite, is especially appropriate as a means to organization. In love and friendship are comprehended some of the most paradoxical aspects of human life, and the ambiguous yet exact symbols of the mythographers and the neo-platonists—Venus with Mars (a union which produced Harmonia) or with Diana, Venus virgo or armata, the double-natured Cupid—find here their natural place. In *The Faerie Queene* they interact with themes like those of Ovidian, courtly, or Platonic love which are not only literary conventions but assumptions about the nature of human experience. With the help of such traditions the interlocking stories of Britomart, Amoret, Belphoebe, and Florimell are related to a common mythological centre of reference, and patterned in a way that does justice both to the complication of living and to the secret laws which control our experience even when we do not know them.

Of the characters in Book III there is one, Britomart, who knows that such laws exist and that to live in accordance with them requires not so much a detailed appreciation of their working as a sure sense of one's own direction. Constancy and a determined and steady progress are characteristic of her. She goes on her way, and events consequently shape themselves into a pattern around her. Several of the other characters, straying about the forest or the shore, depend on her action to make sense of their experience too, and meaning arises from the elaborate pattern of likeness and contrast in which she plays an important part. So in considering the third book it is as well to begin with Britomart, and with her most striking quality, her completeness as woman and warrior, an armed figure like Minerva or Venus armata, in whom feminine and masculine qualities are balanced. Spenser handles her character with a very sure touch, and makes her convincing and, usually, rather endearing. She manages her unusual situation with frankness and good sense because she sees nothing odd about it. She never exploits her femininity, though she will use her double identity with ingenious humour where necessary, as when, at the beginning of Book IV, she claims the rights of both woman and knight in order to win lodging for a stranger. This occasion is one of several which demonstrate the mastery she has attained over both sides of her nature; a mastery now so easy, a concord so complete, that it is accepted with a corresponding naturalness by those who encounter it. When, having conquered as a warrior, she loosens her hair to claim her right as a woman too, the young knight in whose interests she has courteously acted after defeating him is 'doubly overcommen' (i, 15). Britomart's great strength is in her simple and dignified trust in herself and in others; she has none of those feminine fears which bring about the very aggression they imagine, and since she does not exploit she is not exploited, but is accepted on her own companionable terms even by rather coarse-grained characters like Satyrane and predatory ones like Paridell. When in Malbecco's house she casually takes off her helmet her companions in arms are highly pleased both with their 'first error' and with their present knowledge. 'Every one her likte, and every one her lov'd', she is regarded neither as a potential victim nor as a potential tyrant. The poet, with the *Romaunt* and its tradition in mind, compares her to a rose, but a rose whose formidable thorns are noticed at the same instant as her beauty.[6]

> For shee was full of amiable grace,
> And manly terror mixed therewithall,
> That as the one stird up affections bace,
> So th'other did mens rash desires apall,
> And hold them backe, that would in error fall;
> As hee that hath espide a vermeill rose,
> To which sharpe thornes and breres the way forstall,
> Dare not for dread his hardy hand expose,
> But wishing it far off, his ydle wish doth lose.

(III, i, 46)

It is because she is both warrior and woman that she is invincible as either.

---

[6] The treatment of the medieval rose symbol here may be compared with that in III, v, 51, where Belphoebe's tending of the rose, though virtuous, seems less well judged. See p. 101.

Britomart is the one person in the third book who has solved the problems of duality in herself, and consequently, in her relations with others. Being, so to say, both masculine and feminine, with the blended power of strength and love, she can act as a point of reference for all those knights and ladies who, singly and jointly, fail to achieve concord. Such a central figure is necessary to the significant patterning of the book, but the danger is that in making success seem so easy experience may be falsified. Spenser guards against this by showing us, briefly, the effort which has made her. She has had difficulties like Amoret's, but she has dealt with them positively and has made them contribute to her present wholeness. Her previous history is given us in the second and third cantos. When she first idly looked into her father's magic glass—which was made by Merlin but is also called 'Venus looking glas'—and fell in love with Artegall's image, she gave way to the exaggerated feminine terrors of an Ovidian heroine. What is important here is not only the 'naturalness' of her childish and bewildered response but the literary associations which the poet exploits. The exchanges between the girl and her nurse are based on the Virgilian *Ciris*, but they also follow very closely Ovid's story of the unnatural passion of Myrrha, and Britomart sees herself as one of these passive victims, driven, by a brutal and perverted power beyond her own control, to guilt and death. Glauce draws our attention to the Ovidian context of perversity and pain by sharply denying its relevance. Britomart, she says firmly, is no Myrrha or Biblis or Pasiphae; her love may be unusual, but it is not unnatural. 'Why make ye such monster of your minde?' she says, and the astringent, commonsensical phrase, and all the old woman's homely, church-going, comforting activities, set a norm of health and sanity against which the monsters of Britomart's mind, and of Amoret's later, can be seen for what they are—fictions made by our own unbalance, which misunderstands the nature of love.

Britomart needs, however, more than the robust sense of reality which Glauce represents; she needs also the knowledge which Merlin, the maker of the mirror, can supply. What Merlin teaches her is that love is not a thing to be passively suffered, but an opportunity for responsible action and personal growth; not a disease contracted through the pointless cruelty of a Cupid who delights in suffering but part of a coherent divine plan. 'Well did antiquity a god thee deeme', says the poet to Love;

> The fatall purpose of divine foresight
> Thou doest effect in destined descents,

(iii, 2)

and this is the burden of Merlin's prophetic revelation. Britomart has learned to love by 'fatall lore', and has seen Artegall's image not by the chance of a wandering eye but by divine guidance.

> It was not, Britomart, thy wandring eye,
> Glauncing unwares in charmed looking glas,
> But the streight course of hevenly destiny,
> Led with Eternall Providence, that has
> Guyded thy glaunce, to bring His will to pas.

(iii, 24)

Britomart's mistake is understandable, for the mirror in Elizabethan symbolism could be of a kind to reflect false unreal shadows. But it could also be the mirror of truth, penetrating the false appearance of things, and is often an attribute of pictured Truth herself. Britomart's mirror is identified for us as being of this kind when we are told of its power to uncover deceit, 'what ever foe had wrought, or frend had faynd', while its spherical shape, 'Like to the world it selfe', further emphasizes its nature. The globe, a sign of power over the world, is another attribute of Truth.

Thus in seeing Artegall in the armour of Achilles Britomart sees not an illusion, as she supposes, but a truer vision of his essential quality than she could gain from a sight of the man himself. Love is to be a formative experience, not the destructive horror she first thought it, and her task is to accept the divine purpose and her own duty. So Merlin tells her:

> Therefore submit thy wayes unto His will,
> And doe, by all dew meanes, thy destiny fulfill.

(iii, 24)

Destiny is firm, and man's part is to co-operate with it by doing his best with the job in front of him.

> Yet ought mens good endevours them confirme,
> And guyde the heavenly causes to their constant terme.

(iii, 25)

94

It is to explain Britomart's destiny and duty that Merlin pro
phesies the future of her royal descendants. Throughout the
prophecy he stresses the workings of the divine will which deals
with the Britons as did Jehovah with the Hebrews, supporting,
checking, punishing to bring about its own purposes. For any
one of the human links in the chain of divine causation those purposes could not have been easy to see. God's ways are slow. But
overall direction is visible, as much in human error as in human
goodness; the justice and care of heaven are shown in much the
same way as in Shakespeare's history plays. Gormond the Norse-
man overruns 'holy church',[7] Ethelred massacres the monks of
Bangor, in the next generation the wrongs of the Britons are
avenged by Cadwallin upon the Saxon Edwin. But the traitor
Penda, Cadwallin's 'fatall instrument,/T''afflict the other Saxons
unsubdewd', marches to Hevenfield against God's good King
Oswald, who,

> indewd
> With heavenly powre, and by angels reskewd,
> Al holding crosses in their hands on hye,
> Shall him defeate withouten blood imbrewd.
>
> (iii, 38)

Cadwallin, presumably, should have accepted this as a sign of
divine intervention and left Oswald in peace, but instead he goes
out in wrath to 'crowne with martiredome his sacred head'.
Oswald's brother Oswin addes to the prevailing atmosphere of
desecration by buying his kingdom with the Judas-like 'price of
silver' and Penda by further treachery. After Cadwallin, heaven
and destiny see to it that the British power wanes. Cadwallader,
intending to return from Brittany to save his people,

> Shalbe by vision staide from his intent:
> For th'Heavens have decreed to displace
> The Britons for their sinnes dew punishment,
> And to the Saxons over-give their government.
>
> (iii, 41)

---

[7] Religion in this book has a kind of homeliness, with 'holy church'
accepted as a comfortable certainty. It is the simple religious feeling of
people who are too much preoccupied with getting over the next difficulty
to indulge in speculation. The sense of destiny which gives Britomart and
Glauce an unquestioning perseverance in their duty however complicated
the situation appears, is entirely appropriate to the atmosphere of the book.

So the tale goes on, until the Welsh house of Tudor reclaims the throne of Britain.

> Thenceforth eternall union shall be made
> Betweene the nations different afore,
> And sacred Peace shall lovingly persuade
> The warlike minds to learne her goodly lore.
>
> (iii, 49)

The eventual union of Briton and Saxon under the Welsh and English Elizabeth depends upon the union of Britomart and Artegall, and this in its turn depends upon a union of powers in Britomart herself. She must accept that her love for a mirrored image is part of the creative purpose of a providence whose instrument she must fit herself to become. Thus she learns from Merlin that no personal situation is merely personal, but may have results that go far beyond ourselves. Rash action, undertaken with no thought further than the moment, may affect many other people too. This is something that the whole book reinforces; thoughtlessness in Amoret or Marinell may spark off a series of events for others. Britomart's actions turn out uniformly well for herself and others because she has a clear sense of purpose and knows that her purpose contributes to a greater one which is God's. In her story the theme of concord is taken beyond the realm of the personal, for what others in the book cannot even attain is for her only a first step. Because she interprets love responsibly it changes her from a hysterical girl to a woman with a fine sense of personal relationships. She will not be deflected from her destined search for Artegall, but on the way she can show love in various forms from comradeship to protectiveness. She is strong because she is loving and loving because she is strong, and her irresistible spear is surely something more than a magic of chastity. It is a sign of the power that integrity gives, and related to her Minerva-like wisdom and singlemindedness. Stephen Batman tells us that by Minerva's long spear is signified 'the foresight of things to come',[8] and Britomart has been provided by Merlin with this knowledge and the certainty which accompanies it.

Since she solves the problems of reconciliation and understanding which the third book sets, Britomart is its dominant

---

[8] *The Golden Booke of the Leaden Goddes* (1577), p. 5.

figure. Around her are grouped others, male and female, who cannot solve those problems or cannot solve them without her help. Meaning emerges chiefly through the comparisons implicit in such parallel stories as Britomart's and Florimell's, such parallel persons as Britomart and Marinell. Several characters are shown in roughly similar situations and the significance exists in the likenesses and differences we are compelled to see in their behaviour. Often the differences are slight, for a rich concord of qualities may be hard to tell apart from a precarious and imperfect balance, although their consequences are so different. It is the narrow borderline between the true concordia and the many false ones that makes the terms of mortal state so tickle. Such material has to be flexibly handled, and Spenser brings mythology to his aid to achieve an ordering which is an expression at the same time of complexity and of the delicacy of discrimination which that complexity necessitates. Myth in this book is pervasive and its function is structural. Venus plays a large and varied part, as might be expected, and also present are her counterpart Diana, her son Cupid, and her lover Adonis. Mars does not appear in person, nor does he need to. For a Renaissance reader he would be hauntingly present as part of the pattern of love and war, life and death, creation and destruction, which is outlined by the other gods. Venus and Diana have, also, their representatives in their wards Amoret and Belphoebe, and are both present in Britomart, whose 'Dian/Was both herself and Love',[9] whose appearance and actions demonstrate 'chaste affection', and who shares her name with the chaste nymph Britomartis, later the goddess Diana Dictynna. Others too are present by implication, much as Ulysses and Hercules are in the second book; certain of the knights recall Hercules and Achilles, who have their own ambiguous relationships to love and war.

For of course the pagan gods and heroes did not merely survive through the Middle Ages, they were put to new uses. The moral débats between Venus as Love and Diana as Chastity are an obvious example, living on into the Renaissance and into Spenser's poem. In such figures as these the poet had a flexible and adaptable language which the reader had no need to translate, so accustomed was he to its use. Spenser can, if he wishes, go right back to the classical beginnings—to Lucretius's Venus,

[9] Helena's words, in *All's Well That Ends Well*.

97

Virgil's Venus virgo, Ovid's Diana—or he can adopt the different Venuses or Cupids, celestial or terrestrial, of the neoplatonists; but he can also make use of the gods as they appear in the conventions of Renaissance love poetry,[10] widespread everywhere but perhaps most ingeniously expressive in the sonnets and epigrams of the Pléiade and the plays of John Lyly. Never before or since have the gods been able to express so much, grouping themselves into endlessly suggestive arrangements. For example Spenser's encounter between Diana and Venus exists in a rich growth of traditional meanings. The meeting of the goddesses had come to be expressive of more than a plain moral opposition between the sensuous and the ascetic. The intense and subtle contemplation which late medieval and early Renaissance poets devoted to the subject of love suggested to them that Diana and Venus were not only obviously opposed but also in various curious and hidden ways connected. So too were Diana and Cupid. Venus's loss of her runaway son, used by Spenser to motivate the adoption of Amoret and her twin sister Belphoebe, goes back to the classical poets, and there are straightforward Renaissance versions of it like Marot's *Amour Fugitif*, but it is the looser handlings of the incident that are more relevant to Spenser. Lyly's version of it in *Gallathea* affords a particularly useful comparison, for Lyly takes such delight in punning and word-play that he brings together many of those antitheses which are dispersed throughout Elizabethan love poetry. He also makes them very clear, indeed too clear, for their power lies in their ability to express emotional complexities which in logical terms appear contradictory. Alongside Shakespeare's thoughts of love and strife and death in *Romeo and Juliet*, or Spenser's in *The Faerie Queene* or even in the less masterly *Amoretti*, Lyly's treatment merely skims over the surface of very deep waters. But the very lightness of his movements keeps him from sinking, and his clarity is useful as well as charming.

Lyly's runaway Cupid does exactly what Spenser's Venus suspects he may have done: he disguises himself as a nymph and proceeds to throw Diana's followers into confusion. For our

---

[10] A similar expressiveness demonstrated in the sphere of painting, by Professors Panofsky and Wind and others, has enabled us to see more clearly how the poets too could express philosophic and imaginative conceptions through the manipulation of mythological figures.

purposes the plot (which involves a dispute between Diana and Venus) is less informative than the dialogue, and a few extracts from the speeches may suggest the kind of issue which was implicit in the goddesses' quarrel. Cupid threatens so to deal with Diana's nymphs 'that while they ayme to hit others with their Arrowes, they shall be wounded themselves with their owne eyes', and the love-struck Telusa laments that Cupid's 'feeble shafts headed with feathers' can pierce deeper than Diana's headed with steel, and that 'the Game I follow is the thing I flye'. A second nymph indulges in two familiar puns at once in this sentence:

> I will followe Diana in the Chace, whose virgins are all chast, delighting in the bowe that wounds the swift Hart in the Forrest, not fearing the bowe that strikes the soft hart in the Chamber.[11]

The chase of chastity and honour, on which Diana is engaged and to which, in *The Faerie Queene*, she brings up her ward Belphoebe, can merge very easily into Cupid's hunt of love, 'Diana's chase become Venus courte'. Diana's nymph both follows and flies; Diana's arrows can become confused with Cupid's. Spenser's translation of Marot's epigram *De Dyane*, printed after *Amoretti*, is a neat rendering of the same well-worn theme:

> As Diane hunted on a day,
> She chaunst to come where Cupid lay,
> His quiver by his head:
> One of his shafts she stole away,
> And one of hers did close convay
> Into the others stead:
> With that Love wounded my loves hart,
> But Diane beasts with Cupids dart.

Cupid shoots with the arrows of Diana, Diana with the arrows of Cupid; a complicated and hidden interchange is set up in which chastity becomes a weapon of love, or uses love as a weapon. Ronsard uses the same convention in *Les Amours d'Eurymedon et de Callirée*; Callirée's sonnet *Contre la Chasse* makes a close connection between the pursuit of beasts and the pursuit of nymphs. The armed Venus, too, can readily become part of this nexus of meaning, and though like Diana she can make very

---

[11] *Gallathea*, Act I, scene ii.

trivial appearances, in such slight pieces as Timothe Kendall's two epigrams *Of Venus in Armour*, she can also be profoundly philosophical, or tragic as in Statius's *Thebaid*: 'sed fallit ubique mixta Venus, Venus arma tenet, Venus admovet iras'.

So by causing his Venus to remark upon the likeness between her own son and Diana's nymphs, and upon the possibility that he is hiding among them, Spenser points at once to the ambiguousness of the hunts of love and chastity; and the quarrel with its sly comic spites and jealousies ends neither in defeat nor, properly, in reconciliation. It gives the impression rather of an armed alliance in which either goddess will, watchfully, use the other for her own ends. Searching for Cupid, they find instead Chrysogone's twins, born 'unspotted from all loathly crime,/That is ingenerate in fleshly slime' (vi, 3), free from inherited sin as their mother was free from pleasure or pain in their conception and birth. Their creation, of sun and dew, is a kind of perfection of natural processes, and they share between them 'all celestial grace'. But what they are not able to do is to share it with each other, for they are separated at birth, one going to Diana and one to Venus, and these two goddesses are themselves only partial manifestations of the totality of human potentiality. Britomart, in her "chaste affection", honestly combines what each of them stands for, but Amoret and Belphoebe themselves remain separated, brought up according to two rigid and exclusive codes whose non-human quality is emphasized for us by the twins' simple and sinless birth. Yet like their foster-mothers they retain a queer concealed relationship as if, doomed to incompleteness by their separation, they move surreptitiously and unconsciously towards each other. Belphoebe's chase of honour leads her first to Braggadocchio, in the second book, and later to Timias, whom she has followed thinking his track of blood is that of a beast she has struck with an arrow. Both Braggadocchio and Timias address her in terms obviously reminiscent of Aeneas's speech to his mother, and in Book III Belphoebe's identity as Venus virgo is further developed. Possibly too (for this is an area of the poem where Ovid is omnipresent) the poet is remembering a different hunting Venus, who in the tenth book of *Metamorphoses* takes to dressing like Diana to accompany the hunter Adonis.

There is, of course, no question of Belphoebe's nobility. In herself she is admirable and delightful; her intentions are excellent and she is as radiant, and as comically sententious and high-minded, as ever. None the less, in curing the wound Timias has received in the thigh[12] through following Florimell's foster, she

> hurt his hart, the which before was sound,
> Through an unwary dart, which did rebownd
> From her faire eyes and gratious countenance.
>
> (v, 42)

The love she causes is specifically sensuous (v, 50), and her 'earthly paradize' is planted with Venus's myrtles as well as with the laurels which are associated both with chastity (through Daphne) and with honourable achievement. Like Britomart, she tenders dearly the symbolic rose which 'The girlond of her honour did adorne', but set against each other the two stanzas (i, 46 and v, 51) afford a good example of significant variation on a conventional theme. Britomart's rose is straightforwardly at one and the same time beautiful and formidable; Belphoebe

> lapped up her silken leaves most chayre,
> When so the froward skye began to lowre:
> But soone as calmed was the christall ayre,
> She did it fayre dispred, and let to florish fayre.

The description sums up rather accurately her behaviour as the inaccessible ideal of love poetry, her bestowing and withdrawing of favour. Timias must expect no return for his devotion, but the devotion must be complete; she interprets his love for Amoret as a betrayal of herself and turns away like Dido from Aeneas.

> 'Is this the faith?' she said,—and said no more,
> But turnd her face, and fled away for evermore.
>
> (IV, vii, 36)

Timias eventually regains her favour through the agency of a dove, which is the bird of Venus as well as of constancy and peace and which carries back to Belphoebe her token, a ruby shaped like a bleeding heart. She is touched by the devotion manifested in his pathetic appearance and allows him to attend her once more, but though he lives happily enough his life is as wasted as it was when he lived alone in the forest, miserable and dumb. Following Belphoebe he is 'mindelesse of his owne deare

---

[12] Presumably a wound of lust merely, since his heart was sound.

lord' and thus of his duty, which is to attend Arthur on the quest for glory.

Belphoebe's pursuit of honour, though successful for herself, does not result in honour for those more ordinary people who come in contact with her. At home in her earthly paradise in the midst of the forest of the passions, and excellent in her own strange kind, she is set apart in her noble simplicity from erring and complex humanity. Even her speeches show her lack of comprehension of those born of fleshly slime, and her inability to imagine how Diana may shoot with Cupid's arrows. Her conquering radiance, her funny and rather touching lack of understanding of others, the degraded misery to which these qualities of hers reduce Timias, are all part of Spenser's comment on the worship of the lady as ideal. It is a sympathetic comment, but it is also ruefully amused and sceptical. Devotion to an ideal good is excellent; when the ideal is thought of as embodied in a lady of remote but demanding purity pitfalls begin to open before the admirer's feet. Elizabeth, who as queen knew perfectly well what she was doing in exploiting her potentialities as Venus virgo (the connection is made explicit in the *Aprill* eclogue) would no doubt feel justified in accepting the compliment to her chastity and honourable achievement, and to her power to inspire devotion. A sovereign may use fleshly Timiases for her own exalted purposes. But in relation to the poem as a whole Belphoebe operates rather differently.

Belphoebe has her connections, clearly, with that exaggerated adoration and idealization which was one aspect of the literary tradition which has come to be called Petrarchan. Her twin sister has her connections with another, and complementary, aspect of that tradition, the attempt at mastery which the demeanour of the slave serves to conceal. The sisters come into each other's presence only once, when in the fourth book Belphoebe kills the monstrous 'greedie Lust' who has captured frail Amoret, and then finds Timias comforting and, according to the verse which introduces Canto VII, loving her. Timias's 'new lovely mate' has been wounded not only by Lust but by his own rash hand as he tries to save her—Timias's encounters with the representatives of lust are always disastrously clumsy. The occasion is hardly propitious for a meeting of the sisters. Belphoebe's anger and disdain are so intense that she scarcely restrains herself from piercing them both with the same arrow that has just killed greedy Lust, and she flies from her one sight of her sister, her other self, in outrage and disgust.

But this is very late in Amoret's painful history. It begins in the garden of Adonis, the paradise where Venus lives when she is on earth. The Garden symbolizes many things; it relates to its false imitation, Acrasia's Bower of Bliss, in a way that Professor Lewis long ago taught us to see, and to a body of closely inter-woven philosophical and theological conceptions.[13] Most obviously, it is the focus for several paradoxical aspects of our world of generation, and for the moment we may consider it in relation to our present concern, the nature of Amoret who is brought up in it under the tutelage of Psyche. What is most relevant to Amoret is the Garden's identity as Venus's paradise on earth, a counterpart to the remote glade in the forest, the paradise inhabited by the other sister, Diana's ward. Either goddess has a 'paradise' in the sense of a place enclosed, where all that would be inimical to her own nature is shut out. As a place of free natural generation the Garden is good of course; it is the source of the world's life, a true creative Eden where Acrasia's was a false. The Bower exists in a strained extended moment of inten-sity, the Garden attains a truer perpetuity through the acceptance that all things must pass, to return in due time in their cycle. In it God's command to living things at the time of their making is kept,

> for of their owne accord
> All things, as they created were, doe grow,
> And yet remember well the mighty word,
> Which first was spoken by th'Almighty Lord,
> That bad them to increase and multiply.
>
> (III, vi, 34)

In the Garden sensuality is as happy and as blameless as in unfallen Eden,

[13] Of the many useful discussions of the Garden's significance (several are given in the *Variorum* Spenser) I will note here only one of the more recent, that by Robert Ellrodt, *Neoplatonism in the Poetry of Spenser* (Travaux d'Humanisme et Renaissance, XXV, Geneva, 1960), because as well as being valuable on its own account it considers earlier discussions also.

Franckly each paramor his leman knowes,
Each bird his mate, ne any does envy
Their goodly meriment and gay felicity.

(vi, 41)

All sorrows, save that of Time, are non-existent for the natural creatures living and growing here, and even in Time's depredations individual decay is transcended through Adonis, subject to mortality yet eternal in mutability, 'And by succession made perpetuall'. The boar, once fatal to him as the destructive aspect of love,[14] is now imprisoned under Venus's mount; love has become 'eternal blis' and death a condition of endless renewal. This Adonis is the dead but living god of the world of generation, father of all forms and pledge of continuity, 'Thammuz yearly wounded'.

The god of love himself is present in the Garden, but only in his most benevolent form, laying his sad darts aside after fulfilling his more destructive role as the Petrarchan tyrant in 'the world' of human reality.

Who, when he hath with spoiles and cruelty
Ransackt the world, and in the wofull harts
Of many wretches set his triumphes hye,
Thether resortes, and laying his sad dartes
Asyde, with faire Adonis playes his wanton partes.

(vi, 49)

For Psyche too all trouble is now past, and she lives forgetful of the tyrannies of love with Cupid and their child Pleasure;

Fair Psyche to him lately reconcyld,
After long troubles and unmeet upbrayes,
With which his mother Venus her revyld,
And eke himselfe her cruelly exyld:
But now in stedfast love and happy state
She with him lives.

(vi, 50)

[14] The moralisers of the myth generally give Adonis's boar rather limited and dogmatic meanings where Spenser's are more inclusive and less arbitrary; but the frequent identification of the boar with lust or lechery points towards Spenser's more imaginative treatment. The boar is, too, sometimes equated with chaos, which also seems to point towards the meaning of the Garden. Chaos is at once hostile to the eternal mutability of the Garden and essential to it. In both these aspects of its significance the boar's presence, imprisoned safely under the mount, is fitting.

Psyche here can scarcely have, I think, the Platonic meanings seen in Apuleius's original; this, after all, is Venus's earthly home, her centre as Venus genetrix. Rather, Psyche's function seems to be to complete the picture of innocent security and total devotion to love. She brings up Amoret 'in all the lore of love and goodly womanhead' with Pleasure as her companion. But like Adonis, and Cupid, and the boar, and Time, she reminds us that there is another side to experience though one so far kept from Amoret: she is 'lately reconcyld' but she has been long persecuted and separated from Cupid, not only through his anger and Venus's jealousy but to some extent through her own fault. It is to be so with Amoret also. Excellently trained in the 'lore' of love and womanliness but trained in nothing else, ignorant of the complementary realities of Diana and the martial Cupid, her story becomes one of misunderstanding and pain. The 'everlasting joy' of Adonis and Psyche has not come easily to either of them, for pain and trials and personal weakness have had first to be overcome. The Garden is a place of deep and complete delight, it is joyous and safe and good, but whether it is likely to provide a quite adequate training for life among human beings is another matter. Love, like Cupid himself, can assume a very different face in 'the world' from that which it wears in this secure garden which is, in one aspect, so like the heaven of love, the dream of the agonized human lover, evoked in *An Hymne of Love*.

The human reality is explored in Book IV, when Scudamour tells how he captured Amoret as his prize from Venus's temple. Venus there is hymned as the great Lucretian goddess of generation, life, and joy, but there are wretched and frightened lovers as well as happy ones in her temple, and the whole dubious place has in it as much of menace and treachery as of delight. Concord keeps the gate, but Love and Hate keep it with her, half-brothers of whom Hate is the elder, though Love is the stronger. For this is 'the world', where love is also war and fear and betrayal: where the boar is not imprisoned: where the necessary contraries of love and strife may only too readily slip out of Concord's controlling hands and end in confusion. Scudamour sees his winning of Amoret as a conquest—the word is used in the quatrain prefacing Canto X and is implicit in the whole perilous enterprise. Amoret and the Shield of Love go together as a 'renowmed prise' bringing honour to the winner, and the way to the temple is guarded by those personifications of the lady's wary and purposeful hostility which are familiar in the tradition of the Rose. Scudamour is a devotee of the destructive Cupid of the world, who changes his aspect so completely in the simple and happy Garden of Adonis. On Scudamour's shield is depicted 'Cupid with his killing bow/ And cruell shafts' (IV, x, 55), and it is with this shield that he terrifies Amoret's protector, Womanhood, into submission.

Scudamour's rather brusque behaviour is a natural enough reaction to a situation that he clearly feels to be obscurely unfair. He is behaving according to the rules, as he understands them, and he thinks he is doing right, yet Womanhood is contriving to put him in the wrong with her rebuke for being overbold (the phrase is foreshadowed in the words 'Be bold, be bold, be not too bold', with their bloodcurdling fairytale provenance, in Busyrane's house). He feels a kind of guilt, but the tradition of courtly love in which he has been instructed demands agression, however concealed beneath adoring deference.

> For sacrilege me seem'd the church to rob,
> And folly seem'd to leave the thing undonne,
> Which with so strong attempt I had begonne.
> Tho, shaking off all doubt and shamefast feare,
> Which ladies love I heard had never wonne
> Mongst men of worth, I to her stepped neare,
> And by the lilly hand her labour'd up to reare.
>
> (IV, x, 53)

Blamed for laying hold on a recluse virgin 'That unto Venus services was sold', he replies sharply that such service ill befits such a goddess,[15] and his answer gets near to the heart of the matter. The temple's appurtenances—the white-robed virgin priestesses, the danger and the sacrilegious excitement, the modesty and exclusive femininity—are devised to draw in 'Cupid's man', representative of the destructive Cupid who in person is so pointedly excluded, to be replaced by his harmless cherubic little brothers. The statue of the all-powerful goddess, veiled, androgynous, mysterious, smiles at Scudamour's sacrilege of her own temple, despite the terror and the tears; and in her figure is all the dubious power and ambiguous promise of the

---

[15] Marlowe's Leander uses the same argument to 'Venus' nun' Hero.

poetic love tradition. As the great natural creative power of the universe Venus is not concerned with individual human happiness, and so for the fulfilment of her purpose she is ready to depend upon hostility, the weapons of Diana and the spoils of Cupid, exclusiveness set as a snare for violence. Amoret may be conquered, but Scudamour is trapped; small wonder that for neither of them was there a happy hour 'since the day that first with deadly wound/My heart was launcht'.

Scudamour compares his rather doubtfully victorious escape from the dangerous temple to Orpheus's rescue of Eurydice from Hades, and the comparison is ominous enough. Eurydice's death from the bite of a snake in her heel was glossed by some mythographers as being, like Achilles's death from a similar wound, an allegory of the destructiveness of fleshly appetite, and was linked with the fatal femininity of Eve, whose descendants' heels shall be bruised by the serpent. Eurydice, some said, died on her wedding day, and Orpheus's rescue of her turned out to be only temporary. On *her* wedding day, Amoret is to fall into the death of her imprisonment by Busyrane, who will nightly tear out her heart. Amoret's mentor Psyche is relevant here too. Apuleius's story is told as part of the adventure of the girl who was stolen by armed thieves on the day of her marriage. Psyche herself went to her wedding with black torches, and some said wearing a shroud, because she understood love to be death, and Cupid to be a monster.

Amoret's own captivity is a kind of living death, an imprisonment within her own mind, a misapprehension like Psyche's. The inwardness of the experience[16] is marked by the sulphurous flames which choke the entrance to Busyrane's castle 'with griesly hate/And dreadfull horror' and keep Scudamour shut out; by the oppressive silence and darkness, with no living person to be seen or heard; by the childish 'Be bold, be bold, be not too bold' which sums up the ambiguous lore Amoret has learned and whose consequences fill her with mindless terror. The Maske of Cupid which stole her on her wedding day and still holds her enthralled perfectly expresses a morbid emotional condition

[16] I have examined the Busyrane episode more closely in 'Venus and Diana: Some Uses of Myth in *The Faerie Queene*', ELH, XXVIII, 1961. See also Thomas P. Roche, Jr., 'The Challenge to Chastity: Britomart at the House of Busyrane', P.M.L.A., LXXVI, 4, 1961.

through the manipulation of a literary convention. The personifications which in Scudamour's adventure at the temple and in all the courtly tradition stand for the lady's defensive (but also entrapping) devices against the lover are in Amoret's mind turned vengefully against herself and are revealed as slippery, tyrannical, and frightening. Her own weapons of Cruelty and Despight lead her, like 'deathes own ymage', in the grisly but unreal procession. For of course it is all her fancy. The Maske is a shadowy dumb show like that in a theatre, the figures of Strife and Anger and Death which follow it are fantasy,

> So many moe, as there be phantasies
> In wavering wemens witt, that none can tell,
> Or paines in love, or punishments in hell.
>
> (III, xii, 26)

And Britomart, when she saves her, must not kill Busyrane but make him reverse the bloody lines of his charms. What has held Amoret in prison is an obsession, a distortion of reality through a misunderstanding of it. But though what she fears is not wholly real the fear itself is, and so is the torture. This is the most hopeless captivity of all, and one of the most terrible of Spenser's evocations of a state of the mind.

Its exact nature can be approached only by drawing attention to the images which define it, above all to the images of what is monstrous and deathly. Eurydice's anguis in herba lurks in the arras on Busyrane's walls where gold glints

> Like a discolourd snake, whose hidden snares
> Through the greene gras his long bright burnisht
> back declares.

The arras shows the mighty power of Cupid, the wretchedness he can cause, his huge massacres and enthralled kings,

> And eke all Cupids warres they did repeate,
> And cruell battailes.
>
> (xi, 29)

They are indeed cruel wars, predatory, treacherous, often bestial. The beasts of the passionate forest here rush as rams, bulls, stags or more monstrous shapes of centaur or satyr. Phrases of pain and death and desire accumulate: 'So lovedst thou . . . Yet both are of thy haplesse hand extinct', 'Whens dearely she with death

108

bought her desire', and most suggestive of all 'Yet was thy love her death, and her death was thy smart'. Everywhere is portrayed the mutual misery of a situation in which each punishes and is punished in Cupid's wars. This is what fills Amoret's mind, the 'thousand monstrous formes' of love, the whole centred upon the altar and the golden image, the triumphant Cupid of Petrarchan tradition.

But Spenser does not, I think, intend particularly to condemn 'Petrarchan' love or 'courtly' love, any more than he means to condemn the 'Platonic' aspect of Petrarchism in Timias and Belphoebe. The literary themes are expressions of attitudes which have always existed; through them Spenser examines, with sensitive understanding, the tensions set up and the mistakes made in the dealings of human beings with one another and, too, in the managing of those conflicting impulses within ourselves which must somehow be made to cohere. From the first century to the nineteenth the literature of destructive love owes its power to its expression, however distorted or partial, of the enduring truth that in intense personal relationships there is an element of hostility. Concord depends upon both Hate and Love, and though Love must be stronger Hate is the elder, and it was said that love between two persons is born in discord, though it is established in concord. The growth of concord between lovers who are warriors, tyrants, hunters, traitors, is the theme of *Amoretti* and of many a sonnet sequence, but there are other handlings of the theme in which love stops short of concord, and the warfare and the chase are perpetual and mutual; each feels and inflicts pain in revenge for the wound received. And of course this distortion, this failure, is equally true to human life and is portrayed by Spenser with equal insight.

The great poet of this kind of love is Ovid, the master beside whose painful reality the medieval and Renaissance conventions can seem mere pretty evasions; and to Ovid we are directed by Amoret's tormentor Busyrane. He, who sacrifices Amoret to the destructive Cupid, is presumably named from the treacherous Busiris who made human sacrifices to his own god in Egypt and was eventually slaughtered on the same altar. Spenser could have read of him in the mythological commentators and in Diodorus and Apollodorus, but his most relevant appearance is in *Ars Amatoria*, where his story illustrates the theme that love is the result of deceit, which should be avenged by deceit. For Ovid, indeed, love *is* deceit and hostility, and 'concordia' only the momentary defeat of one cruelty by another in a process of continuing strife. 'Fallite fallentes; . . . in laqueos, quos posuere, cadant': the woman must feel the pain of a wound she first inflicted. *Ars Amatoria* and *Metamorphoses* are documents as essential to Spenser's treatment of love as any of the Italian Platonic dialogues, and they are the best guide to Amoret's conviction that because she loves Scudamour she must suffer in Busyrane's house. All our literary expressions of love as hostility and fear, the age-old 'Odi et amo', are shadowed in Ovid and are relevant to the loves, whether tortured or happy, of these two books.

It is not, here, a matter of simple right or wrong, but rather of adjustment and understanding. If it were necessary, as it is not, to label Amoret and Scudamour in such a way one would unhesitatingly call them good and well-disposed people. But something has gone amiss, and even after her rescue by Britomart Amoret remains over vulnerable, fearing her own emotions and those of others, fearing her inability to control either. She is frightened and suspicious where there is no need to be, and goes in terror of Britomart's 'will'[17] until she finds that Britomart is a woman; and once alone she falls victim to the most frankly repulsive of Spenser's embodiments of excessive and monstrous lust. But her unbalance is a consequence of her birth and background, and she is unfortunate in meeting with a correspondingly faulty training in Scudamour, who has 'heard' that lovers ought to be aggressive, and who assails Busyrane's gate in a complicated state of greedy will and envious desire, threatening pride and burning torment. Amoret is by nature incomplete; her submissive womanliness is delightful but it wholly lacks those complementary qualities which are isolated in Belphoebe. She has learned, in the untroubled Garden, only the gentleness and easy courses of love, and the snares and captures of Venus's temple and the passions of the wedding masque are to her frightening treacheries and brutalities, for her part in which she must expect 'paines in love, or punishments in hell'. Like Britomart who had expected the fate of a Biblis, she makes a monster of her mind, and Scuda-

[17] Presumably the word carries its frequent Elizabethan connotation of sensual passion.

mour's well-meaning but conventionally conquering attitude can only encourage her obsession. Thus despite—or rather in part because of—genuine passion they cannot meet. The second thought which made Spenser cancel their union at the end of the third book seems altogether true to their situation. The hermaphrodite image which originally closed the book is an image of union in marriage, of course, but as such it is an image of much more also, an ancient symbol of the uniting of contraries, the achieving of completeness. And this is a state these two are not ready, yet, to attain.

Britomart can save Amoret from Busyrane (though only the momentary presence of her sister's militant chastity can later save her from greedy Lust) because she provides the perfectly balanced chaste affection which Belphoebe and Amoret divide between them in a rather ambiguous way, Belphoebe arousing love and Amoret being uneasily conscious of her involvement in the Ovidian strife and snare. But still more important to Britomart's success on Amoret's behalf is the fact that she has mastered a similar distortion in her own mind, and can show Amoret the difference between it and the truth. Her experience of exaggeratedly submissive femininity has been made part of her own completeness, her strength, and her ability to help others, but in her first adventure, in Malecasta's house, it is still a potential weakness and she is taken by surprise and slightly wounded. Such weakness as Britomart has—and like all the knights she has some —is on her feminine side; no knight can interrupt her purposeful advance, but a woman can appeal to her through pity and fellow-feeling, and a shared experience of unhappiness. This is so even of a cardboard woman like Malecasta, who is not capable of real emotion but is very well able to simulate it in the pursuit of pleasure. Malecasta's castle is well placed for her aims, not in the forest where the dangerous beasts are but near enough to it for its perils to bring enjoyment, 'plaste for pleasure nigh that forrest syde'. Within, it is dominated by the third (in order of importance but not of narrative development) of the variations on the loves of Venus. The walls are spread with costly cloths of Arras, in which is cunningly portrayed

> The love of Venus and her paramoure,
> The fayre Adonis, turned to a flowre.

(i, 34)

In Castle Joyeous Adonis is not wickedly and deliberately degraded, as in Acrasia's bower, he is only trivialized. The god who later in the book is to appear as the symbol of the perpetuity of life, the creative father of all forms, is here even in death an adjunct to sentimental sensuality, languishing before 'a great wilde bore' with the blood showing up his snowy skin, daintily transformed into a flower. The blend of commonplace prettiness and sensationalism is a good deal nastier than anything in Amoret's story; the key word of Castle Joyeous is not passion of any sort but a singularly trivial and vulgar 'pleasure'. The tapestry Venus, begging Adonis 'to refraine/From chase of greater beastes', to follow no boar or savage creature, is like Malecasta herself, living for pleasure close, but not too close, to the forest, and a practised pretender to the death wish of a hopeless passion. Britomart believes that she recognizes a genuine emotion like that she has felt herself, and through the consequent lack of care her feminine side takes momentary control so that she has to defend herself without her armour and suffers a skin wound from Gardante's arrow of sight. But this is her only mistake.

One more interlocking story, Florimell's, completes the general structural pattern of the book of Chastity. It is held closely to the others by parallelism. Florimell is searching for Marinell as Britomart is searching for Artegall, while the details of her imprisonment are like those of Amoret's torture in Busyrane's house, and the poet compares her griefs and Amoret's. The stories are linked also by the relation of all the characters to the literary themes of love and war and the chase, and to the personages of myth and legend who enact these themes. Florimell's adventures broaden the individual problems of Amoret and Britomart into a general view of the nature and effect of feminine grace. As 'beautie excellent' she moves in the non-human as well as in the human world, and through her and Marinell the consideration of 'beauties chace', its discords and its eventual concord, can be taken further. In the course of their reconciliation their elemental nature is developed, but this process is, very properly, delayed until the book of Friendship, and in the third book their primary function is to complete, through a kind of abstraction or generalization, the human pattern. Florimell is all femininity; the dwarf tells Arthur he will gain renown 'Of all good ladies through the world so wide' by helping her. Everything about her seems calculated to divest her of Amoret's or Britomart's individual human warmth. She can appear anywhere, affect anyone, and her shifting loveliness like falling light, her flowery quality, her white and gold, make her seem like beauty itself, or beauty's attractive power. Indeed the way that Spenser uses the word beauty in connection with Florimell practically identifies the two.

Florimell was brought up by the Graces on Mount Acidale, the haunt of Venus and also, we find in Book VI, the home of poetry. The Graces are the givers of all such incalculable and irresistible charm as Florimell casts over the forests and seas of Faeryland, and in the tradition of Ficino beauty is defined as grace; the link with poetry's delight and power is a natural one. Leone Ebreo calls beauty, whether of natural or artificial things, 'Formal grace, which delights and moves him who apprehends it to love'.[18] But in relation to Amoret and Britomart Florimell is primarily important as showing the appeal of feminine beauty. 'None alive but joy'd in Florimell', but in practice their delight in her takes the form of pursuit with a view to possession. She is everybody's prey, compared to a hind or hare or dove, with even Arthur and Guyon joining in the hunt. On the other hand she herself does something to initiate the hunt by always running away, for to her almost anything has the nature of the hunting beast, and she is as ready to flee from Arthur, or from the sound of a leaf moving, as from the foster. If she is always in flight because always pursued, it is equally true that she is always pursued because always in flight, bringing about the chase it is her intention to escape. Of course there is nothing here of hypocrisy or coquetry. Spenser is concerned with impulses at once more delicate and more deeply rooted in mental regions where distinctions like these are not yet made. Deliberate provocativeness and falsity belong only to the witch's simulacrum of Florimell, a body made of snow and controlled by a fallen spirit. The true Florimell's behaviour is part of her nature as the transient gift of beauty, gratuitous and shifting as light, bestowed by the Graces on whatever and whomever 'they list so to grace'. Considered as a person, a character acting in the narrative, she must necessarily appear insubstantial, incomplete, lacking in self-awareness. Being what she is, the attraction of all beauty, she exists primarily in her effect on others, and so must seem changing and ambiguous;

[18] Op. cit., p. 386.

beauty is part of the terms of mortal state. And in so far as she images the specifically feminine loveliness which 'draws us with a single hair' to follow it, she is set alongside Amoret and Britomart to suggest the strength and weakness of the wholly feminine, powerful and powerless, attracting and retreating, its weapons softness and fearfulness and the expectation of capture. In the impression she makes there is something of the long line of literary nymphs, ever fleeing, ever pursued.

> Jamque latet, latitansque cupit male tecta videri,
> Et fugit, & fugiens pervelit ipsa capi.[19]

Florimell is engaged on a search for Marinell, but when she enters the poem her search seems already to be more like a mindless flight, in marked contrast to Britomart's steady forward progress on the quest for Artegall. There is a difference too between Britomart's serviceable armour and the costume of beaten gold in which Florimell takes to the road, her flying hair dressed 'With golden wreath and gorgeous ornament'. Much has been made of the impercipience of those characters in *The Faerie Queene* who fail to distinguish between the true Florimell and the false, and of course this is important. But perhaps it is also important that so many do fail, including even Marinell; the imitation is convincing to almost everyone. The wicked spirit summoned to animate the snow body knows passing well 'All the wyles of wemens wits' (viii, 8), and though the false Florimell's coyness is a parody of the true Florimell's feminine appeal there is something there to be parodied. The situation is different from Una's, where the shock to Red Crosse is that the impersonating spirit, who it seems must be Una, behaves in a way quite alien to her, and where something other than the characters of women is the matter at issue. Again, while it is the false Florimell who promotes discord, the true one can produce confusion, distracting even Arthur's mind from devotion to his supreme earthly good, Gloriana. For he does not simply mistake the flying Florimell for Gloriana, rather he wishes, in a muddled sort of way, that Gloriana were like Florimell.

> And thousand fancies bett his ydle brayne
> With their light wings, the sights of semblants vaine;
> Oft did he wish that lady faire mote bee

[19] Milton, *Elegia quinta* (*In adventum veris*), ll. 129–30.

His Faery Queene, for whom he did complaine;
Or that his Faery Queene were such as shee;
And ever hasty Night he blamed bitterlie.

(iv, 54)

Love does not hold him long, for a spirit brave as his is roused to
'the highest and the worthiest' rather than to 'sensuall desire',
but he has been drawn away for a while from his first pursuit,
and when he takes horse again after a grumpy night outdoors,
unvisited this time by Gloriana, it is

With heavy looke and lumpish pace, that plaine
In him bewraid great grudge and maltalent.

(iv, 61)

It has been pointed out, too, that Florimell is spoken of in a
way that hints at the fatal beauty of Helen, that other 'flowre of
beautie excellent'. Of course she causes no such tragic disasters
as Helen did, and she is worlds away from such figures as Hellenore, petty domestic Helens who cause small and squalid miseries.
Florimell brings about nothing worse than the dispersal and disorder of Gloriana's knights (viii, 46) and jealousy among those
who resent Satyrane's possession of her girdle and so take part
in the rather discordant tournament of Book IV; but if they had
known of her sufferings her knights would, in their burning fury,
have ruined towers, cities, and kingdoms. She shares with Helen
the fatal quality of great beauty and desirability, and her afflic-
tions are of the kind that such a quality might be expected to produce. She seems to attract trouble, or to run into it by running
away. Continually deflected from her own purpose and deflecting
others, she takes with her an atmosphere of the helplessly
mutable, a pathos which is a great part of her charm. Her worst
problems begin when, after her ill-judged stay with the witch and
her son, she is pursued by the witch's beast, 'That feeds on
wemens flesh, as others feede on gras', a swift spotted creature
most like a hyaena. The hyaena was described with unanimous
loathing in the bestiaries for its habit of feeding on human
corpses, so it is an expressive emblem of the greed which sees in
beauty only something to devour. But it is also emblematic of
fearfulness, of change, and of instability,[20] and is one of the

---

[20] Its meaning of instability was based on the belief that the hyena was
at one moment male and another female, thus its character changes too.

many illustrations of the changeable nature of things in the fifteenth book of *Metamorphoses*.

The beast devours the palfrey on which Florimell has long been carried with great speed but small sense of direction. It also causes her to lose her golden girdle, which falls as she runs away. The girdle, we are told later, was Venus's, worn only when she was behaving in 'wively sort' and at other times laid aside, and Florimell brought it from Mount Acidale where she was raised by Venus's attendant Graces. It is able

> to bind lascivious desire,
> And loose affections streightly to restraine,
>
> (IV, v, 4)

and when it is worn by anyone lacking in 'chast love/And wivehood true' it falls from her waist, either loosened or broken. Nothing is said of the seductive charm conferred by the original cestus, but we are told that the belt 'was Cestus hight by name' and we are clearly meant to recall it; as so often, Spenser is going out of his way to remark that delight is none the less delight for being good. But the girdle is involved in an uncommon weight of symbolic action, which it can successfully carry only if its implications whether of chastity or of seductiveness are not pressed too hard. Like Florimell herself, it seems made to suggest the faintly ambiguous quality of untempered femininity rather than to state positives and negatives; it partakes of the nature of undifferentiated experience, where all possibilities exist. Thus it is used to bind the reluctant beast until the creature gets free, yet the beast has been the cause of Florimell's losing it, and it can hardly have escaped the poet's notice that she is without its protection during the worst of her trials. She escapes from the hyaena into the fisherman's boat, to find herself in a situation even more degraded than that in the witch's cottage. It is a pathetically convincing result of her helpless charm, her lack of judgment, her way of throwing herself on the wrong people's mercy, that she is so

---

See J. Pierius Valerianus, *Hieroglyphicorum Collectanea* (Lyons, 1626), Liber XI, caput xxiv. The hyena appears also in T. H. White, *The Bestiary* (New York, 1954). *Appelles Symbolicus* (Amsterdam, 1699), Liber V, caput xxiv, takes the hyena to signify insatiability and also to be, in virtue of its change of sex, 'Imago hominis e cordato in meticulosum transformati'.

often in the hands of the basest. She is flung now among the fish-scales, and her golden robes are filled with the squalid residue of Venus's fecund creatures, born like Venus 'of the fomy sea'. Again she escapes, but as usual into another danger, and becomes the prisoner of Proteus.

Proteus is another image of change, interpreted by some mythographers as the flux of changeable passions which must be bound if stability is to be attained, while to Ovid he suggests the accomplished lover, ready to assume many parts in pursuit of his predatory aims.[21] Such meanings hang about Proteus here. He is part of the whole atmosphere which surrounds Florimell, an atmosphere of the irrational, the directionless, the incomprehensible, full of shifting appearances and of possibilities not seen or not understood. Florimell's story points to the strangeness of human personality and the strangeness of all our experience. In Proteus's cave under the sea Florimell, no longer able to take flight, for the first time stands and thinks for herself. Her methods are feminine still, but resourceful. She counters each change on Proteus's part with a change of position on her own, but it is purposeful and considered change. She is able to resist, the poet tells us, in her faithful love of Marinell, as Amoret resists the obsessive 'odi et amo' of Busyrane in love of Scudamour. Each finds her only strength and stability in the longing to reach her lover, her counterpart, yet for each this longing is the cause of all her pain and imprisonment. Suffering arises from their very efforts towards unity, completeness of being. But Florimell, at least, will attain it within the confines of the poem.

Given Florimell's nature, Marinell whom she seeks has exactly the qualities one would expect. Where she is soft and appealing and a born victim, he is hard, aggressive, grasping and egotistical, though equally caught in the world's ambiguities. He is, too (and this seems equally natural), completely impervious to Florimell's appeal, the one alive who does not 'joy' in her. In human terms he, and his relation to Florimell, are very recognizable. His nature is revealed by the vivid and economical method which prevails in this book, the inter-relating of characters through their common connection with figures of myth. Marinell, son of a sea

---

[21] In the same passage Ovid compares seduction with the catching of fish, for which also versatility is required. Possibly the comparison may be relevant to Spenser's fisherman and fish scales.

nymph, is connected with Achilles; so is Artegall, and they are both overthrown by the woman warrior Britomart, with lasting results in the course of their lives. Achilles had become over the years a double-natured figure, rather like an effeminate Mars or like Hercules in the power of Omphale, swinging between extremes of sulky aggression and passive submission. In Comes, and in the non-Homeric versions of the siege of Troy, Achilles's languor had become at least as important as his wrath, and in medieval Troy stories he may be discovered wallowing on a Turkish lounge in all the self-indulgent grief of the contemporary literary lover, while the moralizers take him as an example of the dangers of sensuality and make much of his vulnerable heel. But the process had begun long before the Middle Ages, and the basis for it is already in Homer. Several classical episodes lent colour to the picture of Achilles as an unstable warrior. There was his subjection to Thetis his mother, and the consequent disguise among women; his slavish passion for Polyxena, leading to his murder by the effeminate Paris (by 'weapon womanish', says Arthur Golding). In the *Achilleid* Statius elaborates at length the Deidamia episode and the girlish and uxorious ways of the young Achilles, and again there is the famous episode, for which Apollodorus is one authority, of the Amazon Penthesilea who conquered her conqueror at the moment of death at his hands. And in *Ars Amatoria* Achilles the Amazon-conqueror, the great fighter in the wars of love, is a key figure. It is these moral and emotional complexities, rather than the battles of the *Iliad*, which define the nature of Marinell.

Marinell's history is close to that of Achilles in several obvious ways. Cymoent has heard a prophecy of danger for him and tries to keep him hidden from it, and when it reaches him none the less she laments like Thetis over her son. The cold acquisitiveness which keeps him patrolling the precious shore to 'love him selfe alone' (they are Florimell's words, lamenting her love in Proteus's cave) recalls Achilles's sulky concentration on his own safety and prestige. Later he is twice overthrown by women and nearly dies in a love-languor like the medieval hero's. But until his narrow self-sufficiency is shattered by Britomart's spear he thrives on his selfishness and the sorrows of others. What Britomart calls the 'sea of sorrow and tempestuous griefe' has been to him a source of complacent enrichment

through the overthrow
And wreckes of many wretches, which did weepe
And often wayle their wealth, which he from them did keepe.

(iv, 22)

He and Cymoent try to avoid the sorrow prophesied for him, but their plan, like Thetis's plan for Achilles, plays into the hands of fate. Marinell thinks himself secure in his pitiless defence of himself and his gold against all comers, for it is from a woman, not from another warrior, that his death is to come. He is loved by many, but 'Dy who so list for him, he was loves enimy'. Confident of his safety, he challenges Britomart on the precious shore and is badly wounded in the left side, the heart's side; and this is the turning-point of his existence. Britomart has casually destroyed all his values; far from dying for him she nearly kills him and then rides on, as indifferent to him as she is to his treasured hoard of pearl and gold which he has guarded so jealously. Marinell's cultivated toughness is revealed as self-loving weakness; a nature which develops one aspect of itself in fear of its opposite may unknown to itself be overthrown and enthralled by that opposite, and so it is with Marinell, the 'thrall' (IV, xi, 7) of his protective mother. Only after Britomart has shattered his self-enclosed small world is he able to feel for Florimell rather than for himself, and so in the end to reach with her a productive harmony of qualities, each tempering the other; 'His stony heart with tender ruth/Was toucht', and he overcomes fear of 'his mothers former charge/Gainst womens love' (IV, xii, 14).

Thus Cymoent's endeavour to control fate only makes her its instrument. 'Weening to have arm'd him, she did quite disarme', for the ways of eternal fate are as impossible to frustrate as they are to understand. No one can deceive his destiny, and it is High God who steers Marinell's course and Florimell's, by the agency, in each case, of Proteus. Through the changing sea and the uncomprehending, incomprehensible sea god providence makes its imperturbable moves. The ways of our own nature are just as puzzling, but here too there are secret rules, and Marinell who thinks himself in command is conquered and saved by them in spite of himself. The puzzles and paradoxes of the third book are brought home in this strange and oddly beautiful story: it is hard to know what we are and what we should do, and the only answer is to try to co-operate with the purposes of life and not to force them to our own ends, not to exploit. It is the difference between Britomart's perfect balance of action and acceptance and the impulsive rashness and extremism of Florimell and Marinell in their different ways. There is more than this, of course, to the story, but its implications beyond the human sphere to which I have confined it are best related to the resolutions which are emphasized in the book of Friendship.

Indeed the third book is so extraordinarily full, even for Spenser, that inadequacy and schematism are particularly hard to avoid. There is much that can only be touched upon: for instance the recurrent note of good-humoured laughter, needed to balance Ovidian obsession, Platonic aspiration, genuine suffering, and to give a full picture of 'How diversly Love doth his pageaunts play'. The good Sir Satyrane, who will not be bothered with courtly services, is just the character to supply it. He has the kind of cheerful robustness suggested by his satyr ancestry and his rugged steel armour and escutcheon of a satyr's head. He respects Florimell as he did Una, or any worthy thing, but he will take nothing over seriously. His comic binding of the trembling, grumbling hyaena in Florimell's belt of chaste wivehood, or his amusement at the silly situation that the Squire of Dames has got into, provide a necessary point of view. Love may be lord of the universe, but it is a help towards health and balance if he can be regarded sometimes as rather a joke. One should perhaps remember that it is Britomart and Artegall, the successful lovers, and not the desperately solemn failures, who are affectionately presented as a little absurd. On the other hand, it would be unlike our sage and serious poet not to show, in the shape of the unnatural and bestial giantess, the equal dangers which lie in wait for honest, laughing, coarse-fibred knights like Satyrane and fashionable lightweights like the Squire of Dames. What may seem normality, or robustness, or healthy cynicism can be as one-sided an attitude, and as inadequate, as any other; and responsibility to the complex truths he knows requires that Spenser should undercut even the undercutting cheerfulness of Satyrane.

Again there is the fine, many-toned episode of Malbecco and Hellenore, which shows, especially in what Miss Tuve has called 'the insidiously flippant scene of Hellenore's seduction by Paridell',[22] what deadly singleness of purpose exists beneath the charm of cynical 'learned lovers' like Paridell or, in his simpler way, the Squire of Dames. Paridell has his own comment on the code of knightly romance; he devotes his time, he tells Britomart, to 'faire ladies love and glories gaine'. The same chivalric words can cover a multitude of meanings. As for Hellenore, she ends with the satyrs in a life degraded for her though innocent for them, and we remember the half-satyr Satyrane and place him more exactly in the poem's scheme. Comedy serves moral realism again in Braggadocchio, the false imitation of manly force and glory, and the snowy Florimell, the false imitation of submissive feminine grace. They are natural mates, and they parody with excellent pomposity other more exalted unions, but their parody reflects upon themselves too, they deflate by the comparison but they are also deflated. The effect produced is extraordinarily complete. Nothing about ourselves and our emotions must be taken too seriously, but everything in the end is profoundly serious. Laughter is good, but good chiefly as a means to self-knowledge and a sense of proportion, the way perhaps to that freedom in which responsibility must begin. For Spenser, love is a subject that leads to the roots of human behaviour; it is not surprising that in the Proem to Book IV he takes issue with the 'rugged forehead' who had reproved him for 'magnifiying lovers deare debate'.

[22] *Elizabethan and Metaphysical Imagery* (Chicago, 1961), p. 221. I do not think anything need be added to Miss Tuve's treatment of this fine episode.

Chapter Four

INVIOLABLE BANDS

THE concerns of the third book are further developed in the book of Friendship, and it is hardly possible to treat either book without moving between the two. But it is at least approximately true that while the third book concentrates on the examination of conflict, separation, complication, the fourth concentrates on their resolution, and the slight but sufficient adjustment of view produces a corresponding modification of form. Both legends involve a number of characters with their separate stories, but the stories here have a greater tendency to merge and the characters to meet, joining forces on the road or encountering at Satyrane's tournament. People who in the third book are searching for each other or trying vainly to find their right path now move further towards a resolution; Britomart meets Artegall, Florimell wins Marinell, and even Amoret and Scudamour, though still parted, have a truer knowledge of themselves and of their predicament. The book is built, accordingly, around a series of meetings or assemblies, notably the two tournaments—that for Canacee and that for the girdle of Florimell—the marriage of Thames and Medway, and the temple of Venus; and whereas the third book is dominated by Britomart, others being implicitly compared and contrasted with her, in the fourth there is no dominant knight through Britomart has still a part to play in the various meetings and partings.

The legend is named after two knights, Cambell and Triamond, fittingly enough since they are most perfect friends, one the husband and one the brother of Agape's daughter, who has the attributes of an emblematic Concord. But the knights' actions do not dominate, and there is no quest for them to go on. Rather, Cambell and his neatly interlocking group, held by the double bonds of marriage and of blood, go placidly about, contrasting with other groups who have come together not out of like-mindedness or kinship but out of self-interest or even for the mere pleasure of having someone always at hand to annoy or otherwise make use of. As with love, such friendship 'is hate'. Similarly the pointless discord of the muddled tournament for Florimell's girdle, where Ate, Duessa, and the false Florimell set the tone, is contrasted with the battle for Canacee, ritual-like in its orderliness, where the four-fold friendship is established through the action of Cambina, Agape's daughter. This battle has taken place before the action properly opens, and it does not forward the events of the book but presents in little, and more formally, the significance implicit in the narrative's comings and goings. Its rather static quality is part of its effectiveness for its particular purpose, and the calm movement of its plot, in which character falls into place with character in a perfectly chiming order, is well suited to a formal explication of the nature of friendship, conducted through the familiar topics of love and war. The sure, quiet concord which Cambell and Triamond achieve is developed from an original hostility, but the hostility of Satyrane's tournament has no such productive and positive outcome.

But while one recognizes the decorousness of the Cambell episode in view of its purpose and its kind, that kind is necessarily low-pitched; it has something of the effect of an extended emblem, and it pales beside the richer harmonies of more memorable passages. Cambell and the three brothers his foes 'the fellonest on ground' are not shown as feeling personal enmity for one another, and they have no reason to; they merely illustrate discord by the formal act of fighting for Canacee. The nature of discord and concord is stated rather than revealed; we recognize a theoretical formulation which never becomes a living human truth because it is not developed in terms of feeling. Triamond is the survivor of the three brothers, Agape's sons, who 'unfold' her nature in what is, as Professor Wind remarks, a somewhat pedantic exercise. One may admire the skilled precision with which, in the second canto, Priamond, Diamond, and Triamond, 'three faire branches budding farre and wide' from one root, are differentiated in a way that only emphasizes their unity, but they have no more vitality than an animated theorem. Only with the arrival of Cambina, descending like the mother goddess in a masque, in her chariot drawn by tamed lions, is there something of the Spenserian richness.

Cambina, Concord, and Venus divide among them the possibilities of concordia, and where Concord's aspect is cosmological and philosophical and Venus's mysteriously creative, Cambina's is human and maternal. Her appearance and actions are emblematic, indeed, but they carry age-old suggestions of comfort and release from care; she has meaning in herself and is not simply illustrative of meaning. She brings her cup of Nepenthe, with balm for the troubled mind, and Mercury's rod, the sign of peace, its two wise dangerous snakes curved quietly and symmetrically about it. According to Valerianus[1] Mercury had found the snakes fighting and had separated them, as Cambina does Cambell and Triamond, and the entwining serpents are also said to be male and female,[2] so that the caduceus image is repeated in the double marriage of the brothers and sisters, with love, friendship, concord knit up inextricably between them. The symmetrical arrangement is reminiscent of those erudite, perhaps rather self-consciously sensitive, discussions which so delighted the Platonists, about the number of persons that exist in true mutual friendship or love: two people who love each other can be one person, Ebreo's Philo tells Sophia, or they can be four,

> Each one being transformed into the other becomes two, at once both lover and beloved; and two multiplied by two makes four, so that each of them is twain, and both together are one and four.[3]

All this, even with Cambina's warm maternal presence to enliven it, is still an abstract rendering of truths which are more vital elsewhere. We feel the presence of friendship more richly in the unphilosophical, untheoretical gallantry of Britomart helping Scudamour, protecting Amoret, fighting Artegall, than we do when it is isolated and explicated by Cambell fighting in Triamond's armour and Triamond in Cambell's, or by the mutual

---

[1] Op. cit., Liber XV, caput xlii, caput xlv.
[2] Richard Linche, *The Fountaine of Ancient Fiction* (London, 1599), under 'Mercury'.
[3] Op. cit., p. 260.

sacrifice of Amyas and Placidas, identical in body and single
in soul. These are direct demonstrations of ideal friendship
achieved, rather than records of the process of achievement;
inevitably they lack actuality compared with the efforts of those
questing knights and wandering women whose actions dramatize
our mental and emotional life. Cambell's, Triamond's, Placidas's
friendships are illustrations, not enactments, and as such they
have a perfectly legitimate place. So have the equally formalized
bickerings of Satyrane's tournament, which is a humorous presentation of the compulsive grudges of those whose egocentricity
incapacitates them for generosity, and which contrasts sharply
with the forms of friendship:

> But after that, the judges did arret her
> Unto the second best, that lov'd her better;
> That was the Salvage Knight: but he was gone
> In great displeasure, that he could not get her . . .
>
> But Blandamour thereat full greatly grudged,
> And litle prays'd his labours evill speed,
> That, for to winne the saddle, lost the steed.
> Ne lesse thereat did Paridell complaine,
> And thought t'appeale from that which was decreed
> To single combat with Sir Satyrane.
> Thereto him Ate stird, new discord to maintaine.
>
> (v, 21–2)

But it is the enactments which best develop the realities of Faeryland, its tensions and balances and precarious securities picturing
our own and so striking home to our experience. Amyas and
Placidas are interchangeable identities; the friendship we know
is that which Concord, Venus's gate-keeper, images in her tense
pose of sustained control over the forcibly clasped hands of Love
and Hate. Implicit in the three is the difficult progress from
initial discord to a concord maintained in difference. Love and
Hate still keep their separate identities, for to merge or con-
fuse them is to slide into the complicated Ovidian travesty of
concordia which Phaedria, Acrasia, and Busyrane follow in their
different ways; but they are clasped together to give the goddess
her power to hold the universe in its living, tensely balanced order.
This is what the world consists in, as we experience it in these
two books; from it, meaning generates itself. All the possibilities,

for good or ill, are present in it, and to these potentialities we may relate the happenings in the temple of Venus and all the interlinked stories which tell of the search for concord and the pitfalls which beset it.

Scudamour, as the conscientiously conventional courtly lover, exemplifies some of these difficulties as he pushes on to the temple, relying in his uncertainty on those facile theories and patterns of behaviour through which error is perpetuated:

> Whom soone as I beheld, my hart gan throb,
> And wade in doubt, what best were to be donne:
> For sacrilege me seem'd the church to rob,
> And folly seem'd to leave the thing undonne,
> Which with so strong attempt I had begonne.
> Tho, shaking off all doubt and shamefast feare,
> Which ladies love I heard had never wonne
> Mongst men of worth, I to her stepped neare,
> And by the lilly hand her labour'd up to reare.
>
> (x, 53)

Even to get in to the temple at all is hard enough. Literary tradition had evolved a set of remarkably flexible symbols for the dangers which meet the plucker of the rose, and there could be no better expression of the tentative way into that alien territory, another person's mind and feelings. All the sudden distrusts and hostilities and withdrawals are there, and feminine puzzles like the Gate of Good Desert whose function is to keep out cowards. The way familiarizes us with Amoret's frightened mind and with Scudamour's confused one, determined to brazen out what he does not understand. One is hardly surprised that these two learn so little from the figure of Concord, which might have instructed them. Many have fared no better, for within the temple there are the failed lovers, tormented—'Some fearing fraud, some fraudulently fayning'—in the best Ovidian manner. And in the midst of them all is the statue of Venus on a 'faire and brickle' altar, as mysterious and as doubtful as anything in this strange but familiar place. She is veiled, and Scudamour is not very sure why. 'The cause . . . was hard to know',

> But for, they say, she hath both kinds in one,
> Both male and female.
>
> (x, 41)

Scudamour is perpetually puzzled, and seems never to know more than what 'they say', but the guess he hazards here is right enough. For this is the ancient hermaphrodite Venus, complete in herself as the spontaneous source of all life.[4] And in practice it is upon this secret, double-natured Venus, rather than upon the single-natured friends Triamond and Cambell, that the book is felt to centre. She is veiled and mysterious because all creation is so, and Scudamour's hesitancy about this enigmatic smiling statue points to the incomprehensibility of the great forces of nature when we have to apply them to the human case. As such a force, Venus's doubleness is a sign of her completeness, and the snake which winds about her marks her as enduring while time endures. But for us the search for wholeness, while it is a law of our being, is both perilous and hard. The hermaphrodite image with which the third book originally ended points forward to the veiled Venus and back through centuries of symbolism to the Platonic androgyne and the double-sexed Adam of the Biblical commentators.[5] But in the second version Amoret and Scudamour are not united, and of course are never so in the six books we have. The concord which the natural universe naturally achieves is not easy for man, split and discordant ever since Eden. Venus herself is the uniting of contraries in the generative world, but that is a world to which human beings do not wholly, or do not only, belong. Scudamour's actions under her guidance are only a desperate hacking at the knot of ambiguousness in which he finds himself tied.

In Venus's temple we recognize our own internal world and all

---

[4] She was a figure well known to the Renaissance from reports of ancient legends, rites, and statues [e.g. Cartari, *De I Dei De Gli Antichi* (Venetia, 1556), p. 117, 'Venere con la barba', and other accounts of hermaphrodite gods] and perhaps chiefly from the commentaries of Servius, Donatus, Landino, etc. on the Venus of Virgil and the phrase 'ducente deo'. Plutarch's Isis, well known to Spenser, is double-sexed too.

[5] I take for granted here, of course, that the narrative function of the hermaphrodite image is to indicate sexual union, but the poem is an allegorical one and, as Professor Lewis has put it, the allegorist does not say 'A is B', but something more like 'A is like B; therefore quite possibly like C, D, and E as well'. The hermaphrodite is an ancient, familiar, and inclusive symbol, and moreover what has prevented the union of these two characters has been developed through the book in moral, emotional, and psychological terms.

the difficulties which, in spite of ourselves, we set in our own
path to love and friendship. It is these troubled and puzzled
people, doing what they can amid dangers, who fully explore the
realities of friendship, not as a philosophical concept or a standard
of right behaviour but as a way of living which they must find or
stay lost and searching for ever. Scudamour continues his
baffled search for Amoret, and she too is still in anguish even
after her release from Busyrane. Wandering away from Britomart's chaste affection she is caught by 'greedie Lust', an embodiment of elemental appetite, boar-tusked, hairy, and carrying a
sharply knotted club. This creature really does bring about a
horrible death. Amoret is now in the clutches of the kind of
thing she has obsessively feared. Dread of such monsters formed
part of her imprisonment; but greedy Lust itself, all-devouring,
primitive, and murderous, and the gross brutalities of its cave,
are very different from the refined agonies of imagination and
conscience in Busyrane's house. The monster

> came rudely rushing in
> And spredding over all the flore alone,
> Gan dight him selfe unto his wonted sinne:
> Which ended, then his bloudy banket should beginne.
>
> (vii, 20)

Very different, indeed, from the golden statue of Cupid, and the
the majestic gold-embroidered tapestries of the loves of the gods;
yet they have something in common.

Amoret runs, and is saved; so is Amyas's love Aemilia. Aemilia
had been captured when, going to meet Amyas, she found Lust
in his place. Amyas, similarly, had found instead of Aemilia the
giant Corflambo, who ruins both men and women, 'strength and
beautie'

> By casting secret flakes of lustfull fire
> From his false eyes, into their harts and parts entire.
>
> (viii, 48)

So too Amoret, straying from the sleeping Britomart, finds not
Scudamour but a sudden consuming appetite, from which it
requires Belphoebe and Arthur to release her and Aemilia. For
Timias to attempt it is disastrous; so closely (if temporarily)
identified are Amoret and her captor that her body screens his,
and in trying to help her Timias himself wounds her. The whole

episode has a powerful emotional realism. The good and loving Amoret can, in her isolation from Britomart and from Belphoebe her twin, be overwhelmed by such primitive urges as this. Both Scudamour and, less directly, Amoret have much to do with Concord's enemy and opposing principle, Ate, who is active in spreading suspicion and jealousy among the knights and their ladies. She, and her dwelling hard by the gates of hell, are given a set description which places her, as 'mother of debate' who lives on the seeds of discord as on bread and sucks life away, in opposition to Concord the giver of strength and fullness of life. Yet characteristically the borderline between them is very fine: not only is Hate, or strife, a necessary component in achieved concord, but in the temple where Concord keeps the gate there are lovers 'Some fearing fraud, some fraudulently fayning' who have failed in love and friendship almost as badly as Ate's 'deare lovers, foes perpetuall'. It is in the encounters of Britomart and Artegall that the narrowness of the line between discord and concord is best seen in practice. The success of these two does not make their story any less alive and actual than that of the unhappy Amoret and Scudamour. Britomart rides seeking her love who is also her foe; she

> Upon her first adventure forth did ride,
> To seeke her lov'd, making blind Love her guide.
> Unluckie mayd, to seeke her enemie!
>
> (v, 29)

Their battles, each a stage in understanding, contrast with the aimless groupings and regroupings of Satyrane's tournament where enmities are as meaningless, incalculable, and brief, as lacking in genuine feeling, as friendships. When Britomart and Artegall fight their actions are expressive of a real and intense hostility, a real and passionate attraction. There is a vitality here which is absent in the battle of Cambell and Triamond, ended by Cambina's ritual magic; their hostility, having its source in the reluctance and resentment of love, moves naturally towards a surrender to love, and the birth of concord from discord engages the emotional truths we know. Britomart's spear and armour become the proper weapons and defences of love, the right version among so many—Amoret's Danger and Doubt, Marinell's defence of the 'spoyle of all the world'—which are wrong.

It is partly because Britomart has been so fully developed as an acting, thinking, feeling, and responsible being that we so readily accept her battles as enactments of emotional and psychological occurrences while they remain actual battles between two angry knights and indeed owe their expressiveness to their remaining so. We do not translate them from physical to mental, they are both in virtue of their intensity. Britomart's first assumption of arms, in which she abjured girlhood and immaturity, her fighting journey and its further armings and disarmings, bring an accumulated symbolic weight to her warlike meetings with Artegall, so that the poet's comment is received not as an interpolation for our guidance but as an expression of our own response.

> Unluckie mayd, to seeke her enemie!
> Unluckie mayd, to seeke him farre and wide,
> Whom, when he was unto her selfe most nie,
> She through his late disguizement could him not descrie!
>
> (v, 29)

The narrative develops their love in terms of war. Britomart first attacks Artegall 'in middest of his pryde' as supreme victor at the tournament; like Hercules or Achilles he is overthrown at the height of his power. He bitterly resents this defeat, inflicted in the name of the knights of Maydenhead, but his attempt to avenge himself by gaining the mastery over her leads to a fuller submission. Their second battle does not, like Cambell's, have to get its meaning and its peaceful conclusion from outside itself, for the growing concord of mutual passion is implicit in every blow they strike. Artegall's anger at his earlier defeat is felt by the reader as resentment at a feared loss of freedom, his waylaying of Britomart as a last effort to impose his will. The words—'despitous ire', 'spoyle and vengeance', 'felonous intent', build up to his astonished and ridiculous upset when

> Unawares his saddle he forwent,
> And found himselfe on ground in great amazement.
>
> (vi, 11)

But he deprives Britomart of the enchanted spear, and she has for once to dismount and fight hand to hand, not from the heights of her indifference, the single-minded detachment which made her invincible by all but Artegall. The battle ends on almost equal terms; it is for Britomart to accept Artegall's fealty, but each is unable to use the sword on the other, each conquers and is conquered, the relationship is established and acknowledged. Through an intensely individual encounter a general truth—the development of concord from the discord in which it potentially exists—is brought home.

Since it is a successful meeting of love, it is also a meeting of friendship. Taught by love, Britomart has already become a complete person, the woman as knight, and the same process is now to begin, through her, in Artegall the aggressively masculine. Neither in the marriage of persons, nor in the marriage of qualities within the mind, is the meeting enough; Spenser is concerned to show the necessity for effort and growth. Britomart here has the advantage of Artegall and is further along the way. She has already been searching for the ideal figure of Venus's mirror, and when she recognizes him in Artegall and knows their enmity to be one of attraction, she has few adjustments to make to the new situation. But Artegall has had no picture of her, or anyone, in his mind, and the attraction which made him wait to challenge her on her way from the tournament was entirely unrecognized. Like Marinell, he has no place in his mind for women, though his motives are less dubious. Marinell is prompted by weakness and fear of loss, he hoards himself as he hoards his jewels and as his mother hoards him. Artegall is simply busy about other things, and finds women a nuisance and love a waste of time. As Glauce wisely puts it, he is 'rebellious unto love'. It seems natural, so exact is Spenser's narrative in these things, that only Britomart, who is as practical and competent as he is, and can work alongside him in comradeship, could defeat Artegall just as only she could defeat Marinell. Her womanly qualities are of a kind that takes them unaware, with all their generalizations suddenly inapplicable; they find themselves 'on ground in great amazement'.

Up to a point, Marinell and Artegall are two of a kind, held together by their common relation as warriors to Britomart who defeats them both, and held together also by the firm pattern of mythological reference which exists in these books. Spenser's handling of the varied resources of myth is commonly very exact. Myth defines meaning but is in its turn defined, as to its central and particular meaning, by the precision of its context. Thus when in Book II Guyon's voyage to the Bower of Bliss is seen as an Odyssean journey the context in which the comparison is made shows us that we here have to do with the moralized Ulysses, the type of temperate and steadfast wisdom. Spenser knew as Shakespeare did that Ulysses was famous for other things too—for slippery and even treacherous cunning, for his ability to make the worse appear the better reason—but these are not relevant to the immediate purpose and our attention is not directed to them. Similarly the Herculean overtones in the same book relate strictly to the moralized hero whose labours are the conquering of the passions and whose famous 'choice' of virtue had and was still to have a long emblematic life.

But there was more to Hercules than this, and in the fourth and fifth books Spenser exploits other connotations which are as much psychological as moral. Hercules, on the one hand a just and noble conqueror of the passions, was on the other an example of great strength conquered by those passions. Diodorus Siculus remarks that the power of love is mighty to trip up those who are proud of their bodily strength, and that for this reason the ancient writers have represented Hercules, otherwise invincible, as being conquered by the might of love. Natalis Comes too writes of the shameful indignities which Hercules underwent through love after a noble and virtuous career, though as usual he converts an interesting psychological generalization into a moral lesson: appetite lies in wait for the good man whose eyes turn for a moment from the sight of virtue. The episodes in the hero's life which lent colour to such interpretations were those involving Iole and Deianeira, who jointly brought about his death; the Amazons; and, especially, Omphale. This relationship, with its transposition of the usual male and female roles, carried a note of portent for Bernard de Montfaucon, as late as the eighteenth century: 'Yet Hercules spins, while Iole and Omphale wear those Arms, formidable to all the tyrants and Monsters both of Earth and Hell.' Looked at from one point of view, the conquering of the unconquered hero becomes the crucial situation in his history, and his adventures with the Amazons and Iole and Deianeira, who was said to be also a fighter, seemed all to be versions of the victory of Venus's warrior, Omphale. Hercules is, in this aspect, another Achilles, and both heroes are drawn upon for the characterization of Artegall.

It is as Achilles that we see him first in Britomart's magic glass.

His crest was covered with a couchant hownd,
And all his armour seemd of antique mould,
But wondrous massy and assured sownd,
And round about yfretted all with gold,
In which there written was, with cyphres old,
Achilles armes, which Arthegall did win
(III, ii, 25)

At this point the near identification with Achilles works to establish Artegall as a supreme warrior and hero, worthy to bear the armour of the greatest of the Greeks, a trophy his survivors had competed for. Old as it is, the armour is 'wondrous maasy and assured sownd', its qualities, of solidity and a strength rare in the modern world, pass over to its owner, and he becomes a figure out of the superhuman past of the great ancients. Two cantos later Achilles is further developed as a point of reference, though in relation not to Artegall but to Marinell; and when Artegall comes before us again, in the fourth canto of the fourth book, we are ready to catch other overtones. Artegall enters the lists against the knights of Maydenhead in armour as striking as that in the magic glass and in a way like it, for it is expressive of an Achillean savagery.

For all his armour was like salvage weed,
With woody mosse bedight, and all his steed
With oaken leaves attrapt, that seemed fit
For salvage wight, and thereto well agreed
His word, which on his ragged shield was writ,
Salvagesse sans finesse, shewing secret wit.
(IV, iv, 39)

Whatever it may show of secret wit, the rough motto certainly sums up Artegall's behaviour at the tournament. He charges the first rider he sees and topples knights over in what seems a random way until his spear breaks, when he draws his sword, 'The instrument of wrath'[6] and goes on

like a lyon in his bloodie game,
Hewing and slashing shields and helmets bright,

[6] That the sword should be chosen for this resounding phrase has implications, of course, for Artegall as champion of justice. The sword of justice is here the sword of wrath. But this significance becomes overt only when we look back from the fifth book.

133

And beating downe what ever nigh him came,
That every one gan shun his dreadfull sight,
No lesse then death it selfe, in daungerous affright.

(iv, 41)

This is something more deadly earnest than the chivalric exchanges to be expected at a tournament. The Salvage Knight rides to 'tyrannize', as the poet puts it, to bend to his will; he rides in the wrath of Achilles. Unhorsed by Britomart in the midst of his pride he is still like Achilles, grudging and furious in disgrace. 'Thereat greatly grudged Artegall', and he leaves the tournament in great displeasure because he has not won. Like Marinell, Artegall is successful and powerful, but within very narrow limits; his success is at once ensured and circumscribed by the fact that he leaves so much out of his considerations. He is brave, but also ruthless, aggressive, and 'tyrannous', with none of the softer qualities which customarily go to make a chivalrous knight or, for that matter, a civilized and well-balanced person. In terms of the poem's fiction all this is suggested in Scudamour's joking comment on Artegall's amatory defeat by Britomart:

Certes, Sir Artegall,
I joy to see you lout so low on ground,
And now become to live a ladies thrall,
That whylome in your minde wont to despise
them all.

(vi, 28)

The tone is light, but the choice of words points to a capacity for submission, in Artegall, which we remember later when he does become 'a thrall',[7] and 'louts low' to Radigund as Hercules to Omphale. Britomart, of course, will take no unfair advantage when he drops his 'powrelesse arme, benumbd with secret feare', but his response to her does none the less foreshadow his later situation, and does suggest what proves to be his danger. What he has ignored or despised gains in its isolation an exaggerated power. The step is easy from exerting tyranny to being its willing victim. But if the soft enslavement of the wrathful Achilles and the formidable Hercules lies like a shadow behind Artegall, it is so far a shadow only. Britomart's armour is a sign of inner strength, not of mastery; and her behaviour, the poet's comments,

[7] Marinell is a 'thrall' too, to Cymoent.

and even old Glauce's forthright advice, establish the rightness
of this victory which, because it is Britomart's, is Artegall's also.
Glauce interprets Artegall's defeat as the completion, rather than
the disgrace, of his knighthood:

> Ne henceforth be rebellious unto love,
> That is the crowne of knighthood, and the band
> Of noble minds derived from above,
> Which being knit with vertue, never will remove.

(vi, 31)

This meeting is only the beginning of a relationship which
becomes increasingly significant in the fifth book, and there we
find that the connections of Britomart and Artegall with Diana
and Venus, with Mars and Achilles and Hercules, can contribute
to our understanding of justice as well as of friendship. Artegall
in Book IV is not yet known to us as the knight of justice; he
is part of an intricate structure of stories and characters through
which relationships between persons and between qualities are
developed and clarified. But Hercules and Achilles were heroes
of justice too, and the associations accumulated in the book of
Friendship have a further part to play. One 'virtue' leads naturally
to another, since it raises issues which can be resolved only by
looking at experience from another standpoint. Problems posed
in the consideration of chastity have to be further explored in the
book of Friendship, and it is inevitable—or Spenser makes it
seem so—that these books should, because of the subjects the
narrative engages and the atmosphere it carries, raise the question
of justice. The setting is one of uncertainty; things may or may
not be what they seem, and characters search for each other and
for their own identities, trying, on the whole, to help each other
and themselves. Most of them suffer, and know that those they
seek suffer. In such a situation men question the justice of conditions they cannot mould to their desires. Why, asks Scudamour,
should Amoret be in such pain, and how can it be right that he,
who means so well, should be the cause of her distress? There
must be something in the nature of things which turns our good
intentions wrong.

It is divine justice that we are likely to question first in such
situations as these, not our own competence, and the greatest
may, under stress, direct their questions thus wrongly. Even

135

Arthur, having made the wrong choice in conditions where choosing is difficult because meaning is obscured, and finding himself alone in the dark wood, cries out petulantly upon the place of night in the established cycle.

> What had th'Eternall Maker need of thee,
> The world in his continuall course to keepe,
> That doest all thinges deface, ne lettest see
> The beautie of his worke?
>
> (III, iv, 56)

Florimell, plaintive in her prison under the sea, gently doubts the gods:

> Ye gods of seas, if any gods at all
> Have care of right, or ruth of wretches wrong.
>
> (IV, xii, 9)

And Scudamour, thinking of Amoret, is bitterly accusing.

> At last forth breaking into bitter plaintes
> He sayd: 'O soverayne Lord, that sit'st on hye,
> And raignst in blis emongst thy blessed saintes,
> How suffrest thou such shamefull cruelty,
> So long unwreaked of thine enimy?
> Or hast thou, Lord, of good mens cause no heed?
> Or doth thy justice sleepe, and silently?
> What booteth then the good and righteous deed,
> If goodnesse find no grace, nor righteousness no meed?
>
> (III, xi, 9)

The sorrowful questioning of the characters is pointed by the sympathy of the poet himself, grieving for Amoret and Florimell, moved to exclamation as he contemplates the brief unhappy lives of men.

> O why doe wretched men so much desire
> To draw their dayes unto the utmost date,
> And doe not rather wish them soone expire,
> Knowing the miserie of their estate,
> And thousand perils which them still awate,
> Tossing them like a boate amid the mayne,
> That every houre they knocke at Deathes gate?
>
> (IV, iii, 1)

The only answer given by way of direct statement to such implicit or explicit doubt of God's justice is Britomart's, when she tries to rouse Scudamour from his abandoned grief.

> Yet if that hevenly grace some good reliefe
> You send, submit you to High Providence,
> And ever in your noble hart prepense,
> That all the sorrow in the world is lesse
> Then vertues might and values confidence.
> For who nill bide the burden of distresse
> Must not here thinke to live: for life is wretchednesse.
>
> (III, xi, 14)

Britomart is the most capable of all the characters, but she has no explanation to give Scudamour, and no comforting certainty that the good, any more than the wicked, will be saved from suffering. Her answer is simply that unhappiness is irrelevant to virtue, that life is wretched and it is weak to expect it to be otherwise. One must submit to the ways of a providence it is useless to question, must endure, and act. This is Britomart's own practice. The one personal complaint she makes during her search for Artegall contrasts with Scudamour's and even Arthur's. Her strong sense of purpose does not make her way easier; there are times when she feels herself to be without assurance, sailing 'withouten starres gainst tyde and winde' on a huge sea of sorrow. But she attributes no blame and asks no questions, but only prays to the god of winds, listens to Glauce's commonsense scolding, and goes on to the next practical step, 'For her great courage would not let her weepe'. The justice of events, she seems to say, is for the gods to manage; our business is with our own justice to one another, with duty, and with affection. This is all that one of the protagonists can say without distorting the experience that these two books present.

But the poet has open to him his own ways of saying that, although we in our world and his creatures in theirs must work in the dark and without hope of reward, in 'vertues might and values confidence', yet in the end Scudamour's accusing questions will be answered. The poet can show, by developing fully the pattern which Scudamour cannot see from within it, that God's justice does not 'sleepe, and silently', goodness will find grace, and righteousness meed. And this is one function of the

137

sea story of Florimell and Marinell, which broadens out the book's individual searches and sufferings to a universal scope, embracing both the generically human and the cosmic. Florimell suggests beauty and softness as they appear analogically in nature, as well as actually in women. Her grace is fleeting, delicate, constantly threatened, like that of the flower with which her name connects her, and her appeal is immediate; 'none alive but joy'd in Florimell'. As for Marinell, he is born half of the sea and lives by the sea's cruelty; the greedy gulf throws up voluntarily for him gold and ivory and pearl,

> And him enriched through the overthrow
> And wreckes of many wretches, which did weepe
> And often wayle their wealth, which he from them did keepe.
>
> (III, iv, 22)

The beauty which surrounds Marinell is derived from the cold impersonal destructiveness of the natural world, and he protects his jewels with a coldness like the sea's. The narrative enacts the union of elemental cosmic opposites, the destructive and the gentle aspects of the natural creation. They are brought together in concord through the Love who first linked contrary dislikes 'with adamantine chaines' and who was often pictured holding a flower and a fish to symbolize his universal power.[8]

The possessive chase from which Florimell flies brings her, too, to the sea, where her flowerlike fragility and her timidity are subjected to the most hostile element and where at last she is saved. It is a sea of sorrow for her as it is for Britomart; 'new waves of weary wretchednesse' are heaped upon her by the avenging queen of love. The image relates her to Psyche[9] and

[8] E.g. Alciati, *Emblemata* (1593), Emblema CVI, 'Potentia amoris'.

[9] The indirect connection with Psyche raises the question of how far Florimell may suggest Platonic meanings of the rational soul caught in the world of sense. Professor Lewis puts it in general and perhaps debatable terms: 'If Florimell . . . willynilly suggests to us the soul lost and imprisoned in the world of matter and change, we cannot be sure that she never suggested this to Spenser.' Part of Florimell's function in the poem would seem certainly to be to investigate the nature of the world of matter and change, to suggest how human beings should respond to and understand it; it may be that the analogy of Psyche, the soul temporarily imprisoned, is present to underline that function. Of all poems *The Faerie Queene* perhaps suffers most from an attempt at definitiveness, and I intend no such attempt.

through Psyche to Amoret; each undergoes a deathly suffering. When Florimell's miseries end at last in unshakable happiness that end is felt to be a law of nature's being and of ours, for what happens for Florimell can happen too for Amoret whom the poet so often couples with her. What Scudamour sees must be only a part of the truth. The magnitude of the step which the delicate Florimell has taken is several times emphasized. Her committing herself to the sea, one of the most familiar and natural symbols of dissolution, is a crisis. She takes to the fisherman's boat in desperation; she has lost her safeguarding girdle of chastity with its associations of magical charm and grace, she is without her palfrey, and she can fly no further. By degrees she is brought to the point where she must stand and, in her own way, resist, and she finds her own strength and the resolution of her difficulties. At first her danger seems greater than ever, but in the end it becomes true that she 'safety fownd at sea, which she fownd not at land'. The place of most peril becomes the place of salvation. The remnant of the persecuting land, the degraded fisherman, who reduces the good things of the ocean to squalor and dirt, causes Florimell's total committal to the sea, and to the long imprisonment by Proteus. And from this point her fate is felt to be divinely directed.

> See how the heavens, of voluntary grace
> And soveraine favor towards chastity,
> Doe succor send to her distressed cace:
> So much High God doth innocence embrace.
>
> (III, viii, 29)

'It fortuned' that Proteus was roving abroad, and Proteus has already established himself as the agent of a purpose beyond his own understanding. His oracular prophecy to Cymoent brings about the very situation that it seems to warn against, and it works for Marinell's eventual good. Now he becomes the means by which Florimell too is tried, and saved, and brought through the sea to Marinell. 'Proteus is shepheard of the seas of yore', and in Florimell's and Marinell's trials he has something of a shepherding function. His own intention, so far as such a creature of nature can be said to have one, is the same as everyone else's, to seize Florimell for himself, but the mythical changes of shape and the undersea setting remove from his actions most of their

139

personal or human content, and the episode is like one of the old fairytales of trial and temptation, seeming arbitrary but leading to wealth and security for the heroine who resists them. Florimell does resist, 'So firmly she had sealed up her brest'. She applies herself with some resource to rejecting the offers which Proteus makes in one form after another, and she will not be intimidated by his more ferocious manifestations, of centaur or of sea-storm.

> Dayly he tempted her with this or that,
> And never suffred her to be at rest:
> But evermore she him refused flat.
>
> (III, viii, 39)

Finally she is flung into a dungeon likened to Hell and imaged as a place of death; horror and darkness dwell there and the seven months of her imprisonment are like a long night.

The seven months are the conventional period for the ritual death which ends in rebirth, the time between the solstices when Proserpine and Adonis and other divinities of the yearly cycle are held underground. Seven is also the number of completion and perfecting, and so is natural for a time of testing such as Florimell seems to undergo. For hers is a dying into life through endurance, and in her, whose nature is sufficiently human and touching to engage our sympathy, the natural cycle is seen as having significance for humanity. Her death and rebirth are not the mere mechanics of vegetative life but analogies for our experience. Not even Amoret's misery is purposeless, since it is the only way to life. Thus Proteus as an agent in Florimell's necessary trial is less a villainous character or an inner evil than a natural process, for this is not a moralized myth but a myth simply. Spenser's choice of Proteus may, none the less, have been influenced by the moralizers, who were almost unanimous in regarding him as the undifferentiated first matter, or chaos, by its nature seeking various forms but continuing the same for all the appearances it assumes. As first matter Proteus has a particular connection with beauty (and so with Florimell) which a passage from Leone Ebreo touches on:

> First matter, in its insatiable desire to partake of divine beauty by the reception of forms, moves continually from one form to another in the unceasing circular motion of generation and corruption.[10]

[10] Op. cit., p. 337.

I do not think that Spenser is expounding the divine beauty of the neoplatonists; Florimell here seems to suggest, or to suggest primarily, the vulnerability and charm of lovely natural things. But the associations which had developed around Proteus may have suggested Spenser's use of him, for they qualify him richly for the part he plays. The particular death Florimell has to endure is that of the mutable natural world; Proteus 'never suffred her to be at rest' until at last he bound her in the cave under the sea.

Enigmatic as ever, like all the ways of the universe, Proteus is a symbol both of change and of constancy in change, and is thus fitted to present a choice to Florimell, who matches him in endurance through change by shifting her ground every time that he does. Through a purposive adaptiveness she remains constant to her one aim, union with Marinell. As her story progresses, it comes to suggest something about the natural world; the impression grows, as we read, that the principle of that world is not mindless alteration but the meeting of the opposites in love, a meeting which makes order out of chaos. Florimell alone is fragile, Marinell alone is hard; each, alone, is pathetic and blind, however beautiful. But they complement one another, and together they become part of the rich productive strength of nature. Change, even the change of death in the dark cave under the sea, is only an expression of permanence, and Florimell lives through the individual destruction inherent in the 'circular motion of generation and corruption' to be reborn in what seems, every year, a miracle.

> From which, unlesse some heavenly powre her free
> By miracle, not yet appearing plaine . . .
>
> (IV, xi, 1)

The miracle takes the form of the coming of Marinell, a guest at the wedding of Thames and Medway. Florimell's pathetic and affectionate lament completes what Britomart's wound had begun, and he too endures a kind of death. 'His cheeke bones raw, and eie-pits hollow grew', he looks like 'ruefull ghost'. He and his mother have attempted to impose their self-centred conception of fairness on a universe which works according to its own mysterious justice, and through this attempt the realities of love and death and life are further explored. Given an apparent choice between life and death they choose what seems to be life but is in fact death, Marinell's cold and detached existence in the lifeless brilliance of precious stones tossed from dead men's hands on to the jewelled shore. From Britomart he receives a 'deadly wownd', a death which, because it is sacrificial, is life-giving. The natural world must die for its own continuance, as the beasts must die sacrificed to the gods for the good of the world. Such dying is sacred, and has its relevance to the life of men.

> Like as the sacred oxe, that carelesse stands
> With gilden hornes and flowry girlonds crownd,
> Proud of his dying honor and deare bandes,
> Whiles th'altars fume with frankincense arownd,
> All suddeinly with mortall stroke astownd,
> Both groveling fall, and with his streaming gore
> Distaines the pillours and the holy grownd,
> And the faire flowers that decked him afore:
> So fell proud Marinell upon the pretious shore.
>
> (III, iv, 17)

As beautiful and ornamental, and as unknowing, as the gilded ox, Marinell is shocked into awareness as he is felled. Throughout his history are heard again and again the words which inform the action, most pointedly in Cymoent's

> I feared love: but they that love doe live,
> But they that dye doe nether love nor hate.
>
> (III, iv, 37)

Marinell has understood Proteus's warning to mean that love would be death for him, but in fearing, hating, and avoiding it he undergoes the sacrificial death which leaves him ready to learn in what sense love really is a kind of death and also in what sense it is life. 'They that love do live'. The words themselves— life, death, love—are flat through long use and misue, and any writer must recharge them if we are to be convinced that he is dealing not in paltry effects of verbal jugglery but in a felt paradox. Spenser does recharge them; they are the explosive point of an accumulated force coming from the finely structured narrative and its images; but one cannot demonstrate this by quotation, only try to suggest the context which gives their full meaning to such drained words as life and death. Florimell uses such words too, as she laments, overheard by Marinell, in Proteus's dungeon. Her speech is poignant and emotionally realistic as she

142

faces the incredible fact of Marinell's indifference to a love that
to her is all important: 'He where he list goes loose, and laughes
at me'. It moves through self-pity, accusation, rebellion, a wish
for Marinell's attention at any cost, and at last to acceptance of
the truth, that wherever he is she can only wish him happy: 'So
over loose, so ever happy be'. It is a speech which convincingly
follows the movements of a mind trying to shake off the bonds of
love while recognizing that they are permanent. At the same time
it is as much a piece of highly formalized rhetoric as is the persua-
sion of Red Crosse's Despair. Its patterned repetition, setting in
developing relationships the ideas of life and death, justice and
injustice, freedom and bondage, carries further the theme which
Marinell and Cymoent have initiated. The words interweave
through three compressed stanzas: 'care of right, or ruth of
wretches wrong', 'I daily dying', 'my lifes deare love', 'Such
thraldome or such freedome',

> And if ye deeme me death for loving one
> That loves not me, then doe it not prolong,
> But let me die and end my daies attone,
> And let him live unlov'd, or love him selfe alone.
>
> (IV, xii, 9)

When Marinell hears Florimell's grief his hard heart is 'toucht
with soft remorse and pity rare', and though he has still to die
another death, and so to loosen the bonds with which his mother's
fear has tied him, the way is now open for him. As his hardness
has been softened, so has Florimell's softness been strengthened,
all in the sea, and at the marriage feast of Thames and Medway,
where their differences are resolved, the sea itself is transformed,
so that the sorrow and death with which it has been associated
are seen to be a part of life and fecundity and joy. The sea which
sends Marinell dead men's goods sends him also Florimell, the
'waift' who according to the strict laws of the ocean must be sur-
rendered by Proteus. Creation and destruction, friendship and
hostility, all are reconciled in these unfathomable depths. The
sea not only kills but redeems. Florimell and Marinell, who
belong in part to the human world and in part to the natural,
turn our minds towards those two essential aspects which we
must reconcile in our understanding of the concord of the universe. We must know that the gentle and the terrible, the lamb

and the tiger or in Spenser's image the dove and the falcon, are necessary for the sustaining of the world; of all the elements it is the sea that can best figure them in their interdependence. The divinities of oceans and rivers passing in procession, the nymphs pressing on one another like waves, chaos almost visibly becoming order; here is the inexhaustible creativeness of the generative world. Water is part of our natural symbolism of dissolution, and also of rebirth; moisture is the source of life, so that the nymphs of the springs 'all mankinde do nourish with their waters clere'; the destroying sea is yet the most fertile of the elements, contemplated by the poet with delight at his impossible task.

> O what an endlesse worke have I in hand,
> To count the seas abundant progeny,
> Whose fruitful seede farre passeth those in land,
> And also those which wonne in th'azure sky!
> For much more eath to tell the starres on hy,
> Albe they endlesse seeme in estimation,
> Then to recount the seas posterity:
> So fertile be the flouds in generation,
> So huge their numbers, and so numberlesse
>   their nation.
>
>   (IV, xii, 1)

Thus the sea with its Protean changes and its 'exceeding fry' of creatures, its endless orderly reception and circulation of waters, is a figure for the generative world. And 'because in this principality is all generation and corruption, the Theologians express it by the Ocean, ebbing or flowing continually: by Neptune understanding the Power or Deity that presides over Generation'.[11]

Therefore, Spenser continues,

>   the antique wisards well invented
> That Venus of the fomy sea was bred.

The rich changing harmonies of the wedding procession, embracing the corners of the world and leading into the resolution in equal harmony of those two contrary aspects of nature, Mari-

---

[11] Edmund G. Gardner, ed., *A Platonick Discourse upon Love*, by Pico della Mirandola. Translated by Thomas Stanley (Boston, 1914), p. 13.

nell and Florimell, assert the essential goodness and final simplicity of the androgyne Venus, 'the root of all that joyous is,/ Great god of men and women, queene of th'ayre', though to men and women she may sometimes seem otherwise. The world is justly made and benevolently sustained, and concord is its universal law. In bringing Florimell and Marinell together in joy through suffering Spenser justifies the sufferings of the rest also; the sea story mirrors the whole living and dying world, built by the meeting of contraries.

Only in the Garden of Adonis, a place inexhaustible in meaning, do we find as satisfying and inclusive a symbol of the concorded opposites of the books of Love; and looking back from the fourth book with Florimell's history in our minds the Garden assumes new richness. In the Garden there is less concern to demonstrate that the paradoxes at the heart of all creation can be seen to work justly and joyously in the world we know, for the Garden of Adonis is not our world, it is the primeval source of natural life. None the less that source is here seen to be, though still paradoxical, ultimately good. And at its centre is, again, the union of male and female principles by which life is kept 'eterne in mutabilitie'. The Garden is predominantly Venus's place, as it should be; in the Adonis myth she is the mother goddess, the central and stable figure, with the young god embodying 'the transitory life which arose every spring and withered away'.[12] But she has none of Acrasia's enervating and corrupting purpose and Adonis none of Verdant's 'effeminate slackness', for the images evoke a rich, safe, creativeness and power. Venus dominates as the goddess of love, concord, and creation, and through her the hunter Adonis, who destroys and is destroyed, becomes part of the perpetuation of life. In the vitality of the mount and the Garden destruction is implicit. Life proceeds in its endless cycle 'like a wheele', and the wheel of generation is turned by Genius, who lets out into the world the creatures grown in the Garden. At unspecified intervals they return, to rest for a thousand years before the process is

---

[12] E. O. James, *The Worship of the Sky-God* (London, 1963), p. 39. For the dominance of the female principle on the mount see C. S. Lewis, 'Neoplatonism in the Poetry of Spenser', Études Anglaises, XIVᵉ Année, No. 2, 1961, pp. 107–116 (a review essay on Robert Ellrodt's book, op. cit.).

renewed.[13] The emphasis is on continuity, but this implies the passing of the individual creature: on creativeness, but this implies, indeed depends upon, destruction.

> Corruption must precede every generation and generation every corruption . . . corruption is produced by the victory of opposites, and generation also is a movement from one opposite to another.[14]

So 'the faire flowre of beauty fades away,/As doth the lilly fresh before the sunny ray', for the enemy of the forms is Time with his scythe. There is no minimizing of the individual losses involved; even Venus grieves for them. But Time is itself part of a nexus of laws which we are not merely to submit to as inescapable but to accept as beneficent. Without Time the cycle would not exist, and the bliss of Venus and Adonis, Psyche and Cupid, is untouched by their pity for 'faire thinges mard',

> For all that lives is subject to that law:
> All things decay in time, and to their end doe draw.
>
> (III, vi, 40)

Just as with Florimell's story of the sea, there can be no life without death. Time, says Leone Ebreo,

> is the cause of generation in this lower world, since things existing in time must needs have a beginning and be generated; and moreover because time destroys the things subject to it, and whatsoever is corruptible must needs be generated. Thus time, symbolised by Saturn, conveyed generation by means of Venus from heaven to the lower world, which is called a 'sea', because of the continual changes of one form into another through continual generation and decay . . . generation in this world originates in destruction . . . For if things were not destroyed there would be no generation.[15]

[13] This movement is perhaps a faint echo of Platonic theory. Again Ebreo (op. cit., pp. 288–9) gives a tidy version: 'For six thousand of the seven thousand years chaos continually brings forth the lower bodies, and when her period is completed, she is said to gather all things within herself, and to rest during the seven thousandth year; and in that time she again conceives a new generation for another six thousand years.' But see, for a detailed discussion of the philosophical problems posed by the Garden, Ellrodt's book and Lewis's review of it, cited above.

[14] Leone Ebreo, op. cit., p. 279.

[15] Op. cit., pp. 150–1. I do not mean to suggest that Spenser intends precisely what Ebreo does, still less that Spenser's poetry is equatable with Ebreo's philosophy, but only that these are some of the ideas and images which were available for the use of this most eclectic but most individual of poets.

Thus 'all that lives is subject to that law:/All things decay in time', but the stanza which follows moves on at once to the joyous life which is dependent upon that law of death. Short of immortality, which is a contradiction of the conditions upon which we have life, there is an untroubled paradisal happiness in the Garden.

> Franckly each paramor his leman knowes,
> Each bird his mate, ne any does envy
> Their goodly meriment and gay felicity.

> There is continuall spring, and harvest there
> Continuall.

(III, vi, 41–2)

But it is in Adonis himself, lying enclosed among the impenetrable trees of the mount, that the paradoxes of the Garden are most richly imaged. The trees in the grove are the traditional myrtles, sacred to Venus and as evergreens associated also with death and rebirth. Such associations ensure our consciousness, as we read, of the Adonis myth, one which caught the imagination of the Renaissance since it contained potentially within it so many of the themes in which their attitudes were channelled. Its inclusiveness enables Spenser to use Adonis as another keystone in the expressive structure of the third and fourth books. He gathers into himself, and thus enriches and clarifies, meanings implicit elsewhere in the narrative. Whereas in Malecasta's tapestry Adonis charmingly dies, to survive only in a flower's prettiness, the Garden builds upon that other version of his fate in which he spends part of the year with Proserpine among the dead and part with Venus in the living world. Spenser would have had also in mind, no doubt, the tradition that Venus hid him among the growing plants that the little potted 'gardens' of his cult are said to commemorate. This Adonis dies only to be reborn, is ritually lamented only to be hailed at his swift return.

Such gods owe their life and creative potency to the fact of their death; through it Adonis is made, not immortal, but perpetual by succession like the yearly grain 'for he may not/For ever dye, and ever buried bee/In balefull night, where all thinges are forgot'. 'For it is the case', says Philo Judaeus, 'both that the fruit comes out of the plants, as an end out of a beginning, and that out of the fruit again, containing as it does the seed in itself,

147

there comes the plant, a beginning out of an end'.[16] Around the mount grow the flowers of other vegetation gods, hyacinth and narcissus; and we remember Adonis and Hyacinthus later, when Marinell revives like a plant in summer at sight of the flowerlike, springlike Florimell, released from her Stygian imprisonment. He banishes sad death, and

> As withered weed through cruell winters tine,
> That feeles the warmth of sunny beames reflection,
> Liftes up his head, that did before decline,
> And gins to spread his leafe before the faire sunshine.
>
> (IV, xii, 34)

Adonis is also the hunter and the hunted, and under the mount lies the boar which wounded him, its malice conquered through the strength of Venus. It lives on, as destruction must while the world lasts, but Adonis and Venus together have made death into life and change into perpetuity. The hunt of death, like that of honour and of chastity, had long been connected with the chase of love, and the two often and ominously merge, as they do in *Sir Gawain and the Green Knight*, with its boar hunt and its mysteriously parallel seduction of Gawain by the lady, or in Ovid's pathetic story of the death of Procris, or in Adonis's own myth.[17] Venus, as Ovid and Shakespeare tell us, begged Adonis to have nothing to do with the pursuit of the great beasts, the boar and the lion, the hunt in which heroes (including Artegall and Tristram) were trained, because in it the destructive forces of nature are unleashed against beauty and tenderness. Spenser does not refer to this motif in the Garden, for he has used it in Malecasta's arras showing 'the love of Venus and her paramoure', where it fittingly suggests the trivial state of affairs in Castle Joyeous, carefully aloof from the reality of the 'greater beasts' of passion deeper in the forest. In the Garden the events leading up to Adonis's death are less important than the mastery of death through love, but the boar (said to have been sent either by Diana or by Mars, both opposed to Venus and both death-

---

[16] *Works*, translated Colson and Whitaker (London, 1949), vol. 1, p. 33.

[17] For the many meanings of the hunt, and their long history in literature, see D. C. Allen, *Image and Meaning: Metaphoric Tradition in Renaissance Poetry* (Baltimore, 1960), and 'On Venus and Adonis', *Elizabethan and Jacobean Studies Presented to F. P. Wilson* (Oxford, 1959).

dealers) is still the destroying aspect of the world, whether chaos[18] or winter or simply death or even a shadow of the great denier himself; 'the devil is that great boar', says Alexander Ross. All these are only partial images of the negation of life and joy, and the boar may be any or all of them.

But in the myth itself the most obvious meaning for the boar was destructive passion, and this too was a familiar association for Spenser's readers and one that the unavoidable comparison with Malecasta's picture makes sharp in the mind. Love, by which Adonis survives death, also delivered him to it. In all hunts there is a fateful intimacy between pursuer and prey, a relationship in which attraction and hostility are mingled, and this mutual fascination is suggested in many handlings of the myth, early and late. In Theocritus's thirty-first idyll the boar pleads that his intention was to caress, not to kill, such beauty; he and Adonis both were betrayed by the great tusks. Adonis and the boar, both equally hunter and hunted, are one centre among several related centres for the chase which works through the third book, accumulating meaning as it goes. Florimell belongs to it, and Marinell the destroyer who is sacrificed like Adonis, and Timias who sees the foster brandishing a boar-spear and follows him only to be wounded in his turn, and Belphoebe hunting too with the same spear. Like all the best myths this of Adonis has many potential meanings, and it brings its own power to Spenser's stories of people—Amoret, Marinell, even at first Britomart—for whom love, and indeed all life, comes to be as death; who do not see beyond to the creation which death must precede. Through the poetry of the Renaissance there echo again and again such words as Passerat's 'Amour et Peur logent toujours ensemble', or the darker saying of Ronsard, 'Car l'Amour et la Mort n'est qu'une mesme chose'. Sayings like these can have many meanings, or no meaning worth expressing, can be trivial, cynical, pretentious, profound. Spenser releases their potentialities in Britomart's girlish melodrama, Amoret's self-destroying obsession, Marinell's negation, Timias's debasement. They all must learn as Cymoent does the truth that they 'that love doe live', although they may have to pass like Adonis through a kind of death in order to do so.

[18] Compare Proteus in Florimell's story, though Proteus lacks the boar's malignancy. The various destructive associations of the boar mentioned here all appear in one or other of the mythographers.

Thus though there is no overt moral or psychological reference in the union of Venus with the reborn Adonis in the Garden, an implicit one arises necessarily through its context among the relationships the poem sets up. From its place at the centre the generative cycle, the law of creation through destruction, moves by analogy into the lives of men. The Garden holds the same kind of assurance as the sea, that we can know concord and order and joy if we accept and work with the laws of all life, although any statement of those laws will remain paradoxical.

> For whatsoever is necessary to the being of the Universe is assuredly good, since the being of the Universe is good. So that evil and decay are as necessary to the existence of the world as are good and birth, for the one prepares the other and leads thereto.[19]

The figure of the living Adonis is not offered as an adumbration of resurrection, as it was to be offered by Alexander Ross, for whom 'Our resurrection in this may be typed out; for although death kill us, it shall not annihilate us'. The books of Chastity and Friendship have to do with such meanings as may seem to cohere in the natural world we live in, not with those revealed from beyond it. But even so, as Britomart's love can seem to her to point to divine direction, as the natural grain of wheat can become a spiritual image, so Adonis may direct our minds to a possible parallel beyond the world of growing things he springs from. When we read of death it is human death we think of, whether the figurative deaths of love and sacrifice or the actual death of the body, and it is human survival we hope for. The questions hinted in the Garden will be taken further in the pastoral of Book VI.

[19] Leone Ebreo, op. cit., p. 119.

Chapter Five

HEAVENLY JUSTICE

IN contrast to the third and fourth books, where the values of Faeryland are felt to be so richly and suggestively present, the legend of Justice is often regarded as a disappointing book; and if we direct our attention too exclusively on the 'naïve' allegory of topical politics it is so. The theory of Renaissance social and political justice is coherent and satisfying enough, but its practice can create difficulties for a twentieth-century reader. Real politics tends to have awkward corners, which refuse to fit into the pattern of an allegorical narrative and which invite extra-literary considerations to intrude into the reader's mind because they have already intruded into the poem. Artegall's freeing of Irena may not refer to Grey, or to Grey only, but it does certainly refer to the freeing of Elizabethan Ireland, and a recent critic sums up the uneasiness in our response:

> Artegall's central quest is the liberation of Irena; and heavens knows what Ireland his Irena signifies, for it seems to exclude the entire population of the land. We cannot but feel that the position is false from the start.[1]

Spenser's prose account of Ireland does not reveal him as the relentlessly cruel colonist he has been sometimes represented as being, but none the less it is not easy to accept affairs in Ireland as exemplifying any viable conception of justice. I do not see how, with the best will in the world and the most understanding use of historical imagination, a modern reader can be quite at ease with

[1] G. Hough, *A Preface to The Faerie Queene* (London, 1962), p. 192.

151

Artegall's quest. Something of the awkward gap between the virtue as contemplated and the virtue as practically applied exists also in the episodes of Belge and of Burbon. Here, certainly, the effect is less uncomfortable, for we do not feel that the contemporary happenings which here so openly govern the fiction deny the justice they are supposed to affirm, but only that their affirmation is neither very interesting nor very revealing. The conclusion to be drawn, one must suppose, is that actual political and social occurrences were no more likely in the sixteenth century than in our own to embody justice, but only to approximate more or less nearly to just action. There is every reason to suppose that Spenser would agree, though as a serious and public-minded man he would have felt impelled by a sense of responsibility to embody his theme in events of the day; but one must regret that he did not, rather, allow the theme to suggest topical happenings lightly where it would, as he does in the other books. The historian, says Sidney, is captivated to the truth of a foolish world, and 'is so tied, not to what should be but to what is, to the particular truth of things and not to the general reason of things, that his example draweth no necessary consequence, and therefore a less fruitful doctrine'.

Necessary consequence is, indeed, what we feel to be lacking. These topical parts of the narrative, while conveying to us the issues of the time, convey little else. Belge, Irena, or Flourdelis do not suggest anything beyond their own story, do not seem importantly relevant to the poem's concerns. They exist for one situation and on one level and do not develop into many-sided meaning. Their stories are for the most part briskly told, but a sharp narrative procedure which would have its virtues elsewhere marks a fall in intensity in *The Faerie Queene*. Typically, the poem's manner is slow and heavily loaded, the references and descriptions look back and forth in a process of encircling and unfolding to which the long serpentine stanza and the leisurely spaces of the canto are perfectly suited. Such a lingering style is an economical way of encompassing Spenser's universe, showing the whole in the part and yet the part contributing to the whole, 'So flowing all from one, all one at last become'.[2]

And yet, to tabulate the weaknesses of the topical allegory is not to say so very much about the fifth book. Our impatient dis-

[2] IV, xi, 43.

appointment at these passages leads us, naturally enough, to see them disproportionately, but in fact they account for comparatively little of the narrative. It is only in the last three cantos that Artegall and Arthur carry out their tasks on behalf of Belge and Irena, and to take these episodes as the essence of the legend is surely as wrongheaded as to take the act of breaking Acrasia's bower as the essence of temperance or the capture of the Blattant Beast as the essence of courtesy. In all the books, even in St. George's, the actual achievement is of less moment than the process of preparation for it, which unfolds to us and to the knight what his 'virtue' really is. In Artegall's case, and in Calidore's, the quest is in the end only half achieved. He is late, almost too late, in coming to Irena's help, and his efforts 'to reforme that ragged common-weale' are interrupted by his recall to court, so that

> of necessity
> His course of justice he was forst to stay.

> (V, xii, 27)

The poem gives us no justification for supposing that Spenser complacently regarded matters of state in his own time as entirely adequate embodiments of absolute justice. Like us, he sees that what is is not quite what should be. We would perhaps explain the failure of Elizabethan policy in Ireland rather differently, but at least the poem does honestly make room for the unpalatable truth that complete public justice is a very rare thing, since its course is deflected by malice, self-interest, and lack of clear purpose. The gap between a noble theory and a squalid practice has been widened for us by the centuries, but some gap there always was in the poem, and apparently by intention. It is so hard to recognize true justice, and to administer it, against the vested interest of humanity, that even Artegall, who is Astraea's own fosterling, returns ingloriously from his uncompleted task with the Beast of shame and slander baying at his heels.

So it is not in the closing cantos of anticlimax, with the knight of Justice scrambling at the last minute to Irena's aid and trailing miserably home, that we can know the virtue as it really is. Except in the one wholly successful piece of historical allegory, the lovely description of Mercilla, justice is hard put to it to survive in the sphere of practical government—whether Elizabethan or Faery—where the real motive force is ambition.

153

Spenser opens the final canto with a passage of grave denunciation. It refers in particular to Burbon ('witnesse may Burbon be') but its sweeping pessimism gives it a wider application. The moral disgust which is one of Spenser's recurrent attitudes towards the places of power is very strong in these last books of *The Faerie Queene*.

> O sacred hunger of ambitious mindes,
> And impotent desire of men to raine,
> Whom neither dread of God, that devils bindes,
> Nor lawes of men, that common weales containe,
> Nor bandes of nature, that wilde beastes restraine,
> Can keepe from outrage and from doing wrong,
> Where they may hope a kingdome to obtaine.
> No faith so firme, no trust can be so strong,
> No love so lasting then, that may enduren long.
>
> (xii, 1)

It is in the nature of men to betray justice as it is repeatedly betrayed through the course of the book, but betrayals and failures do not alter the reality of justice itself. The fable is framed to express this duality. Astraea, in accordance with tradition, fled the 'filth and foule iniquity' of this world ages ago, leaving a mere mortal man to do what he could with the help of Jove's sword Chrysaor and the iron Talus, 'Immoveable, resistlesse, without end'. The proem similarly emphasizes, through the analogy of the world's alteration, the departure of absolute justice. The heavens, established in just order, are strangely altered; Bull and Ram shoulder one another, even the sun has moved since Ptolemy's time,[3] and random movement has become the apparent rule.

> So now all range, and doe at randon rove
> Out of their proper places farre away,
> And all this world with them amisse doe move,
> And all his creatures from their course astray,
> Till they arrive at their last ruinous decay.
>
> (Proem, 6)

The seeming alteration is repeated in the life of man, who created of earth is now transformed to stone, just as the Golden Age is now become a stony one. It is not now as in Saturn's reign,

---

[3] It has been pointed out that, here as elsewhere, Spenser's examples of cosmic change are the old ones, not those of the new philosophy.

when there was universal peace among men and beasts and all things grew freely to nourish them, and when 'Justice sate high ador'd with solemne feasts'. The departure of Astraea is the special mark of our degeneration, for justice is pre-eminently the attribute of God.

> Most sacred vertue she of all the rest,
> Resembling God in his imperiall might;
> Whose soveraine powre is herein most exprest,
> That both to good and bad he dealeth right,
> And all his workes with justice hath bedight.
>
> (Proem, 10)

It is also the attribute of princes, of course, and as God's representatives they are in theory, and in virtue of their office, the fountains of justice on earth. Spenser could do no less than continue, in the same stanza,

> That powre he also doth to princes lend,
> And makes them like himselfe in glorious sight,
> To sit in his owne seate, his cause to end,
> And rule his people right, as he doth recommend.

He could do no less, but he might have done a great deal more. The Virgin Queen was also the Virgin Astraea,[4] returned from the skies to rule England in perfect justice, but she is not so to Spenser although the compliment is one that asks to be made. There is a final stanza of deference to the dread sovereign goddess, giving righteous doom from the seat of judgment 'in th'- Almighties stead' and filling the nations with terror, a final apology from a subject who has dared to deal with her great justice; but this is little enough against the Elizabethan background of praise for the new Astraea. And the last word of all is for Artegall, an instrument of justice who is to finish his quest in disgrace. Throughout, the Proem stresses the absence of justice in a bad modern world, not its glorious re-affirmation in Elizabeth and her government. Right now is wrong, and wrong is right.

> Let none them blame me, if in discipline
> Of vertue and of civill uses lore,
> I doe not forme them to the common line

[4] Frances A. Yates, 'Queen Elizabeth as Astraea', Journal of the Warburg and Courtauld Institutes, X, 1947, pp. 27–82.

Of present dayes, which are corrupted sore,
But to the antique use which was of yore,
When good was onely for it selfe desyred,
And all men sought their owne, and none no more;
When Justice was not for most meed outhyred,
But simple Truth did rayne, and was of all admyred.

(Proem, 3)

Set against this contemporary reality, the compliment to Elizabeth as sovereign, contained in the formal beauty and ritual action of Mercilla's court, is remote indeed. Spenser shows in *Colin Clouts Come Home Againe* that he is as capable as his friend Ralegh of distinguishing between the particular truth and the general reason of things at court, between the poet's image of just and glorious sovereignty and the truth of a foolish world. The fifth and sixth books of *The Faerie Queene* underline his disenchantment. Artegall, operating in the sphere of practical politics, falls short of success, but his failure is only partly his own. It is also the failure of government, and of the monarch whose instrument he is. When we have read the Proem, we can hardly be surprised by the half-heartedness of Spenser's celebration of justice in his own time and realm.

But the absence of Astraea has its effect beyond the political sphere. Artegall's actions and the character he reveals through them are shaped by his isolation, and by his committal to an almost impossible task. Astraea has trained him 'in Justice lore' and has given him Talus with his flail, the power to execute his judgments. But she has withdrawn what he most needs, herself, and he is left to act alone, one just man among many unjust. Artegall, far from being justice itself, is a man working for justice in a world where it no longer clearly manifests itself. Naturally he makes mistakes, and hampered as he is by the injustice which exists all around him he is unable freely and fully to deal justice in the state. But in areas where what is truly just can be known and done by the individual good man, and is not deliberately undermined by others for expediency or gain, he is able to do better.

As is his habit, Spenser indicates at the beginning the nature of the problems which face his knight. But the situation here is unusual. We already know Artegall, and although we know him not as the knight of Justice but as the lover of Britomart and the

156

object of her quest, we are already possessed of certain facts about his nature. He is given to anger and to vengefulness, he has scorned women only to be enthralled by Britomart, he has won the armour of Achilles. And though we may now, in the fifth book, recall that to win that armour was a sign of supreme worth and that the shield pictured human life, including the dealing of justice, within a cosmic setting, we remember also that the hero's most obvious attributes were power and wrath, which have already characterized Artegall, and on occasion effeminate weakness. But it is not to Achilles that Artegall is first compared in Book V, but to Hercules and Bacchus, who together with Osiris were the best known of the ancient heroes of justice.

Hercules was perhaps the most familiar of these exemplars, overthrowing unjust tyrants and re-establishing justice by force. His task, it has been said, was the 'defense of mankind against the forces of the wild', and this is a task which requires violence. Hercules, striding about the primitive west with his 'club of Justice dread', himself naturally shares in the wildness he opposes. His justice operates by vengeance upon the evildoer, eye for eye and life for life. He killed Busiris at the altar upon which that king was accustomed to offer human sacrifice, and his vengeance worked with similar precision and aptness upon Diomedes of Thrace, to whom Spenser refers later in the book. His is a punishing justice, the destruction of wrong that right may be freed, and it is a true justice in a lawless society. Artegall similarly is trained, in earliest youth, to fight against oppression by the forces of the wild. Astraea teaches him the arithmetical precisions of theoretical justice, but in the savage unpopulated places where she rears him he has to practise what he has learned upon the wildest of wild forces, the beasts.

> There she him taught to weigh both right and wrong
> In equall ballance with due recompence,
> And equitie to measure out along,
> According to the line of conscience,
> When so it needs with rigour to dispence.
> Of all the which, for want there of mankind,
> She caused him to make experience
> Upon wyld beasts, which she in woods did find,
> With wrongfull powre oppressing others of their kind.
>
> (i, 7)

The story of Artegall's training would be familiar to Spenser's readers; it is an adaptation of the childhood of Achilles, one of the heroes to whom Artegall has already been related. Comes tells us that Achilles was taught justice by Chiron, and Statius not only makes him say that the centaur implanted in him the precepts of divine justice but dramatizes the process in the *Achilleid*, where the young hero is seen carrying back the lion cubs whose mother he has killed.[5] This forcefulness is what is stressed in Artegall's first lessons. When he grows to manhood men as well as beasts fear his 'awfull sight', 'overruling might', 'the horror of his wreakfull hand' raised in wrath. Justice must first strike terror in the evildoer. But when we meet Artegall in Book IV, he seems to have progressed no further in the understanding of a just man's task than he had during his early days among the animals. He is 'Sir Artegall, the Salvage Knight', in wild disguise of armour covered over with moss and oak leaves, and carrying on his shield his 'word', Salvagesse sans finesse. He 'tyrannizes' among the knights until they fear him as death itself, and when his spear is broken he draws the sword which we later know to be the sword of justice and which already in Book IV we suspect of having allegorical significance from the terms in which it is described:

> His sword he drew,
> The instrument of wrath, and with the same
> Far'd like a lyon in his bloodie game.
>
> (IV, iv, 41)

The danger of a justice which scarcely distinguishes itself from wrath and punishment is that it may begin to participate in the tyranny it destroys. Artegall can kill like the lions he has tamed,

[5] Spenser uses exactly this episode of the cubs not in Book V but in Book I, where Satyrane, followed by a roaring lioness whose whelps he carries in his arms, alarms his mother as Achilles had alarmed Statius's Thetis. Satyrane is taught by his satyr father, a being of the same order—.half man, half beast—as Chiron the centaur, and the parallel helps to define the rough justice, and the recognition and admiration of truth even when it is not understood, which exist among these natural creatures who help Una. But also the parallel Satyrane-Achilles-Artegall helps to define the kind of justice Artegall first learns. It can be rough, and can be violent, but it arises from basic instincts and is a kind of unrefined rightness to be found among the simple and forthright.

and he fights in earnest. The chivalric battle is suddenly a frightening exercise of unrestrained power, and looking back at it from the fifth book we remember Bacon's description of vengeance as a kind of wild justice. But this same sword, which Artegall has seemed to use only as an instrument of his own furious pleasure in fighting, appears in the first canto of Book Five as, in its own proper nature, truly the instrument of wrath. Astraea had taken it for Artegall from Jove's eternal house, where it had been stored ever since the god himself used it against the Titans or giants, pagan shadows of Lucifer's rebels. It is therefore the sword of avenging justice, punishing that aspiring pride which raises itself against the gods and questions divine order. Mutability, with her cosmic questionings, is of Titan lineage, and another questioner, in the fifth book, is a giant too.

The sword of justice is properly to be drawn in defence of that order which is justice whether cosmic or social, just as Talus's flail, 'With which he thresht out falshood, and did truth unfould', suggests not only Hercules's dread club but the threshing floor of the Lord of hosts, where the chaff flies before the wind. Avenging justice has its limitations and perhaps even its dangers in the hands of men, but it is necessary and it has divine sanction. And it comes into operation against all attempts to usurp a higher place than one's due in the universal order. These twelve stanzas serve to orient us, suggesting some of the issues with which Artegall will be concerned. But so far it is a matter of theory. Artegall has been taught how to use the scales of justice and has been given his weapons, and he has practised upon the wild creatures. Now he is setting out to deal justice among men, and in his first adventure he is faced, as Guyon was, with a situation which sums up the kind of problems he will meet. Among the beasts the tyranny of the strong upon the weak is easy to detect, and there is no more to do but punish and prevent it. In society, where sophistication can complicate the simplest issue, right and wrong are harder to disentangle. Artegall finds that before justice can be done it must be identified.

The real concern of the fifth book is the exploration of justice as it can be perceived, understood, and exercised in the difficult human scene which the Proem describes. Like all Spenser's virtues it is a particular way of comprehending truth, and Artegall's adventures are designed to examine the nature of justice as the truth of the universe. When Astraea was visibly present on earth the identity of truth and justice was clearly seen, but now that identity must be proved and proved again through a series of difficult decisions. The simple tactics of the forest will no longer serve. Thus Artegall's first steps upon his quest bring him to a situation where justice does not immediately manifest itself as truth. Injustice has plainly been done, since a woman has been killed, but where justice lies is harder to discover and still harder to bring home. The squire gives his evidence, that the lady was killed in anger by Sir Sanglier[6] who suddenly tired of her and took away the squire's lady instead, but the knight, brought back by Talus, denies it. Artegall soon perceives 'by signes' in the behaviour of the two that the squire is telling the truth, but to demonstrate this is another matter, and Artegall's task is complicated by the different characters and rank of the two men. Sanglier has every advantage, for as well as being ruthless and shameless he is a knight and a powerful fighter. The squire is truthful but also humble and gentle, and he knows he is no match for the knight in physical combat, so he sees no remedy but to yield himself guilty. Artegall can expect no help from him and so has to 'cast about by sleight the truth thereout to straine'. He has to be devious, and make use of injustice itself so that justice may in the end be done. So he intervenes to prevent the old simple methods of 'sacrament', 'ordele', and 'blooddy fight', each of which he sees must inevitably work out wrongly in a case where unscrupulous force challenges weak honesty. He has recourse to the subtle wisdom of Solomon, and delivers the judgment that, since both men claim the surviving lady and he is unable to resolve the case, she should be divided in equal shares between them. If either dissents, he will thereby proclaim himself the murderer of the dead woman and must carry her severed head for a year and a day in penance and in token of guilt.

Artegall's verdict is based not on the old-fashioned methods of trial by battle[7] or ordeal, or even on the conventional weighing

---

[6] His name suggests both his bloody nature and the boar, symbol of destructive wrath.

[7] The efficacy and the justice of trial by combat would seem to have been a matter of debate in Spenser's time, for one of William Perkins's 'Cases of Conscience' is concerned with it. Perkins denies that 'a Combate

of evidence, but on an instinct for the truth. He relies on his own perception, what he later calls the 'doome of right' within the mind. His move brings the truth demonstrably to light as Solomon's had done, for of course the squire dissents from the verdict, preferring to be branded as a murderer rather than to see the lady killed,

> Did yield, she rather shoud with him remaine
> Alive, then to him selfe be shared dead.
>
> (i, 27)

Justice can be obscured by the goodness of men as by their wickedness, and Artegall has to allow for selflessness and love as well as for deliberate cruelty. In order to save a life, the squire, though innocent, is ready to assume another man's guilt and penance, giving up justice for himself to obtain for the woman a benefit greater than any that justice seems able to bestow. His action enables Artegall, in the end, to deal justly with them all, but Sanglier would have escaped if anyone less than Astraea's pupil had been the judge.

Artegall learns here that self-sacrifice, the surrendering of right in one's own cause through love for another, must enter into the operation of justice in a world where divine Justice itself chose, for the sake of others, to be unjustly condemned. 'True love despiseth shame, when life is cald in dread.' The episode has overtones of the New Testament as well as the old, for though the squire is no paradigm of Christ he does in his humility and love suggest something of what justice must be for men fallen but redeemed through Christ. The suggestion is emphasized in the sudden reference, in the squire's first speech over the murdered woman, to the agony in the garden and Christ's acceptance of sacrificial death:

> That I mote drinke the cup whereof she dranke.[8]
>
> (i, 15)

---

[8] Compare, for example, Mark x, 38; xiv, 36.

---

is a triall of innocencie' on the same realistic grounds as those which influence the squire and (presumably) Artegall: 'For he that is stronger usually overcomes in the combate, not he that hath the more righteous cause.' [*Works* (Cambridge, 1609), p. 139.] Shakespeare dramatizes the debate in *Henry VI*, Part II.

The words shock in their unexpectedness and apparent irrelevance, but their startling quality only gives them added force as they fall into place in the unfolding story.

Later, in Canto vi, the Passion is brought to mind again when Britomart, riding to rescue Artegall, is treacherously attacked by Dolon who thinks her ('by many tokens plaine' including the presence of Talus) to be Artegall himself. She is saved 'by Gods grace, and her good heedinesse', refusing to disarm and watching through the night. When her eyelids droop she rebukes herself into wakefulness with a speech in which the sorrowing tenderness of a lonely lover modulates touchingly into the profounder sorrow and tenderness of the lover of all mankind, addressing the sleepy disciples in Gethsemane.

> 'Ye guilty eyes', sayd she, 'the which with guyle
> My heart at first betrayd, will ye betray
> My life now to, for which a little whyle
> Ye will not watch? False watches, well-away!
> I wote when ye did watch both night and day
> Unto your losse: and now needes will ye sleepe?
> Now ye have made my heart to wake alway,
> Now will ye sleepe? ah! wake, and rather weepe,
> To thinke of your nights want, that should yee
> waking keepe.'
>
> (vi, 25)

'Thus did she watch', and the hushed verse evokes a hushed and waiting night. Then comes cockcrow, which marked Peter's betrayal of his master and which here too heralds treachery. The cock's 'silver bell' is a double symbol: it should rouse good men to their prayers at dawn, but it rouses Dolon to his treacherous attempt on Britomart's life, prevented by her careful watch.

> What time the native belman of the night,
> The bird that warned Peter of his fall,
> First rings his silver bell t'each sleepy wight,
> That should their mindes up to devotion call.
>
> (vi, 27)

Again we are reminded, by this second traditional symbol of Christ's passion, that perfect justice is also love, perpetually betrayed by the wickedness or weakness of man. Spenser has a vivid sense of the paradox that men had brought about the saving death of Justice, and

At length him nayled on a gallows tree,
And slew the just by most unjust decree.
(An Hymne of Heavenly Love, ll. 153–4)

As Robert Ellrodt has noticed, the line from the *Hymne* echoes
the Acts of the Apostles; Stephen accuses his accusers with the cry

Which of the prophets have not your fathers persecuted? and they
have slain them which shewed before of the coming of the Just
One,[9] of whom ye have been now the betrayers and murderers,
(Acts vii, 52)

and Peter preaches the same word:

But ye denied the Holy One and the Just, and desired a murderer
to be granted unto you.

(Acts iii, 14)

No man of Spenser's time could contemplate justice without
remembering 'the Holy One and the Just'; Shakespeare could
not in *Measure for Measure* and *The Merchant of Venice*. The
pagan Astraea only abandoned the world, but in Christ the world
was saved even as it condemned him. Justice cannot be now
quite what it was for the good pagans or even for Solomon, for
the avenging wrath of the Old Testament has given place to the
merciful love of the New, which yet is also justice. To this, human
judgment must do its faulty best to approximate. Justice as
defined by the great authorities of the pagan past, Cicero or
Seneca, is enriched by the revelation which Christian men have
had of its full nature, and so Spenser, in describing the actions
of Britomart and the just judgment of Artegall, refers obliquely
to the passion of Christ, the crucial event through which justice
opened out into another dimension.

The task of those who deal justice in a Christian state is the
more difficult and responsible because they are 'instead of God'[10]

[9] The parallel is more exact in sixteenth-century Bibles, where the
phrase runs 'which shewed before of that Just, of whome . . .'.

[10] Henry Smith, writing (in *The Magistrates' Scripture* of 1590) of the
duty of magistrates and all who deal justice, reminds them that they should,
in all their judgments, 'consider what God would do, because they are
instead of God . . . As we should think how Christ prayed before we pray,
and how he spake before we speak . . . so they should think how Christ
would judge before they judge, because God's law is appointed for their
law.' [*Works* (London, 1866), Vol. I, p. 360.]

but are not God; and this is why Christians especially, in the execution of their laws, must make room always

> for mercie and mitigation, as for Justice and extremitie. This must he doe, because his lawes cannot be as Gods lawes are. Gods lawes are *perfect*, and *absolute*, and of such an universall righteousness, as that at all times, and in all places, they are of equall strength, and of the same equitie in all cases: and therefore are to be executed without dispensation, relaxation, or any mitigation, which cannot be offered unto them, but with injurie and violation. But mens lawes, comming from their own wits, are *imperfect*, and so in all cases, they doe not hold the same equitie, and therefore must needes be executed with a discreet and wise moderation.[11]

Justice must be Christian justice, and equity 'Christian Equitie and Moderation'.

> Men therefore, must consider that they are Christians, and live in a Christian commonwealth: And they must not stand only upon the law, and the advantage that the law gives. As they are men, they have a lawe of the countrie, which may allow extremitie: but as they are Christians, they live under a lawe of God, the eternall lawe, which must judge them at the last day: the righteous law, which no creature shall ever be able to blame of injustice, or of extremitie: and men must know, that God himselfe commands this equitie of one man to another.[12]

The theorists of the sixteenth and seventeenth centuries discussed extensively the laws of the state and their administration, adopting the ancient terms—aequitas, clementia, misericordia.[13] Some kept close to the classical meanings of these words and to the conceptions that lay behind them. But even such a resolutely practical, politic, and secular writer as Sir Thomas Elyot, who follows Seneca closely, recommends mercy not only on the grounds that a lack of it causes other virtues to 'lose their just commendation' but on the analogy of the mercy of God whose representatives princes are.

[11] William Perkins, *A Treatise of Christian Equitie and Moderation*, p. 505. [*Works* (Cambridge, 1609).]
[12] Ibid., p. 506.
[13] See M. H. Parker, *The Slave of Life, A Study of Shakespeare and the Idea of Justice* (London, 1955); E. Kantorowicz, *The King's Two Bodies* (Princeton, 1958).

Let governours, whiche knowe that they have resceyved theyr powar from above, resolve in their myndes in what peryll they them selfes be in dayly if in god were nat habundaunce of mercy, but that as sone as they offende him grevously, he shulde immediatly strike them with his moste terrible darte of vengeaunce. All be it uneth any houre passeth that men deserve nat some punysshement. [14]

While William Perkins makes a more forthright appeal to the Christian imperative:

God sheweth most admirable Equitie and moderation towards us, therefore ought we to shew it, one towards another: It is the reason of the holy Ghost, *Be yee mercifull, as your heavenly father is mercifull.* [15]

Perkins provides a useful and inclusive commentary on the the workings of justice as they appeared to the Elizabethan and Jacobean mind. Like Elyot, he is aware of the necessity for precise distinctions, and his definitions are firm enough. But unlike Elyot, he is interested in defining what it is right for a Christian to do rather than what it is expedient and efficient for a governor to do (even the titles of Elyot's *Governour*, Smith's *Magistrates Scripture*, and Perkins's *Treatise of Christian Equitie and Moderation*, tell their own tale), and he is always mindful of the revelation of justice at the atonement. Justice is not separable, for him, from mercy, and his tone is closer to Spenser's or Shakespeare's than to Elyot's. Thus, though he defines equity clearly as 'a moderation and mitigation of the extremitie of a law, upon honest and convenient reasons, and in such cases, as were not directly intended in the law', he cannot really think of it apart from 'a Christian consideration'. The extremity of the law is the justice of the law only when there is no mitigation,

But when there is good cause, why in a Christian consideration of some circumstances, this justice should be mitigated, and yet is not, but contrariwise is extremely urged, and pressed to the furthest, *then it is extremitie*: Now this extremitie of the law . . . is extreme injurie. And of this doth the holy Ghost meane, Eccles. vii, 7 *be not over just.*

---

[14] *The Boke named The Governour* (London, 1907), II, vii.
[15] Op. cit., p. 515.

Again, though he goes on to discuss the two sorts of men who err in equity, those who, carried away by a certain foolish kind of pity and effeminateness of mind, 'would have nothing but *mercy, mercy,*' and those who cry always '*the lawe, the lawe*: and *Justice, Justice*', it is the second sort that he concentrates on, as enemies to all good government. They forget that Justice always shakes hands with her sister Mercy,

> that Justice will not stay where mercie is not. They are sisters, and goe alwaies hand in hand ... as you cannot hold mercy, where Justice is banished, so cannot you keepe Justice where mercie is exiled: and as mercie without Justice, is foolish pitie, so Justice without mercie, is crueltie.

The remembrance of God's mercy lies behind every aspect of justice in a Christian community, and it is this which is Perkins's deepest concern. 'The more mercifull the better Christian. For he hath tasted deeper of Gods mercies to himselfe, and therefore he is mercifull to his brother.'[16]

Spenser's narrative of Justice must be so framed as to take into account this kind of thinking: the relation of absolute justice to faulty human laws, exercised by erring humans upon their erring brothers; the relation of just wrath to loving mercy; the place of clemency and of equity, the 'softer spirit of the law'. The centre from which these relationships is explored is, as so often, itself a relationship, that of Artegall to Britomart. Nothing in *The Faerie Queene* is more remarkable than Spenser's richly economical organization of his material, and here the two central figures bring with them, to the elucidation of what justice is, all the significance they have already established between them of the softening of hostility in friendship, the tempering of anger by loving control, the growth of maturity and responsibility. Artegall in Book IV is the Salvage Knight and his justice is of the wild avenging kind; only after his destined meeting with Britomart does he properly begin his quest, and even then he is still ready to draw his just sword against a carle like Braggadocchio, although equity forbids it. His entire fulfilment is foreshadowed rather than achieved, in Britomart's prophetic dream of herself as scarcely distinguished from Isis with the crocodile Osiris/Artegall beneath her feet

[16] The passages from *A Treatise of Christian Equitie* quoted in this paragraph are to be found on pp. 502, 504, 514.

166

To shew that clemence oft, in things amis,
Restraines those sterne behests. and cruell doomes of his.

(vii, 22)

It has been foreshadowed also, though more dimly, in Merlin's
prophecy of Britomart's and Artegall's joint future as rulers. The
whole atmosphere of purpose and destiny which surrounds
Britomart makes her a particularly suitable character through
whom to examine Christian justice. In a sense not only she, but
the whole tissue of events she has contributed to in the third and
fourth books, moves inevitably towards the themes of Book Five.
The legends of Chastity and Friendship take place in a blind
world, where people beat impotently against what seems to be the
unfair nature of things as Scudamour does—'Or doth thy justice
sleepe, and silently?'—and as Arthur and even the poet-com-
mentator come near to doing. Justice is often questioned in this
part of the poem, but it is never questioned by Britomart, realistic
though she is about the woes of the world. 'Submit you to High
Providence', she tells Scudamour,

> And ever in your noble hart prepense,
> That all the sorrow in the world is lesse
> Then vertues might and values confidence.

(III, xi, 14)

Artegall's words in Book V to Sir Terpin, who attributes his
shame to fate, have a similar bearing though being Artegall he
expresses himself more brutally:

> Right true: but faulty men use oftentimes
> To attribute their folly unto fate,
> And lay on heaven the guilt of their owne crimes.

(V, iv, 28)

Or there is the opening of Canto xi, where in the recurrent dialogue between the now anxious, now confident poet and his
developing narrative we reach a tentative answer to the earlier
lament for the wronged and lost heroines:

> If oten fals in course of common life,
> That right long time is overborne of wrong,
> Through avarice, or powre, or guile, or strife,
> That weakens her, and makes her party strong:
> But Justice, though her dome she doe prolong,
> Yet at the last she will her owne cause right.

This is true for Belge, but true also for Florimell, whose story is triumphantly concluded in Book V. In fact by the end of the fourth book the narrative has reached a point where we, like the characters and the poet, wonder about the justice of the things that happen, and about the nature of just behaviour. Britomart and Artegall move naturally forward from a book of questionings to a book of at least possible answers. Each has something still to discover about the other and hence about the justice which Artegall champions. The new vulnerability which defeat at her 'womans hand' has produced is as great a potential threat to justice as the wrath which it has replaced, and he leaves her only to fall to her alter ego the Amazon, who with her cruel and unscrupulous feminine wiles[17] presents the darker aspect of the woman warrior. If he had not been subdued by Britomart, Artegall would not have become subject to Radigund, but this is part of the risk involved in enlarging one's perceptions. The new capacity for gentleness can be misunderstood and so misused by Artegall himself, and exploited by others. The just man must avoid both the extremity of severity and the extremity of softness, for 'As mercie without Justice is foolish pitie, so Justice without mercie, is crueltie'. Britomart's influence upon Artegall can figure the tempering of justice by mercy which is essential if human society is to reflect, however dimly, the purposes of God. But like the influence of Venus upon Mars it has its ambiguities and dangers.

The lamentable adventure with Radigund dramatizes these dangers and differentiates, at one and the same time, between foolish pity and mercy and between effeminate submissiveness and the reverence of romantic love. The meeting with Britomart looks forward to justice and the meeting with Radigund looks backward to love. One virtue opens out into another and to understand more of one is to understand more of them all. Thus justice is defined not in legal dicta but in the relation of two people whose humanity is already established. The definition owes a great deal to Britomart, for she contributes not only to a clarification of terms but to a fuller comprehension of what justice has to be and do in the midst of suffering and sin. Artegall's companion

[17] Amazons are frequently moralized as harlots; Britomart's indignant grief at Artegall's entanglement suggests that a shadow of this meaning is present.

might have been the severe and starry Astraea, the immortal Virgo of the Zodiac, if Spenser had conceived of the virtue, and so of the narrative, differently. Instead she is a woman, steadfast and protective and close to human trouble, and with as much of Venus in her as of Diana or Minerva. In this book Britomart is closely associated with Isis, who is the mother goddess in one of her aspects and is also by tradition truth, and (with Osiris) justice. When Artegall ceases to exercise justice she does so in his place and is mistaken for him; and it is she, the true clemency, who has to release him from her false image in Radigund. She can do these things because she can in herself suggest both the masculine uprightness and the feminine gentleness of justice, for her nature as woman knight readily embraces this meaning too. But justice is only fully expressed in both of them together. All the potentialities in the operation of justice must be present, and neither of the two alone can show the extreme of severity or of weakness to which justice, if not rightly tempered, can go.

For Artegall's part in the narrative Spenser makes use of the type figure of Hercules, hero of avenging justice, to whom he is compared in the first canto. Hercules with his 'club of Justice dread' is listed among the heroes,

> And such was he of whom I have to tell,
> The champion of true Justice, Artegall.
>
> (i, 3)

Like so many of those personages of classical myth who had for centuries accumulated meanings and associations around them, Hercules had become a very flexible figure; and in both the fifth and the second books Spenser exploits this richness of suggestion to considerable effect. It is of course precisely the huge force and passion of Hercules, as warrior and as lover, which made him such a convincing example of moderation and just action when the moralists—Sophist, Stoic, or medieval—wished to interpret him so; on the other hand

in spite of allegorical interpretation the stories of Hercules continue to suggest terrifying excesses as well as superb self-mastery. Even Seneca's Hercules Oetaeus achieves control of himself only at the end. In the Renaissance, whenever the myth is treated in any detail, the significance of its hero extends beyond such labels as

169

Ripa gives him, and one sometimes has the impression that a somewhat subversive meaning asserts itself under cover of the respectable official interpretation. [18]

Artegall has already shown a Herculean anger, now he is to show Herculean uxoriousness. The affair of Omphale (here, as often, called Iole) falls very pat to Spenser's theme, and it would seem, from the usual abundant evidence of emblem and medal, to have fascinated Renaissance connoisseurs of psychological and philosophical subtleties expressed in pictorial and verbal images. Hercules, spinning in a long oriental robe while Omphale holds his weapons, is another figure for the shifting relations of love and war, submission and aggression; and the 'womanish weake fight' into which Artegall follows the shamed Sir Terpin continues one of the most productive motifs of the poem.

Radigund is one of Spenser's great Venus armata or Diana figures, handled with that sensitivity to small differences of association which makes his variations on a stated theme so delicate. Her associations are both with Belphoebe and with Britomart, yet she is worlds apart from either, as the perverse exaggeration of a psychological function is close to yet very different from the same function in its healthy state. As an Amazon she is associated with the moon-goddess as the other armed women are, but her moon-shield and her darkened beauty become sinister from their setting. With her moon-shield she has the tucked up camis and the buskins of the huntress, but instead of Belphoebe's fresh radiance there is a sombre Asiatic richness and weight. The camis is purple, not white, there is an Eastern scimitar on an embroidered belt about her thigh, and the shield itself is heavy with clustered consonants as with jewels:

> And on her shoulder hung her shield, bedeckt
> Uppon the bosse with stones.
>
> (v, 3)

She marches 'with stately port and proud magnificence' to the sound of shawms and trumpets; an exotic power whose beauty shines sullenly, like the moon in winter fog. But it is this beauty which makes Artegall throw away his sword as he had done at the sight of the angel's face and gold hair of Britomart, when he has the Amazon at his mercy: and Radigund, unlike Britomart, is

[18] Eugene M. Waith, op. cit., p. 40.

ready to exploit her advantage. So justice sinks into foolish pity—
Artegall flings away his sword because his heart is pierced 'with
pitifull regard'—and only Britomart has the power to correct a
perversion of her own clemency.

For there is no doubt of Artegall's blame in this encounter.
He is as well aware of his own shame as he had earlier been of
Terpin's, and the poet's defence of him is perfectly managed,
persuading us to contemplate his weakness. He has fallen, as
Talus says, by 'his owne doome', and his failure in justice is a
failure of the whole man. His relation to Britomart and to her
shadow Radigund implies that justice in its public sense depends
upon a harmony of qualities in the mind, and that this harmony
is seen in private behaviour and personal loyalties no less than in
the framing of laws and the prevention of wrong. The narrative
is handled so as quietly to emphasize a close connection between
the two women, already suggested by the parallel surrenders of
Artegall. The Amazon is a danger to Britomart also, and is able
to wound her to the bone, which no one else has done. Rather,
perhaps, she is a danger to the justice which exists potentially
between them as 'this same vertue that doth right define'.
Potentially only, for like Artegall Britomart is not perfectly
adjusted at first to the relationship. When Artegall leaves on his
quest she is inclined to sway him with those traditionally feminine
techniques which commentators have found so touchingly realistic. But when she has killed Radigund she behaves with impeccable fairness. She neither upbraids nor cajoles Artegall, and is
anxious for his sense of dignity, she is careful to leave men in
charge of the Amazon kingdom, thereby impressing everybody
with her justice and wisdom, and when Artegall sets out once
more she

> wisely moderated her owne smart,
> Seeing his honor, which she tendred chiefe,
> Consisted much in that adventures priefe.
> The care whereof, and hope of his successe,
> Gave unto her great comfort and reliefe,
> That womanish complaints she did represse,
> And tempred for the time her present heavinesse.
>
> (vii, 44)

At this point in their story another of Spenser's beautifully
gauged comments gathers up the implications of the triangle of

characters. Nothing, he says, has such power as beauty to make
mighty hands forget their manliness,

> Drawne with the powre of an heart-robbing eye,
> And wrapt in fetters of a golden tresse,
> That can with melting pleasaunce mollifye
> Their hardned hearts, enur'd to bloud and cruelty.
>
> (viii, 1)

Samson and Antony and Hercules were fettered, but Artegall
is not to be held, and he goes his way despite Britomart and her
golden hair and the claims that the piercingly languorous lines
make so appealing. All very well; but we have already seen him
fettered so, spinning for Radigund and looking for all the world
like Hercules when he changed his lion's skin for a golden robe

> In which, forgetting warres, he onely joyed
> In combats of sweet love, and with his mistress toyed.
>
> (v, 24)

The effect is to merge the two women, the two temptations, into
one; it is as though Radigund's fetters were Britomart's, and now
that she is gone the golden tresses will not bind him again.

Justice is therefore developed through Britomart as well as
through Artegall; though her appearances are brief, they are indis-
pensable. Acting for Artegall in Dolon's house and in the Amazon
city she realizes for us the particular dangers and responsibilities
—including the control of Talus—which this involves, and
practical experience of what Artegall's task really consists in is
reinforced by what she is shown in the symbolic shrine of justice
itself, the church of Isis, goddess of the revelatory mysteries.
What appears there is ambiguous enough and hard to define.
But if it has the oracular quality of a dream it has also a dream's
atmosphere of genuine and urgent revelation. The fidelity with
which the feel of the Jungian 'great' dream is captured deserves
all the admiration it has been paid; like Coleridge Spenser is a
poet not only of waking dream or reverie but of the true dream
with its vividness and solidity and its power to convince us of
profound though non-logical meaning. Britomart's vision seems
itself part of a larger dream, for Isis Church is as strange as
Xanadu and in both cases the air of significance and intense purposeful activity depends upon a process of synthesis. Isis Church

is built of the learning of Diodorus Siculus, Plutarch, and the Italian mythographers, the exalted knowledge of Lucius's visions, and doubtless much more; for the ancients and the Renaissance alike there was endless fascination in the explicating of pagan cult and ritual. It is only too easy to share the fascination, and to speculate on the possible fusion in Spenser's mind of Plutarch's bisexual Isis, the double nature of Britomart, the relation of them both to the moon (for Britomartis became Diana Dictynna, and Isis 'doth the moone portend,/Like as Osiris signifies the sunne'[19]), and Ficino's linking of justice with the moon and with the two-sexed primal beings. But such possibilities are almost infinite, so complex are the proliferations of the major symbolic themes which the Renaissance inherited from the classical past. The exact sources which set Spenser's imagination working here are probably unidentifiable. What seems certain is that the formative influence in the temple of Isis is Plutarch's, and that the influence is one as much of feeling as of fact.

De Iside et Osiride is still a compelling work because of the sweep of mind which enables Plutarch to relate different religious traditions together so that, far from destroying each other, they appear as partial and interlocking truths, thrown up by the mind of man as he tries to advance towards total comprehension. Plutarch's intelligence is of a kind which justifies, rather than destroys, the mysterious. His syncretism, which appealed so strongly to the same tendency in many a Renaissance thinker, would appeal to Spenser as much as to any; and the fact, noticed by many scholars, that Spenser makes his own blend of the rites

---

[19] Ancient explications (perhaps bearing the mysteries in mind) give Osiris and especially Isis such scope that their physical meaning readily merges into mystical, moral, and philosophical ones. As sun and moon they govern the whole world, according to Diodorus, and Milton retains the memory of this huge inclusive myth of the union of male and female as that which sustains the universe; Raphael tells Adam of suns and moons

Communicating Male and Female Light,
Which two great Sexes animate the world.
(*Paradise Lost*, VIII, 150–1).

Of Isis, who is Diana and Venus and all the great goddesses, Bernard de Montfaucon (*Antiquity Explained*) says that she 'was everything, according to the Notions of some, and comprehended and nourished everything, according to others'. The Isis of the ancients is a figure worthy of the atmosphere of sacred awe which surrounds her in her Church.

and beliefs discussed in *De Iside* and uses some of them in connection not with Isis but with Venus, or with Nature, shows how fully he had absorbed his author's attitudes. All divinities exist in Isis, who united with Osiris is truth under the aspect of justice, and thus the long-haired long-robed moon priests belong as much to Cybele and to Diana as to her; and in their blend of masculine and feminine characteristics, recalling Plutarch's Isis, they underline the mystery which is more sharply figured in the goddess's idol.

As an evocation of justice the temple is one of Spenser's most haunting creations, its details building up a still, sacred atmosphere in which ascetic severity co-exists with a tender and sensuous richness. The central image is that of Isis, crowned with the golden crown of divine power and standing with one foot on the coiled crocodile. We are given two explanations of the symbolism; in one the statue is said to signify that Isis will suppress both guile and open force, and in the other Isis is 'That part of justice which is equity', and

> that same crocodile Osyris is,
> That under Isis feete doth sleepe for ever;
> To shew that clemence oft, in things amis,
> Restraines those sterne behests, and cruell doomes of his.

(vii, 22)

Symbolic statues, like allegorical poems, have more meanings than one; gods, like poets, reveal a polysemous truth. The alternative explications, so easily offered, and the dreamlike strangeness of the temple, convey the mysteriousness of the workings of justice. In Britomart's dream the crocodile is Artegall, while she, first serving Isis as priest, seems to merge with the goddess herself in her crown of gold. The crocodile Osiris/Artegall wakes in fire and tempest, and having devoured these it turns upon Britomart too, but is beaten back by the goddess and sues for favour, 'turning all his pride to humbleness meeke' as Artegall has already done. The Chief priest explains that Artegall will subdue the opposition to Britomart's just inheritance of her kingdom and that they will rule jointly to be succeeded by their lion-like son. The little allegory not only foretells their future, it sums up their present and their recent past.

The manifestation in the temple does not explain justice; it evokes a feeling about it, a sense at once of awe and of warm security. The crocodile is frightening, all the more so since it usually carries meanings of cruelty and treachery, present here in its violent action in Britomart's dream and in the explanation of it as an emblem of guile; in Plutarch it is associated with the destructive Typhon. To have to accept it as Osiris causes a small upheaval in our imaginative response, nor can we quite ignore its aura of destruction when we find that it represents Artegall also. Doubtless we are not intended to ignore it; it is an element present in Artegall and present also in justice. The crocodile is closely involved with Isis, wreathing her body as Venus's snake does in the fourth book but under her absolute control. It is fitting that Isis and her temple should remind us of Venus and hers, for Isis is also Venus, and the discordia concors of justice is also the discordia concors of love. Isis, with Osiris, was regarded as one of the great embodiments of ancient wisdom, a goddess of scope and power as inclusive as that of Dame Nature, and if the point is to be properly made it is she who must be shown as dominant, like Venus over Mars. True justice is a tempering of cruel dooms as love is the establishing of concord over discord, and this is best expressed by feminine dominance.

Thus, though one may think of justice as a stern and masculine virtue, in the temple the force of Osiris, the Herculean hero of Plutarch and Diodorus Siculus, is overshadowed by the gentler power of the goddess. That Britomart should worship Isis and serve her, in vision, as priest, should be favoured by her and assimilated to her, is a wholly convincing and satisfying consummation, for Britomart reconciles within herself the partial truths of other characters just as Isis reconciles all divinities and can be invoked as Minerva, Venus, Diana Dictynna, the Mother. The temple is one of those places, like the Garden of Adonis, where meanings are centred, and like the Garden it is predominantly a feminine place, here perhaps especially a maternal place. The goddess, using her wand encouragingly or restrainingly as circumstances demand, but always benevolently, is like a very august nurse who corrects us for our good. The same benevolent authority is suggested by the demeanour of the priests, by such phrases as 'on their mother Earths deare lap', by Britomart's humility and reverence as she prays, and perhaps most of all by the description of how she rests 'Under the wings of Isis' and

175

in that protection is given her strengthening vision of the future. The essential thing that Britomart learns here is her true function, as an avatar of Isis, in relation to the stern and wrathful Osiris/Artegall; but the whole episode has the unexpectedness, the inevitablity, and the promise of endless significant connections, proper to an experience of this dreamlike and revelatory kind.

Mercilla's palace is a lesser companion piece to Isis Church, but the atmosphere here is very different as dream gives way to a formally idealized reality. In the temple justice is imaged in its own essential nature, deeply mysterious and to be known only through vision, while at the palace we watch the just dealings of ideal monarchy in affairs of state. The setting is more public and particular, emphasizing royal panoply, for while Isis is sacred as the mysterious revelation of justice Mercilla is sacred only in virtue of her office, holding from God the sceptre, 'sacred pledge of peace and clemencie'. The cloth of state above the throne is a reminder of her function as God's vicegerent, and hangs like a cloud or a great brooding bird with the sun glinting at its edges. It is upheld by angels, and more of these divine messengers stand about the throne as in heaven they stand and sing their hymns before High God. The descriptions, and Mercilla's behaviour, constantly emphasize the benevolence and long suffering of justice, its tendency to temper or at least to delay its execution in the hope of reform, to correct or persuade rather than to punish. The sword of retribution, which she can wield strongly at need, rusts by her throne, and the lion, growling, is chained beneath her feet as a reminder of Isis's crocodile.[20] Her attendants are the Litae who 'treat for pardon and remission/To suppliants' and who wait night and day upon Jove's judgment seat to stay his vengeance upon the wicked world.

[20] The lion doubtless signifies power, particularly the power which the Queen of England could exert. But it is interesting, in view of the richness of suggestion in such ancient symbols, to remember other meanings of a beast subdued by a virgin. For example an article in the Journal of the Warburg Institute, Vol. II, p. 219, describes a cameo of the Virgin with a lion under her feet, symbolizing the superseding of the Old Covenant by the New, Justice by Mercy. That Elizabeth in a sense replaced the Virgin as an object of devotion in Protestant England is well known. Una and her lion perhaps relate to the same kind of imagery, and Una, like Mercilla, has her connections with Elizabeth.

Mercilla as sovereign is the source of justice for her people, and in her hands lies not only the guardianship of the laws but, most important of all, the prerogative of mercy; this is the reason for her name. Her rare mercies and clemencies are exemplified in her attitude at the trial and are distinguished sharply from the vain pity (which does not temper justice but negates it) to which Prince Arthur almost gives way when he hears Griefe plead weeping for Duessa. Mercy never subverts justice, but

> seekes to save the subject of her skill,
> Yet never does from doome of right depart.
>
> (x, 2)

The poet sets aside the abstract discussions of the clerks

> Whether this heavenly thing whereof I treat,
> To weeten Mercie, be of Justice part,
> Or drawne forth from her by divine extreate,

nor does he trouble to distinguish the merciful action from the clement one. What is he sure of is that mercy is as high a thing as justice,

> Sith in th'Almighties everlasting seat
> She first was bred, and borne of heavenly race;
> From thence pour'd down on men, by influence of grace.
>
> (x, 1)

Tourneur's Castabella makes a similar connection of ideas:

> O Father! Mercie is an attribute
> As high as Iustice; an essential part
> Of his unbounded goodnesse, whose divine
> Impression, forme, and image man should beare.
> And (me thinks) Man should love to imitate
> His Mercie; since the onely countenance
> Of Iustice, were destruction; if the sweet
> And loving favour of his mercie did
> Not mediate between it and our weakenesse. [21]

Mercy comes to us as a gift from God; through grace we receive infinite mercy and through grace we in our turn can exercise it. It is never far from Spenser's mind, as he contemplates justice

---

[21] *The Atheists Tragedie*, III, iv. It is scarcely necessary to quote the parallels in Shakespeare himself.

in this world, that all the souls that were were forfeit once, and in Book VI he takes further his thinking about mercy and grace. The trial of Duessa is formalized and idealized, but it does not falsify the difficulties inherent in the actual trial of Mary which it interprets. Justice is done, but the doing is hard; the advocates who plead for and against Duessa—Griefe and Pittie, Regard of Womanhead, the Law of Nations and the Peoples Cry—and Arthur's shifting emotions as he listens, dramatize the conflicting issues. The impression which the whole book leaves, that it is difficult for men to identify justice and administer it among themselves, is not denied at Mercilla's court. And Spenser deals just as honestly with the related human difficulty, that of recognizir.g justice in the doings of the universe, beyond man's power to control. There too justice is present, however hard to perceive; slow like the grinding of the mills of God but just as sure, and operating of itself as a universal principle which somehow, and in the long run, works through events and sets all right at last. 'Justice, though her dome she doe prolong,/Yet at the last she will her owne cause right.' Several episodes are shaped to show this principle co-operating with the righteous efforts of men, as in Arthur's overthrow of the Souldan, or working alone and requiring only that men should rightly interpret the judgments brought about through the impersonal motions of the elements and the apparently chance circumstances of every day.

These episodes may illustrate distributive or corrective justice, they may have topical reference to the Armada, the Anabaptists, or the tollbridge monopolies, but chiefly they are manifestations of a changeless inexorable power which rules events as it will. Arthur, it would seem, enters the narrative to strengthen this impression as well as to represent the destiny of Britain and perhaps also for mere variety. It is he who in the later part of the book acts as the new Hercules, here unambiguously the invincible avenger of wrong. Whereas Artegall has to strive to be just in himself and to govern justly, and is hampered in his championship of Irena by his own failings and those of other men on whose co-operation he must partly depend, Arthur's very enemies co-operate with him to their own destruction. In the adventure of the Souldan Artegall takes a minor part, while Arthur re-enacts Hercules's vengeance on the Thracian tyrant Diomedes. He succeeds not because of his personal strength—for the Souldan is out of reach in his high swift chariot and can wound without being touched—but because he unveils his bright shield directly in front of the flesh-eating horses so that in terror they overturn the chariot, tearing the Souldan to pieces on the iron hooks of the wheels.

Arthur's shield has always some connotation of the divine truth, the blinding certainty of a revelation not to be withstood, and it burns before the horses' eyes like the lightning flash, the vengeance of Jove. Thus the horses which were to have been the instruments of Arthur's death are turned upon their owner, as in Hercules's similar punishment of the King of Thrace,

> Like to the Thracian tyrant, who, they say,
> Unto his horses gave his guests for meat,
> Till he himselfe was made their greedie pray,
> And torne in pieces by Alcides great.
>
> (viii, 31)

The Souldan's fate is compared also with that of Phaeton and Hippolytus, both killed by the flight of their own horses in legends which illustrate the inevitability of divine retribution. It is Arthur's cause and its truth rather than Arthur himself that destroys the Souldan:

> But the brave Prince for honour and for right,
> Gainst tortious powre and lawless regiment,
> In the behalfe of wronged weake did fight:
> More in his causes truth he trusted then in might.
>
> (viii, 30)

Truth shines out from his shield, justice inevitably follows, and

> by Heavens high decree,
> Justice that day of wrong her selfe had wroken.
>
> (viii, 44)

The adamantine shield is, again, all that saves Arthur from Geryoneo, son of Hercules's Geryon, and its brightness so dismays the Sphinx of the Inquisition that she turns to fly; compelled to fight, she tries to drag the unbearable shield from Arthur's hand and he has to cut off her claw in order to free it. The Sphinx is an emblem of ignorance, and truth is as destructive to her as to the Souldan, or to Arthur's other great enemy Orgoglio who faced by the shield had 'no poure to hurt, nor to

179

defend'. The knowledge of God shines in Arthur's unveiled shield as blindingly as it did to Saul on the Damascus road. There is no standing against it.

Justice in these adventures of Arthur is inseparable from the Bible truth of Protestantism; justice is done in the power of the Lord. In Artegall's encounters justice is still done, and divinely done, but intervention is less direct. In coming to his decisions he co-operates with or interprets the divine will as it is perceived through the ordinary daily workings of the natural world rather than in that sudden blazing out of truth which compels even the brutes to obey. With Artegall there is a kind of cosmic justice at work, visible in the fate of Pollente, whose corpse is swept away by the same river which he has made use of to extort toll and in which he has planned to drown the knight. Lady Munera too is flung over the castle wall, where her guilty blood is washed away by the stream, and with her her illgotten wealth, first burned to ashes as the golden calf, the sin of Israel, had been burned and ground to dust and cast into the brook that descended out of the mount. The just order implicit in the natural world quietly absorbs those who disturb it, and they become as though they had not been. The giant with the scales harangues from a rock by the sea and is flung down and drowned by Talus, fittingly enough since it is in terms of sea and rock, of elemental injustice, that he has tried to prove the unfairness of the world.

Artegall's exposure of the malcontent giant's efforts brings together in the form of a practical test questions that have half emerged often from the material of the poem. The whole concept of personal and political justice depended upon the existence of cosmic justice with its proof of order at the heart of things, as much as on the shining out of revealed truth. The two 'books', the Bible and nature, support each other in the demonstration of justice if they are rightly read, but in neither case is the reading so very easy or the meaning very plain, and one can make mistakes. Throughout the fifth book Spenser has counterpointed possible readings: has the universe gone astray over the ages, is the world growing more disorderly and human nature worse, is the whole thing running down? Or is this only a misreading, caused by our inability to follow more than a few sentences of nature's book at a time, to see more than a corner of the pattern? Set against each other the poet's own pessimistic Proem, the giant's thesis, and Artegall's refutation read rather like a skeleton version of the celebrated discussion between Goodman and Hakewill in the following century, and the same counterpointing is hinted at here and there in earlier books, to be resolved, or rather transcended, in the sixth book and the fragmentary seventh. It is a theme vital to Spenser's whole 'imitation', and it develops naturally through the poet's and his characters' commentary upon the action.

The function of the egalitarian giant is to set in proportion those doubts and objections about the ultimate justice of things which have arisen throughout the poem, by reducing them to absurdity. He has the clumsy stupidity proper to his kind, and proclaims his gigantic simplemindedness in his first nonsense statement

> That all the world he would weigh equallie,
> If ought he had the same to counterpoys.
>
> (ii, 30)

He is no anarchist; he wants not less order but more, and is indignant because the elements have so shockingly encroached upon each other, the sea wearing down the earth and the fire the air, some getting more than their fair share as a result. This is reflected in the affairs of men, 'And so were realmes and nations run awry', and the giant proposes to suppress tyrants and to redistribute wealth more equally, but his main concern is with cosmic justice, on which all the rest depends. There was (and had been for centuries before Hakewill and Goodman and Burnet) much speculation about the world as it was first created,[22] and the giant appears to adopt the view that it was originally a perfect sphere with no protuberances, the shape most suited to the perfect conceptions of God. But he is not content to leave the matter as one of interesting theory. To him it is not speculative but certain, and he proposes to act upon it.

> Therefore I will throw downe these mountaines hie,
> And make them levell with the lowly plaine:
> These towring rocks, which reach unto the skie,

[22] The history of this speculation has been much discussed from various points of view in recent years; e.g. the full account in Marjorie Hope Nicolson's *Mountain Gloom and Mountain Glory* (Ithaca, New York, 1959).

I will thrust downe into the deepest maine,
And as they were, them equalize againe.

(ii, 38)

Artegall's argument opens with the sensible observation that an attempt to restore primitive order depends on knowing exactly what that order was, which is impossible.

For ere thou limit what is lesse or more
In every thing, thou oughtest first to know,
What was the poyse of every part of yore:
And looke then, how much it doth overflow,
Or faile thereof, so much is more than just to trow.

(ii, 34)

But of course the real objections to the giant's proposal are not so much practical as religious and philosophical. The giant assumes that he can find out what it is not for man to know, and that he can improve on the way not only human affairs but those of the natural order are arranged. The presumption of which Artegall accuses him is that of his classical progenitors; he thinks he can do better than God. Church's comment, quoted in the Variorum Spenser, makes the point briefly with the help of an excellently appropriate passage from Pope: 'To this Circumstance Mr. Pope plainly alludes in those fine Lines, *Essay on Man*:

Go, wiser thou! and in thy scale of sense
Weigh thy Opinion against Providence . . .
Snatch from his hand the ballance and the rod,
Re-judge his Justice, be the God of God!'[23]

The giant's antics with his balance profane not only the traditional scales of justice in whose use Artegall was instructed by Astraea but the weighing and balancing of the Creator himself, and his claims and Artegall's rebuke are in the context of Job and of the God who makes 'the weight for the winds' and 'weigheth the waters by measure', and of Esdras who is reproved by the angel for seeming 'to enter into the profound judgements of God'. The passage is a tissue of Biblical reminiscence, of *Psalms, Wisom, Esdras, Isaiah*:

[23] *The Works of Edmund Spenser, A Variorum Edition. The Faerie Queene*, Book V (Baltimore, 1936), p. 176.

Who hath measured the waters in the hollow of his hand, and meted out heaven with the span, and comprehended the dust of the earth in a measure, and weighed the mountains in scales, and the hills in a balance?[24]

Whereas the poet himself and his other characters have moved hesitantly in the regions of faith and doubt Artegall, as Astraea's pupil, simply knows, and can state with authority that what the giant supposes is wrong. The world was justly made and is justly maintained. His frankly religious terminology and the Biblical overtones of his speech give him a prophet's status as he affirms the divine use of the scales of perfect justice and rebukes the giant's blasphemous intention of going over the Maker's work with his own faulty instrument.

> For at the first they all created were
> In goodly measure by their Makers might,
> And weighed out in ballaunces so nere,
> That not a dram was missing of their right.
>
> (ii, 35)

Moreover—however it may look to us—the just order established at the beginning has not been disturbed among the things 'which the heavens containe, and in their courses guide'.

> Such heavenly justice doth among them raine,
> That every one doe know their certaine bound,
> In which they doe these many yeares remaine,
> And mongst them al no change hath yet been found.
>
> (ii, 36)

Indeed the giant is not fitted to criticize, for he does not know how to use his scales, or what they will and will not weigh. God can weigh the wind, but the giant is not even able, in the proverbial phrase, to weigh his words, nor can he balance the false against the true or the right against the wrong, as he vainly supposes, for such things are not commensurable. All the giant's sweat and labour cannot counterpoise the right with 'so much wrong', for 'all the wrongs could not a little right downe way'. They may seem to do so when we are presumptuous or despairing, but this is because we understand so little, and the lesson

[24] Isaiah xl, 12. The *Variorum* lists a number of these reminiscences.

183

Artegall tries to teach the giant is of the same nature as Britomart's lesson for Scudamour in Book III, 'all the sorrow in the world is lesse/Then vertues might and values confidence'. 'In the mind the doome of right must bee', the findings of the scales must be interpreted by a just mind. The scales will weigh wrongs against each other and show which is the worse, 'But right sate in the middest of the beame alone', for it is the right which regulates the weighing, in the balance as in the mind of man, and it is not itself subject to the process it controls. Thus the use of the scales of justice is equated with the finding of the mean, the right which sits always in the middle of the beam.[25] But the giant

> the right from thence did thrust away,
> For it was not the right which he did seeke;
> But rather strove extremities to way,
> Th'one to diminish, th'other for to eeke:
> For of the meane he greatly did misleeke.

> (ii, 49)

This is his essential error, that he seeks not to find the right but to alter what right depends on, those very 'extremities' through which, by a delicate shifting of weights, divine law operates in nature. By this process, which the giant regards as unfair, the created universe subsists in justice through the balanced opposition of the elements; again the balance or reconciliation of opposites provides a unifying principle, familiar in classical and Christian cosmology[26] and carrying its own Biblical connotations. As the cosmologists had pointed out for centuries and as Artegall explains here, the sea takes from the land in one place but returns what it has taken in another, and to interfere with this movement is to upset the exquisite precision of the relationships through which a stable order is held. For order in this world is not a still perfection but a process, carried on through movement, through strife, through love; and, while God's controlled progress is certain and just, man's wilful 'change is perillous, and all chaunce unsound'.

[25] Aristotle's idea of the Judge, and consequently of 'the Just', as a mean is doubtless relevant here, and is a further indication of that close connection between Justice, as the 'doome of right' within the mind, and Temperance, which the book often suggests (e.g. Guyon with Artegall in V, iii, 36) and which is a Platonic as well as an Aristotelian conception.
[26] See p. 87 above.

The just man is therefore no leveller, but one who conforms to the developing purpose of God in creation, and who understands that even death is ordered change. Even Artegall's brisk practical talk becomes resonant as he voices a theme which has the imagery of the Testaments behind it—'For all flesh is as grass . . . The grass withereth, and the flower thereof falleth away'—and a long line of classical meditation like Lucretius's.

> Haud igitur penitus pereunt quaequomque videntur;
> Quando alid ex alio reficit Natura, nec ullam
> Rem gigni patitur, nisi morte adjuta aliena.[27]

Life and death, gain and loss, power and submission, all are part of the great rhythms God has ordained for the upholding of a justice too vast and too august for the giant to see, and there is no ultimate loss, 'For there is nothing lost, that may be found, if sought'.

> Likewise the earth is not augmented more
> By all that dying into it doe fade:
> For of the earth they formed were of yore;
> How ever gay their blossome or their blade
> Doe flourish now, they into dust shall vade.
> What wrong then is it, if that when they die,
> They turne to that whereof they first were made?
> All in the powre of their great Maker lie:
> All creatures must obey the voice of the Most Hie.
>
> (ii, 40)

Artegall would have understood the eternal cycles of the Garden of Adonis, and would have been an approving spectator of the trial of Mutability; and rightly so, for the cosmic processes are at once a figure of, and an assurance of, the justice he professes. Just as the sea takes away from one part of the earth and washes up what it has taken upon another, so does the Lord give, and take away, and we should no more ask the reason why than do the other creatures.

> He pulleth downe, He setteth up on hy;
> He gives to this, from that He takes away:
> For all we have is His: what He list doe, He may.
>
> (ii, 41)

---

[27] *De Rerum Natura*, I, ll. 263–5.

Later, in Canto iv, the sea is spoken of in suggestively similar terms·

> For equall right in equall things doth stand;
> For what the mighty sea hath once possest,
> And plucked quite from all possessors hand,
> Whether by rage of waves, that never rest,
> Or else by wracke, that wretches hath distrest,
> He may dispose by his imperiall might.
>
> (iv, 19)

This passage echoes, also, one of Spenser's most majestic descriptions of justice, and the echo strengthens the book's association of justice and divine power, with the power of the sea as a figure of them both:

> Most sacred vertue she of all the rest,
> Resembling God in his imperiall might;
> Whose soveraine powre is herein most exprest,
> That both to good and bad he dealeth right,
> And all his workes with justice hath bedight.
>
> (Proem, 10)

In Canto iv the sea is shown at its task of disposing 'by his imperiall might', establishing in the process a justice both cosmic and moral. Artegall here needs only to interpret the judgments which have been made through the natural movements of the elements. The brothers Amidas and Bracidas inherited each an island, of equal size, but the sea has washed away land from Bracidas's inheritance and built up his brother's. As a result Bracidas's betrothed, the rich Philtera, left him for his younger brother, and Amidas's Lucy, in despair at her desertion, flung herself into the sea. But instead of drowning, she is washed ashore on Bracidas's island, clinging to a treasure chest which becomes her lucky pilot to safety but which Philtera claims as her own dowry, lost by shipwreck. The dispute between the brothers turns upon possession of the treasure, for Bracidas's view is that both alike should take what 'or God or Fortune' sends. As he has had to accept the erosion of his land to Amidas's benefit, so Amidas should accept his brother's 'good lucke'.

> What so good or ill
> Or God or Fortune unto me did throw,
> Not wronging any other by my will,
> I hold mine owne, and so will hold it still.
>
> (iv, 14)

186

Artegall's judgment is the same. Amidas holds his increased land by right of the sea, and by the same right Bracidas holds the treasure. Amidas has the land and the avaricious Philtera, Bracidas the treasure and Lucy: each of the four is more suitably matched, and more justly served, than in the days when the islands were equal.

Artegall expounds in legal phraseology the sea's right to dispose, 'As thing at random left, to whom he list', of all it possesses through the action of its waves or through shipwreck, and his words reach back to the sea's function in the fourth book, and to Cymoent's formal complaint that Proteus, in imprisoning Florimell, has violated Neptune's prerogative,

> For that a waift, the which by fortune came
> Upon your seas, he claym'd as propertie:
> And yet nor his, nor his in equitie,
> But yours the waift by high prerogative.
>
> (IV, xii, 31)

Bracidas's Lucy is a waift[28] too, and like Florimell she is saved by the sea which seems bound to destroy her; 'cruell shipwracke' which seems to bring only death and wretchedness brings life to her, and dead men's wealth as a means to life. The sea has given and has taken away, giving their just deserts to the selfish and changing death to life for the innocent and lost. It acts, as in Florimell's story and in that of Shakespeare's Pericles, as the giver of life and death, arbitrary yet ultimately just, imaging the mysterious purposes of God and working through oppositions towards the mean, the 'doome of right', and so towards concord. 'So was their discord by this doome appeased,/And each one had his right'. In this instance justice seems again to establish itself unaided, again 'of wrong her selfe had wroken'.

The sea, then, and the cleansing rivers, are a recurring element in the fourth and fifth books. It is at the Castle of the Strond that Artegall assists at the completion of Florimell's story, when the claimant to her name and her golden girdle, so like her that even Marinell is puzzled, is unmasked as a fair franion. Only Artegall, with his clear perception, can accurately weigh her

---

[28] 'A piece of property which is found ownerless and which, if unclaimed within a fixed period after due notice given, falls to the lord of the manor.' (Shorter Oxford English Dictionary.)

pretensions, and she dissolves into nothing, leaving the girdle empty behind. With her go all the false aspects of Florimell, the calculating charms of femininity, the deceptive and illusory aspects of beauty like the rainbow which looks so lovely but is only a trick of the light in the liquid air. It is proper that Florimell's sea-story, with its undercurrents of the meaning and the goodness of the natural world, should be justly concluded in this book; for despite Artegall's mistakes and his recall to the court before his task is done, the deepest impression left upon us is that, whatever the problems of just dealing in the world, justice itself is an abiding reality, the right which all the wrongs cannot weigh down. And the themes through which this impression is conveyed are in part the themes of the books of love, the reconciliation of those opposing realities which in our daily experience seem often so discordant. Isis and Osiris, Britomart and Artegall, land and sea, all in their harmonious duality reveal a purpose both merciful and just, all are sustained by the High God in whom the ultimate mystery of the 'most sacred vertue' is hidden. The fifth book is not altogether a success, perhaps it is not altogether a unified conception. The justice of Isis Church and of the shore where Artegall refutes the giant is not a felt reality throughout the narrative, the potentialities existing in the key passages are not fully exploited elsewhere. But those passages themselves are impressive and subtle, and they all point to the same conclusion.

> All in the powre of their great Maker lie:
> All creatures must obey the voice of the Most Hie.

In *The Faerie Queene*, really to know this is to know that the justice of God is truth,[29] and the fullest expression of the sovereign power of heaven.

[29] Aquinas, *Summa Theologica*, Quaestio XXI, Articulus ii, Utrum Justitia Dei sit Veritas?

Chapter Six

ALL GIFTS OF GRACE

THE legend of Courtesy arises naturally out of that of Justice, like the continuation of a process of thought. But the thought is continued on another plane, as though the thinker has been lifted above all difficulty and can see the world quite new. One has always, in *The Faerie Queene*, a sense of sameness yet difference, as the familiar stories of romance are deployed in new ways from one book to the next, and fresh significances emerge from the controlling figure of knights and ladies and the union of male and female principles, 'which two great sexes animate the world'. But this sense is particularly strong in the sixth book. There is the impression that this legend is in some way special and that Spenser felt it to be so. It has an absoluteness, a finality of self-existence, which separates it from the other books although it develops their themes so naturally. One aspect of its completeness is the simple perfection of Spenser's use of myth here. Pastorella affects us directly as Proserpine does, not the goddess of the Renaissance with the subtleties of the age heavy upon her but the girl who is yearly taken down to death from the flowery fields of a young world and is yearly reborn. Of course Spenser never does lose sight of the heart of a myth, its essential truth. That truth is what holds together all the potential meanings of his Diana, Venus, Isis, Hercules, so that he can make use of all that the philosophers, moralizers, explicators of the age had detected and can do so without the trivial ingenuity which they too often display. Spenser's Adonis is the centre for many structural themes built upon the development of centuries, but he could not be so,

189

or not successfully and satisfyingly so, if he were not so fully realized as the dead yet living god, with all the moist richness of the earth's growth rooted in his body and Venus's. But in Book VI the heart of the myth is all.

The effect of such simplification, such limpidity after all the complexities and interconnections of the earlier books is in itself striking. For four books (if one omits the orderly first where the One Truth is guide) the knights have been struggling on from one crisis to the next, seeing only from tree to tree of the wood of the world. Suddenly we are out, and we can see what the forest is, perhaps even what it is there for and why we should ever have been in it. There is a feeling of springing freedom, and this feeling mounts through the book. Because it exists everywhere in the characters and their adventures it can be intensely realized again and again in details of physical sensation, like that of Calepine who unencumbered by the customary armour which hinders his liberty is suddenly gloriously free to run:

> Now wanting them he felt himselfe so light,
> That like an hauke, which feeling her selfe freed
> From bels and jesses, which did let her flight,
> Him seem'd his feet did fly, and in their speed delight.
>
> (VI, iv, 19)

Delight and liberty are two of the keywords for this book; for it is words that are keys here, rather than grouped mythological persons with their complex of associated themes. Words, accumulating suggestion as they emerge and re-emerge from the action, articulate the meaning of that action, to express themselves fully at last in Pastorella, in the Graces, in the hermit whose service of God and man is perfect freedom. For if freedom is one of the book's words it is a controlled freedom, or a control which arises from knowing one is free; again Calepine's hawk comes to mind, loosed from bells and jesses but in itself a living symbol of spontaneous and delighted control, like the dancing of the Graces or the stars. The sense of release from tension and difficulty makes the comparison with Shakespeare's last plays unavoidable, especially since Pastorella's story and the attitudes inherent in it are so like Perdita's; and like the last plays the sixth book has a delicacy, and a transparency in its use of mythic figures like Pastorella herself or the Salvage Man, that makes commentary

190

feel itself absurd. There is nothing to explicate in the legend of Courtesy, little to interpret, no need to demonstrate the fineness of its quality. But it may at least be possible to suggest something of what its specialness consists in, to indicate how the ways or romance epic are freshly used to touch on the most delicate of all the virtues.

Calepine's free delight as he runs (What more felicitie can fall to creature/Than to enjoy delight with libertie) is part of the nature of courtesy. Release and relief, like Meliboe's and Calidore's and the hermit's when they leave the great world, are part of what the book is about. Its organization expresses the same joyousness, freedom, and simplicity (though a freedom and simplicity which depend upon a subtly directed art, and the book is about this too), and makes less use of the flexible concept of the reconciling or balancing of opposites which from the second book to the fifth has given shape to the affairs of men and of nature. The opposites belong to man's interpretation of the universe he inhabits, and are part of the structure of his mind as they are part of the structure of the cosmos. In human terms—the terms of mortal state—we make sense of the world and ourselves as discordia concors or we make no sense at all. But there are also God's terms, in whom the opposites are at one, and we may approach a diviner vision by the way of the saint, which Red Crosse travelled, or by the way of the poet. Proper distinctions between poet and saint, Edmund Spenser and George of Cappadocia, do not concern us here though they may well have concerned Spenser. We need only to remember the proud humility of the Renaissance maker of divine poetry, as intense in him as in any man of his time. The true poet, though he does not as poet see the New Jerusalem, may see all things made new. His inspiration is from heaven and for him the dark wood may be irradiated by the heavenly purpose. In preceding books we have been much aware of the difficulty even great knights have in perceiving eternal significance in the lifeless complications or the tight-pulled tensions of human experience. Now the poet is standing back a little from these complications and showing us a world serenely held in the hand of God, and free and joyous in the very fact of death and wickedness.

Without the other books, its effect would be far less. Long effort towards the good and the comprehensible is an essential condition of the vision that lights up the legend of Courtesy; Spenser has brought his people to the point where all they can do has been done, and they have earned the right, or the necessity, to let go. Having let go, they see; the complications become simple, the difficult is easy, they may live, with the hermit, 'like careless bird in cage'. The hermit is a representative figure, one who has earned his serene delight as the poem has earned it. He has been a good knight in his time, and has proved himself in the chivalric fight against wrong, and has come to his hermitage only after long and responsible experience of the weariness of 'this worlds unquiet waies'. Calidore finds simplicity too, and because of this he shares for a moment the vision of the poet who made him, and sees the world turn in order excellent about the Acidalian mountain. It is vision which makes the difference; happenings and persons unchanged in themselves may be transformed to the seer. The window which each of Spenser's virtues opens on the unchanging materials of this world affords here a startlingly fresh point of view upon the familiar.

The conditions of life, for most of the book, are the usual ones, and there are episodes that strongly recall events in Book Five. Most obviously there is the tale that Tristram tells Calidore to explain why he has killed an armed knight. The knight has behaved in much the same way as Artegall's Sanglier. Like him, he has treated his lady shamefully because he has seen one he likes better; he has made her walk beside his horse, punching her along with his spear. But whereas Sanglier was able to intimidate the squire, the knight in Book Six cannot intimidate Tristram. To all appearances Tristram is a weak enough champion of the right, for he is very young, on foot, and unarmed, and so is both untrained and unequipped for chivalric battle. But he is practised in the skills of the noble hunt against the greater beasts, and he has his darts and his boar spear, and he kills the knight like the brute he clearly is. The parallel suggests the difference in tone between the two books. Here weak good does challenge armed wrong, and it wins; in this book things come out right. Where Artegall in a similar case has to arbitrate, and can do so only by the exercise of painstaking subtlety, here it is all clear as daylight, and there is nothing left for Calidore to do beyond commenting on a situation that has worked itself out with the acceptable naturalness of a fairytale. It is in the nature

of things that Tristram should beat the knight, while in Book
Five the squire knew perfectly well that he had no hope of success however right his cause. Calidore accepts it all as the natural
thing:

> 'Now sure', then said Sir Calidore, 'and right
> Me seemes, that him befell by his owne fault:
> Who ever thinkes through confidence of might,
> Or through support of count'nance proud and hault,
> To wrong the weaker, oft falles in his owne assault.'
>
> (ii, 23)

In a sense Calidore does act as a kind of judge here in the particular question of chivalric practice involved, the death of a
knight at the hands of a boy who is not even a squire, but the
case is so clear that his judicial manner seems to serve chiefly the
purpose of underlining the relations between justice and courtesy. Again, the story of Crudor and Briana is like that of Pollente
and Munera, for each pair extorts tribute though Pollente's aim
is simple material gain while Crudor seeks to feed his own pride
and selfhood by degrading and shaming others. But the stories
end differently, as do Sanglier's and its echo. Calidore converts
Briana by being good to her, leaving her 'wondrously now
chaung'd from that she was afore' because she is

> All overcome with infinite affect
> For his exceeding courtesie, that pearst
> Her stubborne hart with inward deepe effect.
>
> (i, 45)

Briana then is capable of responding to good in others, and even
Crudor can be persuaded to behave, while Pollente and Munera
could only be destroyed.

The reforming of Briana is Calidore's first adventure, and it
follows directly upon his meeting with Artegall in the first canto.
In that meeting, a parallel relationship is firmly stated between
the virtues the two knights uphold, much in the manner of the
opening of Book Two. There the Palmer speaks as if Red Crosse
and Guyon have to move along parallel tracks:

> But wretched we, where ye have left your marke,
> Must now anew begin like race to ronne.
>
> (II, i, 32)

193

And Calidore tells Artegall

> But where ye ended have, now I begin
> To tread an endlesse trace, withouten guyde,
> Or good direction how to enter in,
> Or how to issue forth in waies untryde,
> In perils strange, in labours long and wide,
> In which although good fortune me befall,
> Yet shall it not by none be testifyde.
>
> (VI, i, 6)

In the twelfth canto we are again reminded of Artegall by the comparisons which link Calidore's capture of the Blattant Beast with Hercules's conquest of the Hydra and the dog of hell, Cerberus.

The Beast, which follows Artegall on his way back from the Salvage Island and which is the object of Calidore's quest, acts as a link between the knights. It is that impulse of pleasure in negation and in the pulling down of good achievement, that inability to believe in any motive but the lowest, which is a permanent element in human society. Such malice is clearly both discourteous and unjust, and it is fitting enough that a creature so subversive of all good order and so destructive of all trust should be represented as hampering justice and as the chief enemy of courtesy. But this is not a very interesting point in itself; it serves rather to alert the reader to more far-reaching relationships between the two virtues which may be developed as the nature of courtesy is explored. Courtesy is, like justice, a matter of giving each man his due, as the first stanza of the second canto says; to be accused of discourtesy is to be reproved 'for not yeelding what they owe'. It is put here in the appropriate social terms of degree, but in practice Calidore and Calepine show a greater delicacy and awareness than the brief expository stanza would suggest. It is that very delicacy and considerateness that distinguishes courtesy. Justice recognizes legal and moral rights, but in courtesy to yield what one owes means to try to make people happy and easy, and if possible good. Artegall and Britomart establish that mercy is just; to Calidore mercy is all. Courtesy can exist only when justice is established, it is the way everyone would behave in a world where mercy was the law. So Calidore begins where Artegall leaves off, and Spenser's con-

templation of courtesy seems a continuation of his thinking about
mercy as 'of Justice part',

> borne of heavenly race;
> From thence pour'd down on men, by influence of grace.

(V, x, 1)

This natural development is dramatized in the first canto. The
bully Crudor, when Calidore has beaten him and has his life at
disposal, cries out for mercy, and Calidore replies:

> Who will not mercie unto others shew,
> How can he mercy ever hope to have?
> To pay each with his owne is right and dew.
> Yet since ye mercie now doe need to crave,
> I will it graunt, your hopelesse life to save;
> With these conditions, which I will propound:
> First, that ye better shall your selfe behave
> Unto all errant knights, whereso on ground;
> Next, that ye ladies ayde in every stead and stound.

(i, 42)

The stanza ties justice, mercy, and courtesy inextricably together. It is just—'right and dew'—to pay each with his own, and
Crudor who has shown no mercy has in justice no right to ask it.
Yet the nature of mercy, as of courtesy, is gratuitous, and Calidore
grants it on condition that Crudor shall try retrospectively to
deserve it. The courtesy which Calidore sets in motion moves
back through Crudor to Briana, and to himself again as Briana
binds herself freely to his service, and from him to the harmless
couple she has wronged.

As so often, the opening cantos have in them compressed hints
enough to place us, to set us looking into the legend from the right
direction. As we look we find that the flow of the whole narrative,
as well as the meanings which make themselves known through
the separate episodes, contributes to the special atmosphere of
this tranquil and joyous book. One hesitates to speak of structure
here, for it is too solid, too architectural a word for something so
flowing and free. There is not the firm religious or moral progression of the first two books, nor the converging themes of the third
and fourth, locked together by the major figures, nor the counterpointing of mysterious truth and muddled human practice of the
fifth. The waywardness of romance narrative seems at first sight

195

to exist in and for itself, lacking the purpose which vitalizes it elsewhere. Calidore opens the book, but when he meets Calepine and Serena in a courteous interchange they take over the narrative, while he chases the Blattant Beast whose attack Serena has invited. Calepine meets the Salvage Man, but loses both him and Serena; they in their turn meet Arthur and Timias, and the story flows on through further losing and finding and helping until Calepine is reunited with Serena, now healed from the Beast's bite, and Calidore, still pursuing it, takes us into the pastoral where those impressions which have been deepening along the apparently wandering ways of Faeryland are ready to show themselves more fully. The interchanges of courtesy run smoothly from one group or one incident to the next, from Calidore and back to him, all yielding what they owe. The circular movement which the narrative as a whole suggests is repeated in many details, in Calidore's handling of Crudor and Briana, for instance; and it is a movement perfectly suited to the nature of courtesy as Spenser develops it.

What is important in the relation of the episodes in this book is their smoothness and naturalness of transition rather than their order. Courtesy is like love in that it can scarcely be well expressed as attainment of a virtue, a moral life journey in which one temptation resisted or accepted leads to another. Instead, the narrative draws together images of courtesy into the circular movement which is an image itself. One could enter the circle at any point, at nature, poetry, grace, delight, and still return upon one's self. No one of these is separable from the others, so that to begin with the image of controlled freedom must be arbitrary, but it is a convenient starting-place.

This image begins to develop itself from the very beginning. Courtesy, a delicate concern for others, is something inborn, freely given to him who possesses it, as freely given by him to others. The people—Tristram, the Salvage Man, and Pastorella herself—who are nobly born though now of low degree illustrate the importance of natural gifts, not of social rank; the 'gentle bloud' which manifests itself in their behaviour is a symbol of their instinctive rightness of feeling. In Calidore the knight of courtesy 'gentleness of spright/And manners mylde were planted naturall', and it is this inwardness and natural freedom of courtesy which is the essential thing, not the meticulous

etiquette of the manuals, in which Spenser shows little
interest.

> Vertues seat is deepe within the mynd,
> And not in outward shows, but inward thoughts defynd.
>
> (Proem, 5)

Simplicity, 'simple truth and stedfast honesty', is the mark of
the courteous spirit. But this is not quite all, for courtesy is both
an inward and an outward thing. In the closing cantos we seem
to enter, through pastoral, into the most 'inward thought' of the
poet himself to find the profoundest meaning of courtesy there,
but courtesy is nothing if it does not reach out towards others,
for 'the gentle minde by gentle deeds is knowne', and it is at this
point, if its spontaneous goodwill is to make itself known in
delicate and fitting action, that control and 'skill' are needed.

Yet the control is itself the result of the free impulse of courtesy, and cannot really be learned. So the poet says, flatly enough.
'Great skill it is such duties timely to bestow'.

> Thereto great helpe Dame Nature selfe doth lend:
> For some so goodly gratious are by kind,
> That every action doth them much commend.
>
> (ii, 2)

What is merely stated here is imaged again and again in the
joyous mastery of Calepine running as a hawk flies, or of Calidore
'full lightly' sweeping Briana's men away as a steer brushes away
the flies on a hot summer day. And the same happy confident
skill is in the picture of Calidore, 'well skild in fight', easily
holding back his natural power until the right moment to direct
it usefully, like the purposeful damming of a river's flow:

> Like as a water strcame, whose swelling sourse
> Shall drive a mill, within strong bancks is pent,
> And long restrayned of his ready course;
> So soone as passage is unto him lent,
> Breakes forth, and makes his way more violent.
>
> (i, 21)

Another aspect of the same concept is present in the appearance
and bearing of young Tristram, where something like Belphoebe's
blend of careless simplicity and formal elegance is used for a
purpose in some ways similar. Tristram's skill as a warrior comes

spontaneously from his generous indignation at the baseness and brutality of the knight he kills. This unity of impulse and controlled direction, the inwardness and outwardness of courtesy, is expressed also in his dress, the huntsman's Lincoln green and horn, boarspear and dart, the natural and functional clothes for a woodman but elegantly beautified by a tasteful and suitable art. He is a swain, but a 'gentle' one.

> All in a woodmans jacket he was clad
> Of Lincolne greene, belayd with silver lace;
> And on his head an hood with aglets sprad,
> And by his side his hunters horne he hanging had.
>
> Buskins he wore of costliest cordwayne,
> Pinckt upon gold, and paled part per part,
> As then the guize was for each gentle swayne.
>
> (ii, 5–6)

Calidore's address to him is a recognition of his particular quality. It is formally turned, charming, as spirited and as controlled as Tristram himself; a conscious literary version of a hunter's life and entirely suited to this elegant woodman.

> Faire gentle swayne, and yet as stout as fayre,
> That in these woods amongst the nymphs dost wonne,
> Which daily may to thy sweete lookes repayre,
> As they are wont unto Latonaes sonne,
> After his chace on woodie Cynthus donne . . .
>
> But should it not displease thee it to tell,
> (Unlesse thou in these woods thy selfe conceale
> For love amongst the woodie gods to dwell),
> I would thy selfe require thee to reveale.
>
> (ii, 25–6)

Pastorella, dressed in home made green and wearing a crown of flowers tied with ribbons, and 'Environ'd with a girland goodly graced,/Of lovely lasses' in the manner of the pastoral shepherd queen, shows a similar blend of qualities in looks and behaviour, naturally enhancing her natural charm:

> And soothly sure she was full fayre of face,
> And perfectly well shapt in every lim,
> Which she did more augment with modest grace
> And comely carriage of her count'nance trim.
>
> (ix, 9)

Calidore, of course, has these qualities in perfection, for in him

> it seemes that gentlenesse of spright
> And manners mylde were planted naturall;
> To which he adding comely guize withall,
> And gracious speach, did steale mens hearts away.
>
> (i, 2)

But among the shepherds he has to learn a new skill, perhaps the most sophisticated of all though also the most spontaneous, the art of simplicity. The courtly manners with which he expects to please Pastorella make no impression at all, for she 'Had ever learn'd to love the lowly things', and she prefers Colin's carolings to the utmost he can do. So in order fully to express his natural courtesy he must become a shepherd like one of those Colin might himself have written of in the heightened simplicities of pastoral where nature is artfully expressed, a literary shepherd like the poets' Paris, as Tristram is a literary huntsman. He dresses

> In shepheards weed, and in his hand he tooke,
> In stead of steelehead speare, a shepheards hooke,
> That who had seene him then would have bethought
> On Phrygian Paris by Plexippus brooke,
> When he the love of fayre Oenone sought,
> What time the golden apple was unto him brought.
>
> (ix, 36)

In learning the lowly things of pastoral Calidore finds the most fruitful of controlled freedoms, the most subtle interweavings of nature and art: in doing so he necessarily finds poetry. For Pastorella the finest courtesy is in Colin's carolings, and Colin is the shepherd poet, the poet par excellence, who sings purely and spontaneously but whose songs are of the highest art; whose subjects are simple because they are the most essential subjects of all.

Nature and art; the two conceptions twine around each other and through the book, to reach their perfection in each other in the pastoral close and, set within the pastoral, Colin's vision of poetry. The same notes have been sounded at the very beginning in the Proem with its intertwining of courtesy, skill, simplicity, natural goodness, delight, poetic inspiration:

That I, nigh ravisht with rare thoughts delight . . .

Such secret comfort and such heavenly pleasures,
Ye sacred imps, that on Parnasso dwell,
And there the keeping have of learnings threasures,
Which doe all worldly riches farre excell,
Into the mindes of mortall men doe well,
And goodly fury into them infuse;
Guyde ye my footing, and conduct me well
In these strange waies, where never foote did use,
Ne none can find, but who was taught them by the Muse . . .

Amongst them all growes not a fayrer flowre,
Then is the bloosme of comely Courtesie,
Which, though it on a lowly stalke doe bowre,
Yet brancheth forth in brave nobilitie . . .

(Proem, 1–4)

From here the legend moves full circle, returning upon itself and so (in Nature's phrase) working its own perfection. The image of the flower, the springing spontaneous goodness of true courtesy, is present in some form throughout. It is 'planted naturall' in Calidore, as Dame Nature's gift; Tristram speaks of 'the blossome of my tender yeares' and, when he is made squire and his inborn courtesy is free to branch forth bravely, he is glad and joyous

Like as a flowre, whose silken leaves small,
Long shut up in the bud from heavens vew,
At length breakes forth, and brode displayes his smyling hew.

(ii, 35)

Pastorella, who dies and is reborn, is most fittingly a flower; flower-decked, garlanded with shepherdesses, fading

Like to a flowre that feeles no heate of sunne,
Which may her feeble leaves with comfort glade,

(x, 44)

brought back to her parents through the rose mark she has carried from birth. Flowers and green growing things are everywhere in the sixth book, among the shepherds, in the hermit's house 'Deckt with greene boughes and flowers gay beseene', even about his little chapel

Which being all with yvy overspred,
Deckt all the roofe and shadowing the roode,
Seem'd like a grove faire braunched over hed.

(v, 35)

Close to the atmosphere of the hermit's delightful house is that
of the woods where Calepine, growing better from his wound
under the Salvage Man's herbal care, goes out with the convales-
cent's delight in seeing life spring again

To take the ayre and heare the thrushes song.

(iv, 17)

There is such freshness and charm about passages like these
that in relation to them even the ordinary rural comparisons
which may occur anywhere in *The Faerie Queene*—Calidore
fighting (on two occasions) like a steer brushing away summer
flies, the Salvage Man driving Turpine's men like scattered
sheep—make themselves felt, and contribute to the sense we
have of pastoral nature existing as an ideal of behaviour and a
statement of value throughout the book. For though Calidore's
stay among the shepherds takes up only four of the twelve
cantos, the book exists in one's memory as a pastoral one, and in
a sense our memory is sound; not only because Pastorella's story
and setting are in their own right so charming and memorable
but because they owe so much of their perfection to the stories
and settings which have gone before. The pastoral episode
reflects back upon the rest of the book, but it is the rest of the
book that makes it so satisfying and complete. The values which
have been partially exemplified, both positively and negatively,
in the stories of Serena, Briana, Mirabella, Tristram, are here
fully embodied, so that the pastoral interlude is not really an
interlude at all but the point at which the circle completes
itself.

Abstractly considered, there appears to be no compelling
reason why this particular virtue should be thought of in pastoral
terms. After all, courtesy derives its name, as Spenser says, from
the court, and one thinks of it as a chivalric virtue, yet in this
book it seems altogether fitting that Calidore should find it most
fully perfected when he leaves off his armour and his courtly
ways in the only community which knows nothing of the Blattant
Beast he seeks. For each of the virtues can be defined only by its

legend, and one need not read far to realize that Spenser's courtesy has little enough to do with the courtesy books but much to do with nature, providence, love, death, and the generous exchanges of compassion and mutual respect among men, matters with which pastoral is peculiarly well fitted to deal. Without the long tradition of elegy and idyll it is hard to see how even Spenser, or even the Milton of Lycidas and Eden, could have expressed so completely and so movingly the pain of loss and the peace of acceptance in a world where death is, and yet is not, the end of all created things; and these are essential to that view of our world which is open to us in courtesy.

Spenser's understanding of the possibilities of pastoral is evident, of course, outside *The Faerie Queene*, and to isolate certain uses in other poems may help us to understand the sixth book more fully, though it is unfair to those poems themselves. *Daphnaïda* may not suffer greatly from such treatment, for it is an undistinguished poem and often clumsy, but it shows a thorough awareness of the issues implicit in pastoral elegy's griefs and consolations, the way in which its simplicity can reach down to our troubles about our own being and that of the natural world. Alcyon's reaction to Daphne's death is as familiar in pastoral literature as it is in life, and Scudamour and the poet himself have voiced a like distress in *The Faerie Queene*:

> What man henceforth, that breatheth vitall ayre,
> Will honour Heaven, or heavenlie powers adore,
> Which soe unjustlie doe their judgments share
> Mongst earthly wights, as to afflict so sore
> The innocent as those which do transgresse,
> And do not spare the best or fairest more
> Than worst or fowlest, but doe both oppresse?
>
> If this be right, why did they then create
> The world so fayre, sith fairenesse is neglected?
>
> (197–205)

Human death is part of the tragic puzzle of nature, of the universe, and it is by way of nature that pastoral elegy both laments and makes acceptable the unbelievable fact which Alcyon expresses for all mankind, ' "Daphne thou knewest," quoth he;/"She now is dead" '. Desolation and death are shared with all the natural world,

For they be all but vaine, and quickly fade,
So soone as on them blowes the northern wind;

(395–6)

and it is because it shares in our situation that it grieves for our loss, so that birds are silent on the naked spray and there are no flowers, when Daphne dies. This sympathy, at first only an additional grief in its proof of Daphne's value, leads also to the gradual adjustment of the shocked mind to irrevocable loss. Alcyon will travel the world sorrowing, as the mother of the gods sought Euridyce,[1] but flowers and leaves and Euridyce will live again, and this is the ground of our hope.

Daphnaïda is a single-minded poem. In *The Shepheardes Calender* the theme of death, grief, and rebirth is deepened and enriched by being related to other aspects of our dilemma. Man is part of nature, but this world's brief beauty gives him less than he asks, and though he loves it he needs to look beyond it. As lover, poet, priest, or simply as an ordinarily responsible human being, he is presented with the same problem, and the *Calender* faces it in all these aspects. Man belongs to the natural cycle of mutability and death, perhaps he shares also in its rebirth. It is the fading natural world itself which looks towards and is our metaphor for the understanding of death as 'the grene path way to life'.[2] Yet for man rebirth is outside the natural order, and though we may use for it the figure of the sown seed and the springing tree we must not mistake figurative truth for literal. For us the natural cycle is in itself the way to death, and we will gain life only by looking to the cycle's source. Colin's two songs in the *Calender*, the praise of Elisa and the lament for Dido, give between them the whole situation.

The *Aprill* eclogue shows us, in the triumphant figure of Elisa, bright as the sun, adored by shepherds and attended by nymphs, the sum of human felicity in a beautiful and sympathetic world. She sits crowned with flowers like Pastorella, she is fit to make a fourth to the Graces as Colin's other lady does in *The Faerie Queene*. Countering this delight is the monstrous darkness of

[1] Proserpine; this is another frequent confusion of names, understandable since the stories of these two are both about death and rebirth.

[2] On the natural cycle and on the 'way to death and the way to life', see R. A. Durr, 'Spenser's Calendar of Christian Time', ELH, XXIV, 1957, pp. 269–95.

203

November, where all things join in lamentation for the natural yet somehow horribly unnatural death of what is valued and loved, undoing 'Dame Natures kindly course'. Nature mourns this death and all deaths, all her and our ancient loss,

> The turtle, on the bared braunch,
> Laments the wound that Death did launch,
>
> (138–9)

and Colin's grief is in Nature's terms:

> Whence is it that the flouret of the field doth fade,
> And lyeth buryed long in winters bale:
> Yet soone as spring his mantle doth displaye,
> It floureth fresh, as it should never fayle?
>
> (83–6)

The flower will spring again, but 'vertues braunch and beauties budde/Reliven not for any good', and although Dido's body held all that might be in earthly mould that body is buried now. Even Colin's verse falters, for the poet and his singing must die in this world as his subjects must. 'All musick sleepes where Death doth leade the daunce.' But it is at this lowest point—the sinking into earth of the body which itself is earth—that pastoral elegy begins to rise. Dido's body is buried like the seed of the faded flower, but like it she rises reborn, and to a higher rule and joy than even Elisa could encompass here, reigning 'a goddesse now among the saintes,/That whilome was the saynt of shepheards light'. Elisa's pastoral will fade, but our eternal pastoral abides.

> No daunger there the shepheard can astert:
> Fayre fields and pleasaunt layes there bene,
> The fields ay fresh, the grasse ay greene.
>
> (187–9)

It is in relation to this pastoral theme that we must see Pastorella, the fading flower 'That long had lyen ded' and is 'made againe alive'. Her story is introduced in the *Calender's* terminology:

> There on a day, as he pursew'd the chace,
> He chaunst to spy a sort of shepheard groomes,
> Playing on pypes, and caroling apace,
> The whyles their beasts there in the budded broomes
> Beside them fed, and nipt the tender bloomes:
>
> (ix, 5)[3]

---

[3] Compare *Februarie*, ll. 35–6.

and Colin the arch-poet of the *Calender* is here too. The *Calender* as a serious pastoral asserts through the sympathy of man and nature the life and power of all those good things—love, work, poetry—which come within the genre's scope; and it sees them as different aspects of the truth which the natural order, spiritually read, can adumbrate. Heaven is Dido's source and end, and the source and end also of poetry. In the *October* eclogue Piers tries to encourage Cuddie, who has come to regard his singing as only the feckless and unrewarded summer play of the grasshopper, by reminding him how Orpheus his great predecessor tamed the hound of hell and brought back Eurydice from Pluto's kingdom by his music's might. Poetry and love are the conquerors of death. Thus poetry, like man its maker, can share in eternity as well as in the mutability of natural life. 'All thinges perish and come to theyr last end', says E.K. in his last, brave gloss, 'but workes of learned wits and monuments of poetry abide for ever.' 'La mort ny mord' is pastoral's motto, no less than 'Et in Arcadia ego', and the *Calender*, which is 'for every yeare', will outlast 'steele in strength, and time in durance' because it not only follows the natural cycle but sees it in its timeless significance.

In the legend of Courtesy Spenser's method of using pastoral proper as the culmination of the book's whole movement allows him to extend pastoral meanings into areas with which in *The Shepheardes Calender* he is not directly concerned. The basic meanings remain the same; and not in the pastoral only but throughout the legend nature, which affirms death and decay, affirms also life and love and order, for it is after all God's book, meant for man to read, and it does not close with death. Nature is an all-pervading presence in the sixth book, and with nature the natural man, unspoiled by the selfish vices of the competitive world, man who has either regained the pastoral Golden Age, as Calidore, the hermit, and Meliboe have done, or, like the Salvage Man, has never lost it. The good figures co-operate with a sympathetic goodness in Nature herself as in pastoral proper. The Salvage Man enters the poem like a thing of nature; he is invulnerable, fierce as a tiger and swift as a buck, pitying and suffering with the suffering Serena just as the flowers droop and the rain falls in sympathy with the sad shepherd. He expresses his feelings as an animal does, in murmurous sounds 'which Nature did him teach', and she has taught him too the completely natural life. He eats no flesh or blood, 'obeying Natures first beheast', and in return he has Nature's gifts; he knows the healing properties of herbs and he instinctively acts with the compassion and the self-less loyalty of the chivalric ideal. Natural courtesy will make itself known in however 'undisciplyned' a way; the wild man's willingness to help quickly teaches him the skill to do so.

The hermit too has reached, after the long discipline of chivalry, the point where he can parallel, on the higher level of sanctity, the innocent trustfulness and helpfulness of the Salvage Man. His power of healing goes beyond Nature's means, for he adds to the knowledge given through her the gift of spiritual skill which enables him to cure the wound inflicted by the Blattant Beast, the inward bite of shame that cripples Timias and Serena. No one in the whole of *The Faerie Queene* gives so unmistakable an impression of holiness as the hermit, yet his sanctified insight is expressed, just as readily as the Salvage Man's instinct for good, in terms of nature. His house is small but green and springing, his little chapel is like a growing grove, with ivy shading the rood; in this tiny space there is a sense of complete natural liberty. The joyous acceptance of control in which the hermit's perfect freedom consists, his happy discipline of praise, of 'howres and holy things', could scarcely be better expressed than in the twice repeated simile of the caged bird.

> Small was his house, and like a little cage,
> For his owne turne, yet inly neate and clene,
> Deckt with greene boughes and flowers gay beseene.
>
> (v, 38)
>
> And weary of this worlds unquiet waies,
> He tooke him selfe unto this hermitage,
> In which he liv'd alone, like carelesse bird in cage.
>
> (vi, 4)

Salvage Man and hermit alike live in the utmost simplicity and content, and have only the homeliest fare to offer, but their guests accept it gratefully as they ought.

> Yet howsoever base and meane it were,
> They tooke it well, and thanked God for all,
> Which had them freed from that deadly feare.
>
> (iv, 15)

Yet was their fare but homely, such as hee
Did use his feeble body to sustaine;
The which full gladly they did take in gree,
Such as it was, ne did of want complaine,
But being well suffiz'd, them rested faine.

(v, 39)

Such gratitude is courteous not only to one's host but to God
the true giver of nature's goods; thus Timias and Serena
'thanked God for all'. Medieval treatises had stressed the importance of giving thanks, and also of remembering the needy, while
we eat, as a courteous return to a courteously benevolent God,
but thankful contentment and humility are values native to the
pastoral too, and the fine speech of the patriarchal shepherd
Meliboe in the ninth canto is a definitive statement of much
that pastoral and much that this whole legend stands for. Meliboe
expounds the pastoral ethic of the contentment of those 'taught
by nature, which doth little need'. Content with simplicity leads
to independence of all but God; lack of envy and ambition leads
to a willingness to grant others a freedom like one's own. This
state of freedom in virtue, the state truly natural to man, is contrasted with the perturbations which result from selling one's
freedom for money, as Meliboe had sold himself for yearly hire
in the court gardens. Now he has returned from the example of
Cain,[4] who tilled the soil in his eagerness for gain and his lack of
reliance on God, to that of the shepherd Abel who was content
to wait upon natural increase, the divine provider working
through the processes of nature:

The litle that I have growes dayly more
Without my care, but onely to attend it;
My lambes doe every yeare increase their score,
And my flockes father daily doth amend it.
What have I, but to praise th'Almighty, that doth send it?

(ix, 21)

[4] A passage in Johan Huizinga's *Erasmus and the Age of Reformation*
(New York, 1957) is relevant here. At dinner in Oxford 'The discussion
was about Cain's guilt by which he displeased the Lord. Colet defended
the opinion that Cain had injured God by doubting the Creator's goodness,
and, in reliance on his own industry, tilling the earth, whereas Abel tended
the sheep and was content with what grew of itself' (p. 32). For Luther
Abel was the type of faith, or more exactly of 'faithful works', while Cain
undertook works which the Lord does not ask.

Meliboe is able to live in serene acceptance of the natural cycle because he knows what lies behind it and gives it meaning, and because he knows it is in vain that men

> The heavens of their fortunes fault accuse,
> Sith they know best what is the best for them.

Pastoral is the best of all metaphors for a life of such natural holiness, but literal rusticity is not implied; one can live so anywhere, as Meliboe explains to Calidore:

> But fittest is, that all contented rest
> With that they hold: each hath his fortune in his brest.
>
> (ix, 29)

Pastoral is an attitude of mind; the old shepherd's teaching only underlines the impression that this whole book makes upon us, that the way the world looks depends on the seer as well as on the things seen, that, as Meliboe puts it, 'It is the mynd that maketh good or ill'. All the good characters, not only the shepherds, exemplify Meliboe's way of living in their own fashion. Courtesy, it would seem, stems from a grateful acceptance of life as divinely given, a trust in God from which naturally arises a trust in God's creatures and a sense of their individual value. This is the freedom from self-concern, the spontaneous generosity and tact, without which courtesy cannot exist, for it is not etiquette or correct behaviour, 'not in outward shows, but inward thoughts defynd'. For such a definition the gracious natural background of pastoral and the simple truth of the shepherd are in place even if only to distinguish between the outward show of courtly manners and true courtesy's delicate concern. But the pastoral meanings go beyond this to show courtesy, in Spenser's rich sense of it, as natural to man when unspoiled by selfishness (and so equatable with 'humanity') and corresponding to the divine benevolence for which pastoral nature is a metaphor. Piety, poetry, and sympathizing nature, all the resources of the pastoral tradition, are drawn upon to express the divine concern to which our human concern for each other is the only proper response, and to suggest the generosity of the gifts of God which we call fortune or chance.

Nowhere are we more conscious of the help given freely to man. Again and again events are referred to 'Chance' or 'Fortune', and the frequently recurring words direct our awareness beyond the happenings to the purpose which gently and unobtrusively shapes them. Calepine is led to rescue Serena not through some wise decision of his own but 'by chaunce more then by choyce', and is himself saved from Turpine by the wondrous chance of the Salvage Man's arrival. 'Such chaunces', comments the poet, 'oft exceed all humaine thought', fortune passes all fore-sight. Matilda complains bitterly of Fate and Fortune, which have denied her the child needed to maintain her husband's conquest of the evil Cormoraunt, but it is Fortune which helps Calepine to save a baby being carried off by a bear. 'Lo! how good fortune doth to you present/This little babe', he says to her, and the situation is so managed as to make it seem that Fate and Fortune have had everything in hand all the time. A prophecy exists that there shall 'Be gotten, not begotten' to Matilda's husband a son who is finally to defeat the giant; this particular baby has, it is clear, been chosen to perform a particular task. Calepine is conscious of this. Many foundlings, he says, have done great things, as though they were the children of the gods. The little story is so neat and convincing that we recognize with pleasure, as a further proof of Fortune's long and witty foresight, the happy coincidence by which a knight called Sir Bruin is provided with a son through the action of a bear.

Often the intervention of providence is more clearly named. Calidore and Coridon go 'God before' to save Pastorella, and her story is of course the finest example of that purposeful ordering of fortune which is part of the book's theme. She is exposed as a child because of the storms of fortune which fall upon her mother, and Meliboe 'Found her by fortune'.[5] But already the divine care is being hinted at. The maid who leaves the child waits

> To weet what mortall hand, or heavens grace,
> Would for the wretched infants helpe provyde.
>
> (xii, 8)

Similar phrases play through Pastorella's life. Fortune heaps sorrows on her as it did upon her mother, and yet each disaster

[5] The name occurs in Chaucer and Virgil but it was also the name of the shepherd who, in accordance with the purposes of the gods, found the exposed child Oedipus.

takes her further towards release. The Brigant captain views her with lustful eyes, but this is 'as Fortune had ordayned', and it keeps her alive. Her survival as a baby is attributed finally not to fortune but to grace; the heavens have graced Claribell in restoring her daughter 'whom High God did save' (xii, 17). Tristram, sent as a child to the forest to escape death at his uncle's hands, and the baby saved from the bear, are similarly under the protection of a providence which cares especially for the defenceless and oppressed, and all these persecuted children have a purposeful and valuable life to live after their experience of death.

It is in the darkest of these providential episodes, the sacrificing of Serena, that divine grace is most stressed, with a grimly exultant irony. Serena has already resigned herself to 'Gods sole grace' in her terror of the Salvage Man, and has found him to be, against all appearances, the instrument of that grace. Now she is taken by the savages, who are at the opposite pole from pastoral man, for they are not merely bestial but 'damned souls' whose unnatural cannibalism, 'A monstrous cruelty gainst course of kynde', is a sign of their spiritual distortion, their misapprehension of the true nature of the world which pastoral man responds to with instinctive rightness. They have a religion and some notion of superhuman beneficence, but they have distorted this too in the likeness of themselves. Serena has been betrayed to them by false Fortune, the poet says; however this may be, the savages regard it as 'good hap by heavenly grace' to come upon such excellent potential food. But they decide that 'since by grace of God she there was sent' the proper return is to sacrifice her to that god, whom they worship with bloody vessels, holy sacrificial fire, and a wild disordered music in which Nature, horrified and trembling, cannot join, for it is no part of the universal harmony. The stark humour which pervades the account—'For sleepe, they sayd, would make her battill better', 'To dare not to pollute so sacred threasure,/Vow'd to the gods: religion held even theeves in measure'—emphasizes the appalling misconceptions which guide the savages' conduct and are pictured in every detail of their ritual.

The darkness, with a fitful glimmer from the sacred fire and the stars, the shrilling and wailing of bagpipes and horns, the muttering of charms, make the sacrifice weirdly sinister, yet what brings home most of all the hideous unnaturalness of the scene

is the elaborately sensuous description of Serena, with its
reminders of sacred and secular love poetry. The mere presence
of such voluptuous beauty and fullness of life makes absurd the
squalor and the frightened destructiveness of the savage world
and justifies the poet's disgusted laughter. The worst thing about
the savages is that in their perverted nature and perverted
religion they profane (the word is Spenser's) the sanctity of the
human body, proposing to use for themselves, or to give to their
god to use, the astonishing gift of life which is so powerfully
expressed here through the incongruousness of Serena's beauty
and dignity in this sordid setting. They lay her on their altar,
and yet she is already herself an altar, in virtue of her intense
human vitality and of her woman's beauty:

> Her tender sides, her bellie white and clere,
> Which like an altar did it self uprere,
> To offer sacrifice divine thereon.

> (viii, 42)

The ironies built up through the clash of living reality against
the cannibals' impious incomprehension come to a climax in the
sacrificial act itself. For the grace of God does truly attend
Serena, and as the priest's knife descends Calepine, brought by
chance more than by choice, sacrifices him in her place to the
devils he has taken to be God.

> He him preventing, layes on earth along,
> And sacrifizeth to th'infernall feends.
> Then to the rest his wrathfull hand he bends,
> Of whom he makes such havocke and such hew,
> That swarms of damned soules to hell he sends.

> (viii, 49)

Once more there is release from death and evil recoils upon itself.
The savages find the reality, and the god, they have invented.

At once, by the sharpest of contrasts, there follows the shepherd life whose ordered peace is the sign of God's goodness,
expounded by Meliboe, and we begin to see more clearly the
relation between courtesy and grace and pastoral poetry. 'Grace',
in its many senses, is a word repeated often in this book. Sometimes it seems casual enough; when applied in the first and
second cantos to Calidore, for instance, or (ironically) to the disarming flatterer Blandina who pacifies Prince Arthur. But it is

this unobtrusive repetition, with implications gradually revealing themselves through the narrative, that makes possible the rich uses of the word in the sacrificing of Serena and prepares us to see more than conventional meaning in the 'modest grace' of Pastorella. Normally in this book the word implies something given, as even the cannibals thought Serena was 'given' to them and so must be given back to their god. What is given may be Calidore's charm or Mirabella's beauty, or the impressiveness of the hermit whose 'grave beseeming grace' draws into one phrase the divine and human connotations of the word; and in the tenth canto the continual shifting play of 'grace' and 'graces' and 'gracious' settles into one of the richest of Spenser's symbolic pictures, the appearance to Colin the shepherd poet of the Graces themselves. Here both Colin's gift of song and the gift of graciousness which Calidore possesses are seen as, precisely, gifts. They are bestowed by the Graces, daughters of delight, traditionally symbolizing the free flow of benefits among men and between men and the gods. 'Those three to men all gifts of grace do graunt', the poet tells us, 'And all that Venus in her selfe doth vaunt/Is borrowed of them'. And Colin elaborates:

> These three on men all gracious gifts bestow,
> Which decke the body or adorne the mynde,
> To make them lovely or well favoured show,
> As comely carriage, entertainment kynde,
> Sweet semblaunt, friendly offices that bynde,
> And all the complements of curtesie.

> (x, 23)

The Graces were a very popular symbol among artists and philosophers.[6] They can be seen as unfolding the attributes of Venus, thus demonstrating in a variety of ingenious ways the nature of love; they can illustrate the circle of eternity, emanating from and returning to the divine. More ordinarily, Comes reminds us that they denote the fertility of fields and abundance of fruit (so that they are particularly at home in pastoral) and that they are said to be the daughters of Jove because human faculties are not enough to bring them forth. Divine clemency is necessary for the riches of fields and flocks and for all benefits. And always

---

[6] E. Wind, op. cit., Spenser's use of the Graces, and E.K.'s gloss in the *Calender*, are discussed.

they are closely connected with Venus,[7] that is with love and beauty and generous creation, and always they enact, with their interlocking arms, the circular movement of giving and receiving. 'Quam à Deo acceperimus, eadem illi referenda gratia est.'[8] It is this movement that Colin stresses in explaining their appearance, and E.K. has a long gloss on it in the *Aprill* eclogue. Both passages have given rise to much discussion of how, precisely, Spenser was interpreting the morality of giving and receiving, and whether he stood with Servius or with Seneca. But in its place in the vision, in the pastoral, and in the whole legend, this becomes largely irrelevant to the poem however interesting in itself. There is no real question of whether receiving may be more blessed than giving; each depends upon the other, is part of the circle, so that to give is to receive and to receive is to give. Though the letter of interpretation may differ, it is such passages as these from Pico and Ficino (whether or not Spenser knew them) that come nearest in spirit to the imaginative conception which Spenser's Graces embody:

> Of the Graces one is painted looking toward us; the continuation of our being is no reflex act. The other two, with their faces from us, seeming to return; the operations of the Intellect and Will are reflexive: 'What comes from God to us, returns from us to God.'[9]

> This divine quality of beauty stirs desire for itself in all things: and that is love. The world that was originally drawn out of God is thus drawn back to God; there is a continual attraction between them— from God to the world and from the world to God—moving as it were in a circle. This circle may be said to display three qualities: beginning in God, it is beauty; passing into the world, it is love; and returning to unite the creation with the Creator, it is pure delight.[10]

[7] References in *The Teares of the Muses*, 1. 403, and in *The Faerie Queene*, II, viii, 6, suggest that Spenser regarded them as Venus's daughters and Cupid's sisters. In Book VI they have their conventional parentage as daughters of Jove and Eurynome.

[8] Pietri Costalii *Pegma*, p. 285. This is part of an explication of an emblem of the three Graces, in which is stressed the importance of repaying (by way of generosity to dependants and the needy) God's gift to us.

[9] *A Platonick Discourse upon Love* by Pico della Mirandola, p. 35.

[10] Ficino, quoted by John Vyvyan, *Shakespeare and Platonic Beauty* (London, 1961), p. 39.

I would by no means press the comparison, and I would certainly not suggest that in this instance Spenser is doing anything in the nature of a Platonic 'unfolding', though his treatment of Agape's sons in Book IV shows an exact acquaintance with the method. But it is this kind of thinking that best illuminates the Graces here as the image which holds together the various meanings of 'grace', the key to the innermost nature of courtesy. It suggests courtesy's connection with love and delight and beauty —beauty is a certain lively and spiritual grace, says Ficino, infused by the divine ray—and with generosity both human and divine. God's own grace to men is itself a gift, a final generosity beyond their deserts, and in this legend human life is interpreted partly in terms of grace. Human troubles are not ignored, for there is pathos in the suffering and death of the good and even a particularly sinister horror in the capture of Serena, but they are rendered in the last resort impotent by our certainty even while they operate that they do so under control. And it is the poet, present here as the shepherd Colin, whose task it is to apprehend, and to remake, the true meaning of the created world, in a shape and a language which will embody its freedom and fecundity and also the purpose which gives it completeness.

For of course the ordering power of the book of Courtesy, felt by the reader as the divine grace which restores Pastorella to life and saves Serena from immolation and the nameless baby from the jaws of the bear, is really the ordering power of the poet, creator of the small universe of the poem. By tradition the pastoral is the particular domain of poetry, a delicately distanced version of reality where everything is present—love, work, thought, art, death—but in a simpler and more readily comprehensible form and so in a sense a more real form. To Calidore this world's gay shows 'Be but vaine shadowes to this safe retyre/Of life' (ix, 27). The 'rest amongst the rusticke sort' is a smaller, clearer world within that more difficult and complex one of Faeryland which is, for all its fantasy, so close to our experience of living. And enclosed within it again is Mount Acidale, the home of poetry where the Graces bestow their vision, at once infinitely private and overwhelmingly true, upon Colin alone, vanishing when Calidore breaks in upon them, for they come to 'whom they of them selves list so to grace'. It is as though we have moved inwards to the depths of the poet's mind, where the divine gift of poetry is received and from where it rises again into the world.

In one aspect the pastoral passage is Spenser's comment on his own creation, on the kind of strength and the kind of fragility poetry has. He wrecks his inset miniature world twice over, for the Brigants' destruction of the shepherds and their life is foreshadowed earlier in the same canto in the vanishing of the Graces from the Acidalian Mount. Our world depends on the way we see it. But even for the poet, the nature of things can be apprehended only briefly, and his moments of vision are easily shattered by the intrusion of the everyday. Vision fades, when the Graces withdraw from those 'whom they of them selves list so to grace', but it can be eternalized in words, for 'workes of learned wits and monuments of poetry abide for ever'. Fragile though it may be compared with the heavy reality of daily life, it is the golden nature of the poet which convinces us of its greater truth; and Acidale and the dancing figures of Colin's vision are Spenser's most confident and quietly triumphant expression of his belief in the truth of God-given poetry. It uses some of the most familiar images by which the Renaissance expressed its faith in the ordered goodness of even the fallen world, and uses them with superb finality. Acidale is the haunt of the Graces and of Venus because poetry has its own indefinable closeness to love and beauty and vitality, and Spenser seems habitually to have linked them all in his mind. In *The Teares of the Muses* he addresses the

> three twins, to light by Venus brought,
> The sweete companions of the Muses late,
> From whom what ever thing is goodly thought
> Both borrow grace, the fancie to aggrate.
>
> (403–6)

The mountain with its symmetry of trees and water is all poetic paradises reduced to their essential qualities of springing life, the inexhaustible fecundity and the pure stern clarity of nature as it should be and, essentially, is. It seems the most perfect of earth's pleasaunces, made by Nature's deliberate art as a place of total delight,

> For all that ever was by Natures skill
> Devized to worke delight was gathered there,
> And there by her were poured forth at fill.
>
> (x, 5)

It has a silver stream guarded from all noisome things by nymphs who join in the singing of the water and of the choir of small birds in the branches which bud all winter as in summer. High in the same trees there are soaring hawks, for the poet's nature has room not only for the gentler creatures but for those of 'majesty and powre'. Just so Dame Nature, at the trial of Mutabilitie, has the beauty of sternness in her veiled lion's face, but flowers grow 'voluntary' beneath her feet. The likeness of the poetic mountain to Dame Nature's Arlo Hill is the measure of how close the poet's nature is to the true nature of things.

Here Calidore breaks in upon that sight which makes him long to stay near the mountain, 'Nor certes mote he greatly blamed be', for it is the pastoral life that has led him through love to the sight of courtesy. He sees

> An hundred naked maidens lilly white,
> All raunged in a ring, and dauncing in delight,
>
> (x, 11)

and the Graces within the ring in their own interwoven circle, and at the centre of all the single figure of the shepherd's lass, Colin's love, around whom the glorious order of poetry forms itself. He pipes to her alone, not for praise or gain but in self-forgetting devotion to her and to the song, as the good poet must, and so the Graces dance to his piping and his 'love is there advaunst to be another Grace'. Colin's nameless 'love' is everyone's love in poetry, and the poetic inspiration which Calidore is allowed momentarily to see is, naturally enough, something like his first sight of Pastorella sitting

> Environ'd with a girland, goodly graced,
> Of lovely lasses.

Colin's lass and the Graces are similarly engarlanded, by Venus's maidens, and all add grace to one another:

> All they without were raunged in a ring,
> And daunced round; but in the midst of them
> Three other ladies did both daunce and sing,
> The whilest the rest them round about did hemme,
> And like a girlond did in compasse stemme:
> And in the middest of those same three was placed
> Another damzell, as a precious gemme

Amidst a ring most richly well enchaced,
That with her goodly presence all the rest much graced.

(x, 12)

Spenser draws from the figure of the circle all the metaphorical
fullness which can develop the vision's significance. The ring of
dancing living people, naked because they are the pure unveiled
truth, is a natural thing, but it is also an artefact, a jewelled ring
with one woman as the precious gem at the centre of the setting.
Art and nature are one in the living order of poetry, and so it is in
the dance, in which control arises from the first free impulse itself,
as it does in Calidore's and Calepine's joyous courtesy. In the
following stanza the ring becomes a vision of cosmic order, of the
divine art itself, as the dancers move in poetry's re-creation of the
great dance of the universe, circling around the shepherd girl as
the stars 'move in order excellent' about Ariadne's crown set in
the firmament and shining through bright heaven. The translated
crown brings to mind the parallel translation of Ariadne herself;
it symbolizes her death in this world but also her passing to
another, as in Titian's painting of it and in the explanations of
mythographers. (One entry for 'Corona Ariadne' in *Apelles
Symbolicus* is 'In aeternitatem et perpetuitam coelestium gau-
diorum'.) Ariadne is one of the most human and touching of the
heroines of myth, and her tale is one of repeated and undeserved
suffering, of desertion even by the god who saved her when
Theseus sailed away. If in one version she dies in the embrace of
Dionysus, somehow she is also raised to joy and glory as his wife,
and the cluster of stars is there as an eternal reminder of the
apotheosis of human weakness and grief. Whether in reading we
think primarily of Ariadne or of Colin's love made immortal in
poetry,[11] the vision has at its centre the exaltation of a simple
human being, and affirms with all poetry's divine authority the
truth which pastoral hints at and which Pastorella's life repeats

---

[11] Pope can still use this kind of condensed figure (with a light touch
but with a serious intention) at the end of *The Rape of the Lock*, where
Belinda is reminded that she must die but is at the same time assured of
immortality through the poet's celebration of her beauty and her fate:

When those fair suns shall set, as set they must,
And all those tresses shall be laid in dust,
This Lock, the Muse shall consecrate to fame,
And 'midst the stars inscribe Belinda's name.

in narrative form: that loneliness, sorrow, and death are transcended in beatitude, in immortal heaven and in immortal art.

Here, then, is poetry at its task of perceiving and embodying truth, a truth which can be experienced in the poem itself but can be only roughly approximated in such words as order, love, creation, eternal joy, supernatural benevolence joining with human devotion. It is an important part of Spenser's meaning that the truth is revealed to, and through, the good and humble people of pastoral, who live like Meliboe without thought of fame or money as their reward, 'contented to abyde'. Ordinary people receive divine gifts, poetry, courtesy, personal grace, and the power to attract love. But all these gifts carry their responsibilities, and this is one reason why the Graces are present. They 'on men all gracious gifts bestow', they signify the circulation of blessings throughout a beneficent universe, and what they give to men must be passed on, to be given 'in greater store'. The proper duty and courtesy of the poet is selflessly to repay his 'divine gift' of inspiration in deathless poetry, as Piers implies when he apostrophizes poetry in the *October* eclogue:

> Then make thee winges of thine aspyring wit,
> And, whence thou camst, flye backe to heaven apace.
>
> (83-4)

And the courtesy of all good men is similar, to repay God for the good of the world by trust in him and by kindness to others, 'yeelding what they owe'.

In either case life must be lived, as it is by the hermit and the old shepherd, in the thought of the giver of life. The Graces, turning in their circle with arms affectionately interlocked, are the most satisfying of Spenser's symbols of courtesy, but they could not be so but for the many episodes, characters and images which have prepared for them in the larger, looser circular movement of the legend as a whole. Calidore and Calepine and Arthur, Meliboe and Serena, Salvage Man and hermit, all play a part in the continuing circulation of gifts from heaven, among men, and back again to heaven, and opposed to them are those who interrupt the stream or dam it to keep the benefits for themselves. The enemies of courtesy, whose emblem is the snarling Beast of Calidore's quest, are those who unnaturally suppress the spontaneous movement of generosity, and, mistaking what freedom is, seek

218

to establish it for themselves by receiving without giving. They see others as mere objects to be used, all the more so if they are weak, and so their response to love is not to return it, or be compassionate to it, but to take pleasure in having a fellow creature at their mercy. Thus Crudor makes use of Briana's love to further his sense of power through the pointless degradation of his fellow men, and Briana in her turn uses like domestic beasts the men and women whose beards and hair must line a cloak to gain her Crudor's favour. The movement of the circle is here reversed, and it has to be set moving the right way by the spontaneous but purposeful courtesy of Calidore. In this particular episode, one can catch the very moment of the turn; Briana, impelled in the wrong direction by her obsession, passes on her guilt to Calidore in accusations of treachery and threats of revenge; but Calidore refuses to be drawn into the movement of shame which Crudor has begun. 'Not unto me the shame,/But to the shamefull doer it afford', he says, and by granting mercy to Crudor on condition he grant it in turn to all others he sets in motion a circle of benevolence. The effect is seen at once in Briana, who was shamed and scolding but now freely binds herself to generosity.

Again Mirabella, endowed by Nature 'with plenteous dowre/ Of all her gifts', 'gifts of beauties grace', repays the generosity of Nature and the devotion of her lovers with scorn of others and love of herself, and exploits beauty and love to triumph in them. But all is 'repayd with interest againe' through the intervention of Cupid, who sentences Mirabella to make amends through love and pity. Her payment too is a change of direction, an inner adjustment which is dramatized in her punishment by her own pride and her own scorn, qualities in herself of which she must repent. Before she can love others instead of using their love to advance her own sense of triumph there must be a radical alteration in attitude, a turning of attention away from herself. Accordingly she must relive, in reverse, her former course; Scorn laughs at her pain, and the staring giant Disdaine, who is aware of nothing but himself, and who when hauled up again to his golden feet 'lookt againe aloft,/As if he never had received fall' wonderfully expresses the looming egotism, at once terrible and absurd, which was the basis of her maladjustment. Disdaine is 'sib to great Orgoglio' and has his kinsman's stalking step and air of monstrous self-absorption. Both giants are evocations of pride, a concern with self which at last turns upon the mind which nurtures it. Both become a punishment, and Disdaine carries a punishing weapon like Orgoglio's, a club as deadly as lightning and like it a 'dreadfull instrument of ire'. Red Crosse's selfhood and its consequences in self-consuming guilt are fatal to holiness and must be destroyed, but Mirabella knows that she must endure Disdaine; her life and freedom depend upon it. One is reminded of yet another gaoler, Busyrane, who must be forced to unread his spells before Amoret can escape from the prison of her own tortured mind; and in both cases the traditional behaviour of the lady of courtly love, and the personifications which express it, are being used in the representation of a conversion, a readjustment of the mind. Yet Amoret and Mirabella are two very different characters, and the mental and moral processes involved are different too. Spenser understands so clearly what might now be called the psychology of courtly love that he can use it as a many-sided image. Mirabella's endurance is a necessary stage in her growth in courtesy; she recognizes it as inevitable and just and convinces Arthur that it is so. The god of love is here the opposite of the Petrarchan tyrant in his triumphal car surrounded by chained prisoners. He is not the afflictor but the avenger of cruelty, 'myld by kynd' and yielding as judge to even Mirabella's prayer for mercy; for love belongs to the exchanges of courtesy and in this book is closely associated with the Graces. It is only human peevishness which provokes him, only human selfishness which perverts love and all gracious things.

There are other examples of the selfishness which stops the flow of courtesy, from poor Priscilla's venial, fussy inability to love or serve freely because she cannot look beyond her own social standing and good name, to the Brigants' use or misuse of their fellow men by selling them as slaves. The cannibals exemplify such misuse at its most extreme, for they live by preying on the weak, serving 'their owne necessities with others need' (viii, 35), and they distort even heavenly grace itself. They are the book's most horrifying symbol of ingratitude, the breaking of the Graces' circle which takes them to damnation. In such cases, the inescapably faulty justice of the fifth book must be remedied by the courtesy of God and man, the circle must be closed again by the intervention of providence to save the oppressed. The rescue of so many of the weak and suffering prepares us for the apotheosis

of Pastorella, lost child, shepherd queen, and flower goddess, the
Calender's Elisa and Dido in one. Serena is twice between life
and death, but Pastorella suffers repeated 'deaths' after the first
one in childhood from which Meliboe saves her. Her story is
conceived in a way that stresses death within death, she is pitched
past pitch of grief, and yet relief comes. She is imprisoned and
ill in the 'darknesse dred and daily night' of the Brigants' underground cave which is like hell to her, and is caught in the battle
in the cave where steel flies to make a way for Death himself,

> making way for Death at large to walke:
> Who, in the horror of the griesly night,
> In thousand dreadful shapes doth mongst them stalke,
> And makes huge havocke.

(xi, 16)

Later the surviving thieves find her, a 'dreary dying mayd',
pinned to their dead captain under a heap of corpses. They
recover her to life, but a life so wretched that it is a double death,
so that they only renew 'her death by timely death denying'
(xi, 23). Only when Calidore reaches her does she, who has
wished for death so long, begin to feel life stir in a true revival.

> So her uneath at last he did revive,
> That long had lyen dead, and made againe alive.

(xi, 50)

The movement is completed at Pastorella's reunion with her
life's source, Claribell, who finds that what had seemed to be death
is not. The child she has 'thought long dead, she fyndes alive'.

> And livest thou, my daughter, now againe?
> And art thou yet alive, whom dead I long did faine?

(xii, 19)

Further marking the long descent, death below death, and the
ascent from even this depth to fullness of life, there are the
recurrent images of falling and rising, and of dark and light and
fading flowers.

> Her lovely light was dimmed and decayed
> With cloud of death . . .

> Like to a flowre that feeles no heate of sunne . . .

> And forth her bringing to the joyous light . . .

221

The emphasis leaves us in no doubt of Spenser's meaning as Pastorella dies and is 'made againe alive' like Proserpine or like Florimell in her sea change. All the sufferings and salvations of the lesser characters are summed up in the rebirth of the pastoral heroine; the greatest of God's gifts is the transcending of sorrow in eternal life.

Spenser draws here upon the strength of that one of all the myths which is rooted most deeply in our nature, but it is the measure of the greatness of this book, and of its masterly planning, that the pastoral romance, placed as it is, can establish its meaning so simply and acceptably, becoming itself a myth, 'inexhaustible to contemplation'.[12] Because the order and ultimate goodness of the world have so made themselves felt through the whole legend, we accept without trouble the death of the good Meliboe and his people. The poet's confidence, which can envisage even the destruction of Colin and of all the poetic pastoral existence with such complete serenity, evokes a corresponding serenity in us. Colin's world is destroyed by the depravity of man, but we have seen the truth in the Acidalian vision. Poetry has made its assertion of value, and Pastorella and Calidore survive to carry that value into the more complicated situations of the poem as a whole, where it is harder to see. And this the reader must do in his turn, when he passes from the poet's imitation of nature back to nature itself. What Shakespeare does through Prospero, Spenser does in this last peaceful legend; he gives us a new perspective upon the ordered world of his poem and the world of our experience, and upon the relation between them. Poetry itself becomes part of the nature to be imitated.

That this perspective should be achieved in a book about courtesy, generosity, charity, and grace is fitting; for courtesy is 'the poetry of conduct',[13] and two passages from Maritain's *Art and Scholasticism* set up relevant connections:

> Art therefore is the product of a spontaneous instinct like love and ought to be cultivated like friendship: because it is a virtue like friendship.

[12] I take the phrase from I. A. Richards, writing (in *Coleridge on the Imagination*) of the greater mythologies.
[13] 'We are to conceive of courtesy as the poetry of conduct.' [C. S. Lewis, *The Allegory of Love* (Oxford, 1936), p. 351.]

Literature is to art what vanity is to the moral life. Poetry, I have said elsewhere, is to one what grace is to the other.[14]

Courtesy is full 'humanity', the natural and right response to the generosity of God and Nature, man's part in the circling movement of benefits, the receiving and bestowing of grace. In this movement poetry has its place, for it too is divinely given, and all Spenser's poetry is a repaying of the gift above all worldly riches, the 'divine gift and heavenly instinct . . . poured into the witte by . . . celestiall inspiration' which E.K. tells us was described in *The English Poete*. In the book of Courtesy he shows us in what the repayment consists, in the dedicated vision of the shepherd poet who re-creates the benevolent life of the universe in his picture of the Graces, circling in delight in their dance of reciprocal goodwill around a human figure. Courtesy, like the other virtues of the poem, is a way of focusing the attention on the purposes of a divinely ordered universe, and these are ways that 'none can find, but who was taught them by the Muse'.

Although so many stories are left unfinished, although Arthur has not found Gloriana and Cleopolis is still unseen, there could scarcely be a more satisfying close to the poem as we have it than this serene meditation, transcending in peace 'the less or more, the fine balance of right and wrong'[15] with which the book of Justice is concerned. But the two Cantos of Mutability form a coda that one would not willingly lose, and a standpoint from which the whole of the poem may be surveyed.

[14] Pp. 42, 98.
[15] C. J. Sisson, discussing the end of *King Lear* in *Shakespeare's Tragic Justice* (London, 1961), p. 98.

Conclusion

THE LAWS OF NATURE

THE magnificence of the Mutability Cantos in and for themselves needs no remark, but as part of *The Faerie Queene* they develop some of that poem's most important structural themes. As the printer puts it, the Cantos 'bothe for forme and matter appeare to be parcell of some following booke of *The Faerie Queene* under the legend of Constancie', and it seems justifiable to read them, as Professor Lewis has done, as the core or 'central allegorical gable' of a book about change and permanence, no mere fragment but a further stage in the cumulative progress of Spenser's vast consideration of the universe. It is true, of course, that without the book of which the Cantos were to form a part we cannot be over confident about their apparent significance. In each book one episode modifies another and meaning resides in the interrelation of all of them, and this is true even of such central passages as Colin's vision or the Bower of Bliss. For that matter it is equally true that book modifies book, so that the significance of each is deepened by the existence of all; we cannot know how much more would be open to us in the books we have if the legend of Constancy,[1] and whatever others were still part of Spenser's plan, had been finished. But the advantage of a patterned narrative, built up through the manipulation of

---

[1] The name presumably depends upon the publisher's guess, but it is a good guess; 'Mutabilitie' and 'Constancie' are words familiar in the long discussion about the decay of the universe which went on in the sixteenth and seventeenth centuries. E.g. Justus Lipsius's *De Constantia* was englished by John Stradling as *Two Bookes of Constancie* (London, 1599).

structural themes, is that while always developing it is always coherent; and underlying all the intricacy of the six completed books is the problem with which the Cantos deal more openly, the problem of meaning.

The book of Holiness interprets human life in terms of Bible truth; the significance of living must be discovered in the direct relation of man to God. In the following books the characters have to manage the labyrinth without so firm a clue. Only hints of a presiding purpose shine through the wandering wood, but the hints accumulate to the point where, in Book Six, the poet can make his own task of seeing and shaping meaning into part of his poem. He stands back to contemplate the order he has made, but only to return, in the Mutability Cantos, to the complex experience in which the order is implicit. From the serenity of the legend of Courtesy, lit by divine grace, we return to grapple with a life of tensions and flux, but we return knowing that meaning depends on vision, on our ability to see. In the Cantos are present the felt complexity and the felt unity of life, the equilibrium which depends on the existence of opposites, the harmony which depends on many voices, and behind them the 'Sabaoths sight' of wholly clear vision, when we shall no longer see 'like an image in a glass'. The ideas which are dramatized in Mutability's trial are part of the Renaissance synthesis of Plato, Aristotle, Ovid, Lucretius, Boethius, and more recently Lipsius, Bodin, and Spenser's favourite Du Bartas, and being derived from such heterogeneous sources they are not, philosophically, particularly consistent. But as images ('what is usually called an "idea" may be a poetic image also')[2] in the developing meaning of the poem they make impressive poetic sense, accommodating both the appearance of things and that beyond appearance which the poet's faith tells him he will one day see.

The Cantos begin with the image of the circle, but it is the circle as wheel, the frighteningly aimless symbol of Fortune:

> What man that sees the ever-whirling wheele
> Of Change, the which all mortall things doth sway,
> But that thereby doth find, and plainly feele,
> How Mutability in them doth play
> Her cruell sports, to many mens decay?
>
> (VII, vi, 1)

[2] Northrop Frye, *The Anatomy of Criticism* (Princeton, 1957), p. 84.

This is the condition of the world as we find and feel it when we are submerged in it, this is one way of seeing Mutability. What we hear of her first is wholly bad. She has widespread and old-established power, being of antique race and ancient lineage, but it is a menacing lineage since she is descended from the Titans who fought against Jove for heaven's regiment and are a synonym for impious pride, the first of sins. The link with the primal sin which spoiled the world is made firm in the following stanzas. Mutability aspires to dominion so that she may be honoured as a goddess ('and ye shall be as gods', the serpent told Eve) and she has perverted

> all which Nature had establisht first
> In good estate, and in meet order ranged.
>
> (vi, 5)

The fall is lightly but precisely glanced at in lines which tell how Mutability

> made them all acurst
> That God had blest, and did at first provide
> In that still happy state for ever to abide.
>
> Ne shee the lawes of Nature onely brake,
> But eke of Justice, and of Policie:
> And wrong of right, and bad of good did make,
> And death for life exhanged foolishlie:
> Since which, all living wights have learn'd to die.
>
> (vi, 5–6)

She is of earthly lineage and mortal, like earthly men, 'th' Earth's daughter', 'this bold woman', 'thou fraile woman', and Jove (like Jehovah) stays his hand when he is about to hurl his thunderbolt because, if he exerts his full power to strive with flesh, the progeny of man will be rooted out. Mutability is 'the force behind the sin of Adam'[3] and behind the dissatisfied pride of Adam's sons who would dispute the purposes of God. Jove, hearing her speak, recognizes the voice of mortality.

> Will never mortall thoughts cease to aspire,
> In this bold sort, to heaven claime to make,
> And touch celestiall seates with earthly mire?
>
> (vi, 29)

[3] *The Allegory of Love*, p. 354.

226

The fallen cannot storm heaven, but must try to win it back by goodness, from a gracious lord.

> Then ceasse thy idle claime, thou foolish gerle,
> And seeke by grace and goodnesse to obtaine
> That place from which by folly Titan fell.
>
> (vi, 34)

The touching interlude of the foolish Faunus, who like Mutability insults Cynthia, the nearest earth of the planetary gods, repeats the theme of sinful presumption on the level of comedy, with its little motives and little rustic similes of the dairy and the creaming pans, reinforcing the universal by the particular, reminding us 'mongst these sterne stounds' of the 'soft delights' and pathetic losses of home. Faunus's story is modelled on Actaeon's, which was interpreted, obviously enough, as a blasphemous attempt to know more of divinity than a creature should, so that it is something like Mutability's attempt, and something like the fall; and Faunus himself is something like a comic devil with his hooves and horns, the devil as fool, pathetically laughable. As for the consequences of his silly presumption, they are great enough: the ruin of the beautiful symmetrical hill of Arlo where Nature chooses to appear before all the creatures and utter her mysterious truths. The place now lies waste under a curse, like the earth, and when Nature has vanished like the Graces 'whither no man wist' she is not seen again on Arlo hill.

The little story charmingly underlines the nature of Mutability's claim to universal sovereignty: it is a reversal to chaos. She is descended on the mother's side from 'Earth, great Chaos child' and on the father's from Titan, elder brother of Jove's father Saturn. Her line is the elder, as primeval chaos is older than order; but it was the line of Saturn, the god of the Golden Age, which established control over the wild force of the more primitive gods, imprisoning them in hellish dungeons under the earth. The bright heavens are held, says Jove,

> by conquest of our soveraine might,
> And by eternall doome of Fates decree.
>
> (vi, 33)

But the Titaness is strong too. She does not frighten Jove, but the other gods would have broken rank in disorder if he had not

227

forced them to stay still. She is also beautiful and appealing, as earth and its human and animal creatures are, and this is part of her strength. 'Such sway doth beauty even in heaven beare.' She is indeed a more complex figure than her ancestors, finely conceived to combine all the appearances, to its human inhabitants, of the mutable world. Our sense of the fleeting beauty of life, our sense of its unfairness, our injured pride and resentment at what we see as the ever-whirling wheel of change, are all in her. Though her claim is not allowed and Jove is victorious, neither he nor Nature makes any attempt to punish her by casting her out, as her ancestors were cast, from the doings of the universe. For she is part of the universe; unknowing, she maintains it, fulfils the purpose of the god of Nature. She misinterprets her proper function, as we are tempted to misinterpret it while we are carried on the wheel of change, but she performs it none the less. For the wheel where Fortune's victims desperately cling can also be seen as Hakewill was to see it, 'observing a constancy even in turning', and as the circle through which the creatures work their own perfection: a movement made under control. Mutability, caught in her own nature, cannot see herself so; fallen with us she shares our blindness, and like us she will not accept as true what she cannot see. 'But what we see not, who shall us perswade?' she answers Jove; and the words typify her situation and ours, unless 'grace and goodnesse' give us the vision to recognize great Nature, 'unseene of any, yet of all beheld'.

Mutability is oddly convincing in action and speech; she is so, I think, because her character arises so directly out of the fluctuating experience which she personifies. She is as complicated a mixture as one of us, indeed she is one of us, and her attitudes express our own. One reason why she is linked with the sin of the first parents is that she owes her power over our minds to the fall; the universe seems to us to be ruled by pointless change because of the dullness of our understanding. But of course her sway does not exist only in our minds, it is actual and physical, for sin brought also death, and the flawed order and proneness to decay of the sublunary world. Within the regions of time her power is genuine, however tragic the cause, and she advances without hindrance as far as the moon, where Time is the gatekeeper. Her tussle with Cynthia is unresolved, and beyond the moon her claim to power has sufficient appearance of reality to alarm the gods and to be submitted to Nature; for these are the regions, once thought unchanging, where the new star had come and gone in Cassiopeia. The case is strongly put, yet it has in it the duality of Mutability herself, for of the examples she gives of the rule of change many are equally the traditional examples of a universal order based upon balance and alternation. The earth, breeding new things from old so that 'of their winter spring another prime', the constant movement of the waters, the 'reciprocall vicissitude' of the four elements, are symbols either of endless flux or of an intelligible cyclical movement, according to one's point of view.

Mutability seeks to clinch her claim to the earth with a procession of times and seasons, but this is summoned by Nature's servant Order, and the seasons and months walk by in their ancient panoply like the illuminations in a Book of Hours. They do of course demonstrate change, but imaginatively they suggest rather recurrence, stability, for they have their old comfortable human associations, Autumn with fruit and corn, Winter with chattering teeth, March the sower and November come straight from fatting hogs. The familiar yearly cycle is further suggested by the lines which close the procession of seasons. February, coming last, has his plough with him,

> And tooles to prune the trees, before the pride
> Of hasting Prime did make them burgein round.
> So past the twelve months forth, and their dew
> places found.

> (vii, 43)

The end is the beginning, and the Hours too move in a circle, taking turns to watch heaven's gate. Last of all in the processon of time's movement is Death, with Life walking ahead of him, and here the difference between what things are and what they appear to us to be is finely used.

> Death with most grim and griesly visage seene,
> Yet is he nought but parting of the breath;
> Ne ought to see, but like a shade to weene,
> Unbodied, unsoul'd, unheard, unseene.

> (vii, 46)

Death is to us the grimmest figure in Mutability's pageant, yet is he nought but parting of the breath. The quiet negatives reduce the deathshead of tradition to an invisibility; Mutability's climax is not really there at all, and the procession culminates in Life, all joy and delight and hardly distinguishable from love. The stanza, and the consideration of earthly time, ends with a description of him.

> But Life was like a faire young lusty boy,
> Such as they faine Dan Cupid to have beene,
> Full of delightfull health and lively joy,
> Deckt all with flowres, and wings of gold fit to
>   employ.

(vii, 46)

Mutability claims too that the gods themselves are subject to her. Her argument on this score reflects the confusion of human opinion in such matters. She argues on several fronts at once: the gods are taken as planetary powers, whose course in the sky is variable to our observation; and as mythological figures, dependent for their existence upon the wavering thoughts of men. Jove was born on earth, she says, though opinion differs about the exact place; so he is 'mortall borne, and thrall to me'. What emerges is as much the puzzlement of mortal men, looking out across the borders of time, as the universality of change. Mutability closes her case triumphantly with an example as double-sided as any, for the sphere of the fixed stars was a favourite symbol of permanence and order. 'It self is moved', as Mutability says, but the image that dominates the stanza and dominates our response is that of the stability of the fixed stars as against the wandering planets: 'Onely the starrie skie doth still remaine'.

Nature's reply takes up the potential meanings which have been implicit in Mutability's plea. It is a considered answer, for the case is not simple. Nature agrees that all things are changed; and yet 'being rightly wayd' they are not, for change is a condition of their development and of their return 'dilated' to themselves. Their movement is not a wavering line but a circle, a deliberate process by which they make use of change and so work their own perfection. They change, then, but they are not subject to change. That the judgment is gnomic is to be expected, for what only Nature can rightly weigh man can scarcely hope to make explicit; but it would seem to apply to the whole of creation. Even in the sublunary world Mutability works under a control which she does not see. She, who aspires to make all things change, will one day be allowed to do so. But when that day comes, and we shall be changed, her task will be done; she will become her own victim. 'Death, thou shalt die'; these are the paradoxes in which of necessity the divine purpose reveals itself, and Nature, though not God, is a shadow of God, with her blinding light like the sun's that cannot be looked on, and her garment like that of the transfigured Christ. She reminds us of much else too, for Spenser has made wonderfully tactful use not only of the tradition of 'Alane' and his *Pleynte of Kynde*, and of the attributes of the great mother goddesses Isis and Venus, but of the themes of his own poem. The opposites of life and death, the elements on whose balanced conflict the universe is sustained, the circling seasons, all moving before Nature for her judgment on their meaning, gather together the implications of the pastoral cycle, the hieros gamos of Venus and Adonis, and much else with which the poem has been concerned. The marriage of opposites, about which so much of Spenser's imitation has been organized, is identified with the highest of ordering powers below God himself, Nature whose authority not even Mutability dreams of questioning.

Nature is moving and unmoved, seen and unseen, terrible and beautiful, man and woman, embodying all the mysteries in one august figure. She is veiled to shield man from the terror of her lion face, the sun's face with a brilliance that can be seen only in its reflected image; and as it was said of Isis, who lifts her veil sees truth. Alanus, whose Nature is already an ancient figure, strives to express in his elaborately antithetical prose a similar sense of the paradoxical quality of the world as it appears to man. 'The concordant discord, the single plurality, the dissonant consonance, the dissenting agreement, produce the structures of the palace of earth.' The central paradox, and all the lesser ones which branch from it into the individual lives of men, will be surpassed, but only in the 'stedfast rest' of Sabaoth.

In a poem so intricately worked it is not safe to take any passage in isolation, and the opening stanzas of a canto often use personal utterance as a way of modulating into another aspect of a book's subject. Without knowing what the two stanzas of 'The VIII. Canto, unperfite' led to we cannot guess at their full purpose, but as a completion of what has gone before they are wholly satisfying.

The sudden transition from the vast assembly of the creatures, now 'quite dismissed', and the vanished truth of Nature, to the pillars of eternity is one of the most effective of all transitions. The contrast is a poetic statement; the great ordered company on Arlo hill, Mutability, the gods, even Nature herself, will vanish in actuality as in their pictured form in the poem, on the day when 'all shall changed be'. Contemplating this, all the beauty and richness and sadness of the mutable world can only seem vain and transitory. The mind moves naturally in the direction to which Nature's words have pointed it, when change shall be final, and

> all shall rest eternally
> With him that is the God of Sabbaoth hight:
> O that great Sabbaoth God graunt me that Sabaoths sight!

If, as Mrs. Bennett believes, Spenser intends a play on Sabaoth/ Sabbath, he may even here be hinting the mysteriousness of Nature's God, the Lord of hosts, of the conflict of this world, and the God of eternal peace. Whether or not this is so, the last fine stanza is true to the whole poem, though the transcendence of eternity has been glimpsed only once before, in the first book when Red Crosse turns from the world of fruitless joys to the bright towers of the New Jerusalem. Though it has done so by chance, Spenser's unfinished imitation has come full circle, rounding in its own small sphere the complexities of the created world.

Faeryland contains great things and small, huge moral conflicts and little follies and confusions; its fullness is one reason why it is, as it has recently been called, 'so continually and inexhaustibly rewarding'.[4] But all the detail, which might so easily have over-whelmed us in a muddle of vivid impressions, is structured upon the firm basis of the old and all-embracing commonplace of the fluctuating sublunar world, depending upon stress and equilibrium but resting in the last resort on the eternal stability of bright heaven. Ronsard assumes the same nexus of associations in his *Hymne de l'Éternité*, where he considers Eternity herself and Discord her enemy, and generation and continuation in Venus and Nature.

[4] *The Times Literary Supplement*, 14 December 1962, in a review of G. Hough, A Preface to *The Faerie Queene*.

Je veux, s'il m'est possible, attaindre à la louange
De celle qui jamais pour les ans ne se change,
Mais bien qui faict changer les siecles & les temps,
Les moys, & les saisons & les jours inconstans,
Sans jamais se muer.[5]

A commonplace indeed, expressed or implied in a multitude of writings in verse or prose. But nowhere does it shape so organically about it material so voluminous. In this intricate structure there is room for cosmic contemplation and for the most delicate perception of the workings of the human mind. The Mutability Cantos remind us, by allegorizing the very basis of that structure, of the power of imaginative organization which went to the making of such 'order excellent'.

The judicious poet holds all things from the heaven to the abyss within his hands and his discretion, so Giraldi supposed, and Spenser's aim is not much less than this. But his stand is firmly on common earth, and when he writes of great matters the emphasis is always on what they mean to man, how they modify, clarify, complicate our living. The poet is there in the world he has made, wondering or delighted or sad, and in all this representing us. The result has a wonderful verisimilitude, of a certain kind, the kind that one of the finest of Spenser's critics has described in saying of *The Faerie Queene* that it is 'like life itself, not like the products of life. . . . The things we read about in it are not like life, but the experience of reading it is like living'.[6] Because this is so, many readers will find in it many things, and no one can hope to embrace all that is there. It adapts itself to us, and in each reader's experience of it the emphasis will be different. There is no thornier problem than that of just how literature is related to life; but what is most important in this particular poem is perhaps not individual meanings, the precise sense localized in an episode, a reference, an emblem, but the perception of relationships, the unfolding of purpose, an imitation of the kind of meaning we feel in life by living it. The best of all comments on

---

[5] *Oeuvres*, Edition Critique par Paul Laumonier (Paris, 1935), p. 246.
[6] *The Allegory of Love*, p. 358. Edwin Honig has a remark upon allegory which, if one thinks of it particularly in relation to *The Faerie Queene*, points in the same direction: 'Allegory, which is symbolic in method, is realistic in aim and in the content of its perception.' [*Dark Conceit, The Making of Allegory* (Cambridge, Mass., 1960), p. 180.]

the poem's vitality is the one it contains in itself, in the sixth book's interrelation of gift and use, 'Nature's skill', the art which is itself part of the nature it celebrates. For art of a very complex kind creates the poem's sense of spontaneous life. Allegorical poetry, which used to be thought almost a contradiction in terms, as though allegory were a strait jacket on the imagination, is here the expression of joyous free activity in accepted control. This, the poem makes us feel, is what both life and poetry should be, even though both contain sadness and difficulty; and so it is with the sixth book that the last word must be, with the Graces dancing in delight, and with art and nature conjoined on Mount Acidale poetry's home, where is gathered

> all that ever was by Natures skill
> Devized to worke delight.

INDEX

Achilles: subjection to women, 118; in Troy stories, 118; in *Achilleid*, 118, 158; in *Ars Amatoria*, 118; relation to Marinell, 118; relation to Artegall, 130, 134, 135; in Comes, 158; mentioned, 97, 107, 157

Acrasia: and Mortdant, 39–41; and Guyon, 72–78; and Verdant, 76–77; compared to Venus, 76–77, 145; mentioned, 53, 54, 84, 89, 112, 125

Actaeon, 227

Adonis: in the Garden, 104–5, 145–150, 189–90; in Malecasta's house, 111–12, 147, 149; mentioned, 97, 100, 140

Aemilia, 128

Aeneas: descent to underworld, 17, 56; and Venus, 100

Aesculapius, 17–18, 19, 28n

Agape, 122, 123, 214

Alanus de Insulis, 73, 89, 231

Alciati, Andrea, 138n

Alexis, Guillaume, 90

Allegory: implication of order in, xvi, xix; 'naïve' allegory, xvii; aim of, 233n

Allen, D. C., 148n

Alma, castle of, 64–71

Amavia, 39–41, 44, 47, 52, 64, 65, 76

Amidas, 186, 187

Amoret: compared to Britomart, 93; and Venus, 98, 100; and Timias, 102; relation to Belphoebe, 102–3, 111; in Garden of Adonis, 103–5; in Temple of Venus, 105–7; in Busyrane's house, 107–11; compared to Florimell, 112, 113, 114, 139; and Lust, 128–9; compared to Mirabella, 220; mentioned, 85, 91, 96, 101, 110, 111, 112, 117, 122, 126, 127, 135, 136, 140, 149

Amoretti, 98, 99, 109

Amyas, 125, 128

Antaeus, 69

Apelles Symbolicus, 13, 37n, 116n

Apollodorus, 109

Apuleius, Lucius, 105, 107, 173

Aquinas, Thomas, 16, 188n

Archimago: and Red Crosse, 6–9; and Guyon, 36; and Britomart, 83–84

Ariadne, crown of, 217–18

Ariosto, 85

Aristotle, 184n, 225; *De Mundo*, 87–88

Arlo Hill, 216, 227, 232

235

Artegall: image seen by Britomart, 93–94; as Achilles, 94, 133, 134, 157; meets Britomart, 129–35; compared to Marinell, 131, 134; as Salvage Knight, 133–4, 158–9; 166; frees Irena, 151–3; trained by Astraea, 156–8; and Sanglier, 160–2; as Osiris, 166, 174–6; and Britomart, 167; enslaved by Radigund, 168–72; as Hercules, 169–70, 172; overthrows Pollente, 180; and the Giant, 180–5; relation to Calidore, 192–5; and Bracidas, 186–7; and False Florimell, 187–8; mentioned, 53, 70, 96, 112, 120, 122, 148, 155, 159, 162, 163, 168, 169, 178

Arthos, John, 1n

Arthur: rescues Red Crosse, 21–25: fights for Guyon, 62–64; at Alma's castle, 65–71; and the Chronicle, 66–67; fights Maleger, 68–71; meets Britomart, 81; pursues Florimell, 83, 113, 114; and Belge, 153; at Mercilla's court, 177–8; as Hercules, 178–9; and Blandina, 211; and Mirabella, 220; mentioned, 85, 112, 136, 167, 180, 196, 218, 223

Ashley, Robert, 48n

Astraea: flees world, 154, 155; trains Artegall, 156–8; mentioned, 153, 159, 160, 169, 182, 183

Atalanta, 60, 60n

Ate, 123, 129

Atin, 47, 53

Bacchus, 157

Bacon, Francis, 159

Bale, John, 23, 24n

Batman, Stephen, 88n, 96

Belge, 152, 168

Belphoebe: and Guyon, 47; in Book II, 48–52; as Venus virgo, 50–52, 100; and Diana, 98, 99, 100; and Timias, 100, 101–3, 109; and Braggadocchio, 100; compared

to Britomart, 101; and Amoret, 102–3, 111, 128; mentioned, 91, 92n, 170, 197, 110, 149

Bennett, Josephine W., 232

Berger, Harry, Jr., xiii, 5n, 48n

Biblis, 93, 110

Blandina, 211

Blattant Beast, 153, 194, 196, 201, 206, 218

Blenerhasset, Thomas, 24

Boccaccio, Giovanni, 69

Bodin, Jean, 225

Boethius, 225

Bower of Bliss: nature of, 72–78; and Garden of Adonis, 103; mentioned, 53, 64, 71, 131, 224

Bracidas, 186, 187

Braggadocchio: and Belphoebe, 47–48, 100; mentioned, 51, 121

Briana, 193–5, 196, 197, 201, 219

Brigants, 210, 215, 220, 221

Britomart: meets Guyon and Arthur, 81–3; as woman warrior, 91–93; loves Artegall, 93–94; compared to Amoret, 93; and Merlin, 95–96; dominant in Book III, 96–97; compared to Belphoebe, 101; saves Amoret, 108, 111; at Malecasta's house, 111–112; and Florimell, 113–14; and Marinell, 118; meets Artegall, 129–35; mistaken for Artegall, 162; betrayed by Dolon, 162–3, 172; and Artegall, 167, 194; relation to Radigund, 169, 170–2; as Isis, 166, 169, 174–6; in Isis Church, 172–6; and Scudamour, 184; mentioned, 79, 85, 86, 100, 110, 120, 122, 124, 129, 134, 137, 149, 150, 156, 157, 163, 168, 188

Britomartis, 173

Bruno, Giordano, 35n

Burbon, 152, 154

Busiris, 109, 157

Busyrane, 106, 107–11, 112, 117, 125, 128, 220

Calepine: saved by Salvage Man,

209; saves Serena, 209, 211; saves baby, 209; mentioned, 190, 191, 194, 196, 197, 201, 217, 218
Calidore: meets Tristram, 192–3, 198; relation to Artegall, 192–5; reforms Briana, 193–5, 219; taught by Meliboe, 207–8; sees Graces, 214–16; rescues Pastorella, 221; mentioned, 153, 191, 196, 197, 199, 200, 201, 205, 209, 211, 212, 217, 218, 222
Calvin, John, 16
Cambell, 122, 123, 124, 125, 127, 129, 130
Cambina, 123, 124
Canacee, battle for, 122, 123
Cartari, Vincenzo, 65, 127n
Cassirer, Ernst, 77n
Castle Joyeous, see Malecasta
Christ: temptation compared to Guyon's, 56, 57, 61, 64; Passion of, 161–3; betrayed by Peter, 162; and justice, 162–3
Chrysogone, 100
Cicero, 163
Circe, 71, 73
Ciris, 93
Claribell, 210, 221
Claribell (knight), 85
Colin: sees Graces, 212–18, 224; mentioned, 199, 222; in Shepheardes Calender, 203–4, 205
Colin Clouts Come Home Againe, 86–87, 156
Comes, Natalis, 118, 212
Comus, 75
Concord, 45, 79–80, 87, 105, 109, 123, 124, 125, 126, 129
Coridon, 209
Cormoraunt, 209
Crudor, 193–5, 196, 219
Cupid: and Diana, 99; in Garden of Adonis, 104, 105, 146; in Busyrane's house, 108–9; and Mirabella, 219–20; mentioned, 90, 91, 93, 98, 100, 106, 107
Cybele, 174

Cymochles: in Bower of Bliss, 53; fights with Arthur, 62–63; mentioned, 52, 54, 74
Cymoent, 80, 81, 82, 118, 119, 142, 143, 149, 187
Cynthia: and Faunus, 227; and Mutability, 228

Dante, 24
Daphnaïda, 202–3
Daphne, 74
Despair, 25–27, 143
Diamond, 123
Diana: Dictynna, 97, 173, 175; and Belphoebe, 98, 99, 100; and Venus, 98–100; and Cupid, 99; and Britomart, 135; and Adonis, 148; mentioned, 42, 43, 90, 91, 97, 98, 103, 105, 107, 169, 174, 189
Diodorus Siculus, 109, 173, 175
Diomedes of Thrace, 157, 178
Discordia concors, 87–91, 109–110, 125, 175, 231
Disdaine, 219–20
Dolon, 162, 172
Du Bartas, Guillaume Salluste, 90, 225
Duessa, 3, 8, 9, 10, 11, 15, 17, 123, 177–8
Durr, R. A., xvi n, 203n

Ebreo, Leone, 48n, 89, 113, 124, 140, 146
Elissa, 46
Elizabeth, Queen: and Britomart, 96; as Venus virgo, 102; as Astraea, 155; as Mercilla, 156, 176–8
Ellrodt, Robert, 103n, 163
Elyot, Sir Thomas, 164, 165
English Poete, The, 223
Epithalamion, xv
Eurydice, 107, 108, 205
Evans, Maurice, 61n, 63n
Eve, 40, 107, 226
Excess, 75

INDEX

Faeryland, xiii, xviii, 34, 83, 113, 125, 214, 232
False Florimell, 113, 114, 121, 123, 187–8
Faunus, 227
Ficino, Marsilio, 89, 90, 113, 173, 213, 214
Fidelia, 28–29
Flora, 9, 72, 73
Florimell: nature of, 112–15, 138–141; compared to Amoret, 112, 113, 139; and the Graces, 113; compared to Helen, 115; and hyaena, 115–16; and Proteus, 117, 140–1; compared to Pastorella, 222; mentioned, 82, 84, 85, 91, 97, 101, 119, 120, 122, 136, 143, 145, 146, 148, 149, 168, 187, 188
Florimell's girdle, tournament for, 122, 123, 125, 129
Flourdelis, 152
Fowler, A. D. S., 41n
Fradubio, 11
Frye, Northrop, xvii, 225n
Fulgentius, 69
Furor, 47, 52

Gang, T. M., 5n
Gardante, 112
Garden of Adonis, 73, 103–5, 106, 110, 145–50, 185
Garden of Proserpina, 59–61
Gelli, Giovanni Battista, 73
Genius: in Bower of Bliss, 72, 73, 78; in Garden of Adonis, 145
Gerrish, B. A., 6n
Geryoneo, 179
Giant of False Justice, 70, 180–5
Giraldi Cinthio, 233
Glauce, 93, 131, 135, 137
Gloriana, 114, 115, 223
Goodman, Godfrey, 181
Graces: appear to Colin, 212–18; and Cupid, 220; in *Shepheardes Calender*, 203; mentioned, 113, 190, 223, 227, 234
Grylle, 73, 74, 77

Guyon: and Red Crosse, 34–37; and Amavia, 39–43; and the Bloody Babe, 42–44; at Medina's castle, 44–47; meets Occasion, 47; meets Phaedria, 53–54; in Mammon's cave, 55–62; swoons, 61–64; at Alma's castle, 64–68; and the Elfin history, 67–68; at the Bower, 71–78; meets Britomart, 81; pursues Florimell, 83, 113; mentioned, 84, 85, 131, 159, 193

Hakewill, George, 181, 228
Hamilton, A. C., xvi n, 5n, 20n, 36n
Held, Julius S., 9n
Helen, 115
Hellenore, 120–1
Heninger, S. K., Jr., 21n
Hercules: descent to hell, 60; and Antaeus, 69, 70; and Omphale, 118, 132; compared to Artegall, 130, 135; in Diodorus Siculus, 132; in Comes, 132; as hero of justice, 157, 159, 169–70; compared to Arthur, 178, 179; mentioned, 53, 97, 134, 189, 194
Hermit, 190, 191, 200–1, 205, 206–207, 218
Hesiod, 90
Hieatt, A. K., xvi n
Homer, 90, 118
Honig, Edwin, 233
Hoopes, Robert, 5n
Hough, Graham, 151n
House of Holiness, 28–30
House of Pride, 12–15, 16, 21, 59
Huddibras, 45, 46
Huizinga, Johan, 207
Hunter, G. K., 24n
Hyacinthus, 148
Hymne in Honour of Love, 87, 105
Hymne of Heavenly Love, 163

Impatience, 69
Impotence, 69
Iole (Omphale), 170
Irena, 178

Isis: and Osiris, 169, 174, 175, 188; bisexual, 173; as moon, 173; as Diana and Venus, 173n; reconciles all divinities, 175; mentioned, 166, 176, 189
Isis Church, 172–6, 188

James, E. O., 145n
Jonson, Ben, 90
Jove: and Mutability, 226, 228

Kantorowicz, E., 164n
Kendall, Timothe, 100
Kermode, Frank, 56, 62n

Lewis, C. S., xix, 44, 103, 127n, 138n, 145n, 222, 224, 233
Lipsius, Justus, 224n, 225
Lucifera, 12–14, 58, 59, 61
Lucretius, 97, 185, 225
Lucy, 186, 187
Luther, Martin, 16, 27n, 207n
Lyly, John, 54n, 98, 99

Malbecco, 92, 120
Malecasta, 111–12
Maleger, 68–70
Marinell: nature of, 117–19, 138–145; compared to Achilles, 117–119, 133; conquered by Britomart, 118–19; compared to Artegall, 131; compared to Adonis, 148, 149; mentioned, 53, 81, 96, 97, 112, 114, 117, 120, 122, 129, 142, 143, 187
Maritain, Jacques, xviii, 222
Marot, Clément, 98, 99
Marriage of Thames and Medway, 122, 141
Mars: and Venus, 3, 54; and Guyon, 38; and Artegall, 135; and Adonis, 148; mentioned, 90, 91, 97, 118
Maske of Cupid, 107–8
Matilda, 209
Medea, 72–73
Medina, 44–47, 52, 53, 64, 71
Meliboe: compared to Abel, 207;

instructs Calidore, 207–8; finds Pastorella, 209; death of, 222; mentioned, 32, 191, 205, 211, 218
Mercilla, 153, 176–8
Mercury, 124
Merlin, 86, 93–96, 167
Milton, John, 55, 60, 69n, 114n, 173n, 202; On the Morning of Christ's Nativity, xv
Minerva, 91, 96, 169, 175
Mirabella, 201, 212, 219–20
Montfaucon, Bernard de, 132, 173n
Mortdant, 39–41, 44, 47, 52, 54, 64, 65, 68, 76
Mount Acidale: home of Venus, 113, 215; of Graces, 113; of Florimell, 113, 116; of poetry, 214–16, 234; mentioned, 192, 222
Munera, 70
Mutability: trial of, 225, 229–31; nature of, 226–9; mentioned, 159, 186, 216, 232
Myrrha, 93

Nature (goddess), 174, 200, 216, 227, 228, 229, 230–2; in Shepheardes Calender, 204
Nelson, William, 71n
Neptune, 81, 144, 187
Nicolson, Marjorie Hope, 181n
Night (goddess), 17, 19

Occasion, 47, 52
O'Hehir, Brendan, 88n
Omphale, 132, 134; as Iole, 170
Orgoglio, 18–25, 56, 179, 219–20
Orpheus, 107
Osiris, 157, 166, 169, 173, 176
Ovid, 90, 93, 98, 100, 117, 125, 126, 148, 225; Ars Amatoria, 109–10; Metamorphoses, 110, 116

Palingenius, Marcellus, 89
Palmer, 36, 41, 52, 55, 62, 71, 81, 84, 193
Paridell, 85, 92, 121

Paris, judgment of, 60
Parker, M. H., 164n
Pasiphae, 93
Passerat, Jean, 149
Pastoral: in *Shepheardes Calender*, xvi, 203–5, 211, 214–17; in *Daphnaïda*, 202–3; in *The Faerie Queene*, 205–8
Pastorella, 189, 190, 196, 198–9, 200, 201, 203, 204, 209, 212, 214, 214, 217, 221–2
Pegma, cum narrationibus philosophicis, 37n, 73n, 213
Perissa, 46
Perkins, William: *Commentarie upon Galatians*, 24–25; *Cases of Conscience*, 31n, 160n; *Treatise of Christian Equitie*, 164n, 165–6
Peter (Apostle), 162, 163
Phaedria, 53–54, 74, 89, 125
Phedon, 52
Philo Judaeus, 89, 147
Philotime, 58, 59, 60, 61, 66
Philtera, 186, 187
Pico della Mirandola, 89, 90, 144n, 213
Pilate, 60
Placidas, 125
Plato, 91, 225
Pleasure, 104
Plutarch: *Gryllus*, 73; *De Iside et Osiride*, 173–5; mentioned, 89
Poetry, nature of: xii, xvi, 215, 218, 222–3
Pollente, 193
Pope, Alexander, 182, 217n
Prays-desire, 65, 69
Priamond, 123
Priscilla, 220
Proclus, 87n
Proserpine, 140, 147, 189, 222
Proteus: as prophet, 80, 81; captures Florimell, 117; function of, 139–43; as first matter, 140; mentioned, 82, 83, 119, 142, 143, 187
Psyche: and Amoret, 103, 107; in

Garden of Adonis, 104–5, 146; and Florimell, 138, 139
Pyrochles, 47, 52, 62–63

Radigund: relation to Britomart, 134, 169, 170–2; enslaves Artegall, 168–71
Radzinowicz, M. A. N., 41n
Ralegh, Sir Walter, 60n, 156
Red Crosse: as romance hero, 3–6; and Archimago, 7–9; and Sansfoy, 10; and Fradubio, 11; in House of Pride, 12–17; fights Sansjoy, 15–17; and Orgoglio, 18–25; and Despair, 25–28; in House of Holiness, 28–30; fights dragon, 30–31; and Guyon, 34–37, 56; mentioned, 62, 70, 84, 85, 114, 191, 193, 220, 232
Ripa, Cesare, 41n, 69
Robertson, D. W., 61n
Roche, Thomas P., Jr., 107n
Romance, xiv, xv, 1, 2, 3
Romaunt of the Rose, The, 90, 92
Ronsard, Pierre de, 99, 149, 232–3
Ross, Alexander, 60n, 69n, 149

Salvage Man, 190, 196, 201, 205, 206, 209, 210, 218
Sanglier, 160, 161, 192
Sansfoy, 10, 15, 16
Sansjoy, 15–18
Sansloy, 15, 45, 46
Saturn, 227
Satyrane, 92, 115, 120, 122, 158n
Scudamour, 105–7, 108, 110–11, 117, 122, 126–7, 128, 134–7, 167, 184, 202
Seneca, 163, 164, 213
Serena: and Blattant Beast, 206–7; and Salvage Man, 210; and cannibals, 210–11; saved by Calepine, 211; mentioned 196, 201, 205, 209, 212, 214, 218
Servius, 213
Shakespeare, William, 95, 98, 132, 148, 163, 187, 190, 222
Shamefastnes, 65

Shepheardes Calender, The, xvi,
203–4, 205, 221; *Aprill*, 102, 203,
213; *July*, 35; *October*, xii, 205,
218; *November*, 204
Sidney, Sir Philip: on poetry, xii;
on history, 152
Sir Bruin, 209
Sir Gawain and the Green Knight,
148
Sisson, C. J., 223n
Smith, Henry, 27n, 163n, 165
Socrates, 59
Solomon, 160, 161, 163
Souldan, 178–9
Spencer, Theodore, xvi
Speranza, 29
Spitzer, Leo F., 35n
Squire of Dames, 120, 121
Statius: *Thebaid*, 100; *Achilleid*,
158
Steadman, J. M., 31n
Symbolicarum Quaestionum, 60n

Talus, 154, 156, 159, 160, 171, 172,
180
Tantalus, 60
Teares of the Muses, The, 213n, 215
Temple of Venus, 79, 110, 122,
126–8
Terpin, 167, 170, 171
Theocritus, 149
Thetis, 118, 119
Timias: pursues foster, 83; and
Belphoebe, 100, 101–3, 109; and
Amoret, 102; and Blattant Beast
206–7; mentioned, 149, 196

Tourneur, Cyril, 76, 177
Triamond, 122, 123, 124, 125, 126,
129
Tristram, 148, 192–3, 197–8, 200,
210
Turpine, 201, 209
Tuve, Rosemond, 88n, 120, 121n
Typhon, 175

Ulysses, 71, 72, 97, 132
Una, 2, 4, 9, 10, 22, 26, 114

Valerianus, J. Pierius, 116n, 124
Venus: and Mars, 3, 54, 76–77, 91,
168, 175; and Amoret, 98, 100;
meets Diana, 98–100; in Garden
of Adonis, 103, 104, 105; in
Temple, 105–7, 126; in Malecasta's house, 111–12, 148; and
Britomart, 135; and Adonis,
146–50, 190, 231; and Graces,
212–13, 215; genetrix, 79, 105;
virgo, 91, 98; armata, 91, 99–100;
hunting, 100; hermaphrodite,
127, 145; mentioned, 174, 189,
216
Verdant, 54, 74, 76, 77, 89, 145
Virgil, 98

Waith, Eugene M., 71n, 170n
Whitaker, Virgil K., 27n
Whiting, G. W., 25n
Wind, Edgar, 9n, 35, 123, 212
Woodhouse, A. S. P., 5

Yates, Frances A., 155n